PEACE, LOVE, AND BARBECUE

PEACE LOVE AND BAR BE CUE

RECIPES,
SECRETS, TALL TALES,
AND
OUTRIGHT LIES
FROM THE LEGENDS
OF **BARBECUE**

MIKE MILLS
AND **AMY MILLS
TUNNICLIFFE**

FOREWORD BY
DANNY MEYER

INTRODUCTION BY
**JEFFREY
STEINGARTEN**

RODALE

Printed in the United States of America
Rodale Inc. makes every effort to use acid-free ♾, recycled paper ♻.

Book design by Carol Angstadt
All photographs © 2005 Amy Mills Tunnicliffe, except those noted below.
Family photos courtesy of Mills family
Page 21, courtesy of Jackson County Historical Society
Page 83, courtesy of Billy Bones Wall
Page 135 (top right), courtesy of Woody Wood
Page 209, courtesy of A. Vincent Scarano
Page 210 and back cover, courtesy of Blue Smoke

Library of Congress Cataloging-in-Publication Data

Mills, Mike, date.
Peace, love, and barbecue : recipes, secrets, tall tales, and outright lies from the legends
of barbecue / Mike Mills and Amy Mills Tunnicliffe ; foreword by Danny Meyer ; introduction
by Jeffrey Steingarten.
        p.   cm.
Includes bibliographical references and index.
ISBN-13 978–1–59486–109–3 paperback
ISBN-10 1–59486–109–9 paperback
1. Barbecue cookery.   I. Tunnicliffe, Amy Mills.   II. Title.
TX840.B3M54   2005
641.5'784—dc22   2004031087

Distributed to the book trade by Holtzbrinck Publishers

10   paperback

RODALE
LIVE YOUR WHOLE LIFE™

We inspire and enable people to improve their lives and the world around them
For more of our products visit rodalestore.com or call 800-848-4735

In loving memory of Faye and Leon Mills
and my brother, Bob Mills;

And with love and thanks to my brother and sisters,
Landess Mills, Jeanette Hudgins, and Mary Pat Mills.

—M.M.

To Woody and Faye Landess Tunnicliffe, my pride and joy.

—A.M.T.

DEFINITIONS
JUST SO WE KNOW WE'RE ALL TALKING ABOUT THE SAME THING

secret

1. Something kept hidden from others
or known only to oneself or to a few

2. Something that remains beyond
understanding or explanation; a mystery

3. A method or formula on which success is based:
The secret of this dish is in the sauce.

tall tale

An improbable (unusual or incredible or fanciful) story

outright lie

1. A false statement deliberately presented
as being true; a falsehood

2. Something meant to deceive or give a wrong impression

Contents

Acknowledgments

FROM MIKE: My lifelong friends, Jean and Jim Tweedy, have been with me through thick and thin, and Dana and Jim Ritcheson add a little color to my life. Dana is also a recipe tester extraordinaire, and she contributed several of her own family recipes for the cause. Many opportunities came my way because of Pat Daily, Tom Viertel, and Gerry Dawes. I treasure their friendship.

I couldn't do what I do without the unfailing support of the management and staff at 17th Street in Murphysboro and Marion and at all of the Memphis Championship Barbecue locations in Las Vegas, particularly Paula Baldi, John Farrish, Troy Harris, Scott Lee, Brent Marrs, Laurie Neff, Steve Overlay, Becky Streuter, Bob Striegel, Gary Strothmann, and Rob Weisen. Extra special thanks to Becky Streuter, who developed and wrote recipes, tracked down information, and kept me organized. The Las Vegas operation wouldn't be possible without my partners Dick Hart, Carlos Silva, and Dan Voland. John Hatfield and Dr. Jim Stalker lent expert advice about spices and recipes.

To Jeffrey Steingarten and Danny Meyer, my gratitude for friendship and opportunities beyond my wildest dreams. To the entire Union Square Hospitality Group—especially Paul Bolles-Beaven, Jenny Zinman Dirksen, Michelle Lehmann, Michael Romano, and David Swinghamer—I admire your passion. Thank you to the entire Blue Smoke crew, especially Kenny Callaghan, Jennifer Giblin, Selby Ham, Jr., Mark Maynard-Parisi, Todd Mott, and the rest of the gang—for always welcoming us with open arms.

And last but not least, my deepest gratitude to our many barbecue friends, pitmasters, police, and evangelists, who graciously shared their stories, reluctantly parted with their recipes, and answered innumerable questions throughout the writing of this book. It's an honor to be your friend.

FROM AMY: Because this book is a celebration of family and friendship, the gratitude must start with the family without whose support this book would be impossible: Woody and Faye Landess Tunnicliffe were extremely patient during the past year when this book was the focus of our household. Woody cheerfully trekked to dozens of barbecue joints, even though he much prefers fine dining. Many of his keen observations found their way into this book. Faye Landess has possessed an incredible palate since she was tiny, and she participated in this project with great gusto. "What are we going to try next?" was her constant refrain.

Jeanette and John Hudgins added detailed memories and treasured recipes. More recollections were provided by Landess Mills and Mary Pat Mills. Chris Mills, Barb and Dan Benz, and Libby Steigman sent much emotional support my way.

My grandmother, Mama Faye Mills, was my personal hero and role model—a wonderful mother, ingenuous provider, and bright inspiration to her family. I missed her physical presence while writing this book. She would've had lots of opinions to offer.

Who would've thought we'd find an agent who's not only a barbecue aficionado, but Memphis-bred as well? This book would not have been possible without Janis Donnaud's enthusiasm, tenacity, advice, and friendship. Thanks to Carolynn Carreño for introducing us and for her friendship as well.

We feel incredibly lucky to be published by Rodale; working with this outstanding team has truly been a delight every step of the way. Many thanks to the discerning Margot Schupf and to Sara Sellar, Kevin Cooper, and Megan Phillips. An editor like Miriam Backes is every writer's dream—I deeply appreciate your ideas, expertise, and enthusiasm! Thanks to Andy Carpenter and the talented and oh-so-patient Carol Angstadt for the inspired design of this book and its cover. Thanks to Nancy Bailey for expertly ushering this project through editing and production and to Roy Finamore for his eagle eye and recipe-writing lessons.

The best friends in the world were always there with words of encouragement: Pamela Copeman, Nida and Todd Mudd, Amanda Walker, Susan Suarez and Doug Brown, Jane McMurry, Peggy Walrod, Joanna McGee, Meredith Graves, Mary Kay Burnett, Marybeth Desai, and Jami Gregory.

Many people endured my fact-checking phone calls, but Elizabeth Karmel, Carlene Phelps, Kell Phelps, and Carolyn Wells helped way beyond the call of duty.

The following people provided many kindnesses along the way: Peter Comrack, Jack Dickerson, Peter Farrar, Mary Jane Hanron, Jeff Harmon, Susan Kagan, Emily McCary, Stephanie Middleton, Michael Obel-Omia, Kathleen O'Shea, Gus Pena, Sally Sampson, Mike Taylor, and Kerry Weiss.

Not many people have the opportunity to write a book with their father. Spending so much time together and seeing a different side of my Daddy was truly a gift. Falling back into our father/daughter pattern, though, was inevitable, and he never missed an opportunity to revisit any childhood lessons he thought I might have forgotten. During several particularly trying periods, he reminded me, in his inimitable fashion, "Just remember what I've always told you: If it was easy, everybody would be doing it."

I guess the same could be said for barbecue.

Foreword

Sometime around the summer of 1999, I remember getting a call from Rocco Landesman—a great theater man and, like me, a native St. Louisan and passionate Cardinals fan. Rocco started the conversation by asking if I liked barbecue. I laughed.

"Why do you want to know?"

"Because a good friend of mine from the theater world—Tom Viertel, who's a true barbecue aficionado—knows this world champion pitmaster from Southern Illinois whose ribs will knock your socks off. And we want you to taste those ribs." My ears perked up, and I laughed again.

"What's so funny?" he asked.

"Not only do I adore barbecue, but I've been thinking about how I could create a business to share my passion with even more people. And selfishly, to figure out a way to get decent barbecue right here in New York."

Rocco launched his assault. "What do you say I introduce you to Tom and we all eat a bunch of ribs and pulled pork together? Tom thinks these ribs are so good they ought to be served in New York. He wants you to get to know Mike Mills and build the restaurant."

"I'd love to taste those ribs, Rocco, but I can't open another restaurant now."

"That's okay," he said. "Just taste the ribs. We'll pick a night when the Cardinals are on TV, and you'll come over to Tom's place. I'll bring the Budweiser." He had me hooked

Danny Meyer, David Swinghamer, and me at the Food and Wine Magazine Classic in Aspen, June 2002

with that perfect trifecta: baseball, barbecue, and beer. In a matter of a week or two, I had a barbecue epiphany. Mike Mills's ribs—frozen, shipped overnight, thawed, and reheated—were just about the best baby backs I had ever tasted in my life.

I won't bore you with the details of the nearly year-long cat and mouse game I played in my own mind (and with Tom Viertel, Rocco Landesman, and my partners) as to whether or not we could possibly open another restaurant. Suffice it to say that no matter how often my brain told me that it would be unwise to pull this off, it was impossible to get Mike's ribs out of my head. One way or another, I was going to figure out a way to make this restaurant happen. It was only a matter of time.

Tom gently coaxed me into inviting Mike for a visit. "Even if you don't end up doing this restaurant together," he said, "you two really should know one another." Mike journeyed to the Big Apple (not *that* big of a stretch; Murphysboro *is* known as Apple City, after all), and we spent two or three days talking pig. He was the real thing, and I knew it. Behind this man whose touch with pork was so heavenly was a human being with a heart the size of a ham.

We embarked upon what would be a two-year courtship before opening Blue Smoke. Mike hooked me up as a rib judge at the Memphis in May World Championship Barbecue Cooking Contest and lovingly taught our team (just about) everything he knew about barbecue. With the exception of his sauce and dry rub recipes, he shared what he knew and was also gracious enough to introduce us to dozens of other wonderful pitmasters, who—thanks to the entrée Mike gave us—were willing to share many of their secrets and best practices. There was no question as to our easy personal chemistry or to the genuine mutual respect and common outlook of hospitality we shared about restaurants.

Mike is my favorite kind of cook: He has dedicated himself to a journey of excellence for the singular purpose of delighting others. And through it all, he possesses the kind of self-assured humility that is such a rare combination in cooking professionals. He knows he's good, and he knows he can always do better. Mike measures his success by the number and arc of the smiles in his dining rooms. And best of all, he surrounds himself with the nicest, most generous people you can imagine. In the end, I had no choice but to work with Mike to bring real pit barbecue to New York.

By writing *Peace, Love, and Barbecue,* Mike has broadened his lifelong desire to provide pleasure through barbecue. Like most good pitmasters, Mike is a great storyteller and if this book strictly was *his* story, it would be a juicy read. What makes it succulent is that Mike has chosen to tell the story of barbecue in the United States, sharing his megaphone with dozens of the pit personalities he believes form the fabric of this great American culinary tradition.

— DANNY MEYER

Introduction

This is the last cookbook you will ever need.

Sure, its coverage of European and Asian food and that of Latin America, the South Pacific, and Australasia might be considered superficial. But you could spend the rest of your natural life cooking what Mike Mills has to teach you about barbecue. And then you might not want to cook anything else.

I was amazed when I first read the chapters that follow—and, yes, not a little wounded. I remember years ago when I first asked Mike for the ingredients in his Magic Dust. He first replied that nobody has the entire recipe; each member of the Apple City team knows only three ingredients, which they add to the pot when none of the other team members is present. Next time he said yes, he had the recipe written down, and he was willing to tell it to me, but then he'd have to kill me. As I was very new to Southern barbecue, I took Mike's answers as signs of great wit and originality.

Now turn to Chapter 1 (or wait until I'm finished), and there they are, Mike's mopping sauce and his mentor, Mr. Whitt's, barbecue sauce, among other treasures. You'll have to wait all the way to Chapter 2 to find his recipe for Magic Dust. Later, Mike tells you how to create your own dry rub and a million other things. There they are for all the world to know them. *And all this from one of the greatest barbecue cooks of all time.* A few months from now, I expect to have acquired a barbecue pit for my backyard in Greenwich Village, and then I will attack the creation of barbecue in earnest. Until then, I'll be content with several of the side dishes Mike has collected—Vencil's pinto beans, the Pig Pickin' Cake, maybe Mike's cole slaw. The first of these is made completely from scratch. The second includes instant pudding, two canned products, and a pound of frozen nondairy topping. I'm sure it is scrumptious.

Even in this age of heightened barbecue awareness, many Americans still misunderstand the word "barbecue." Can you blame them? The American language practically requires such confusion. "Barbecue" has four essential meanings, of which three refer to grilling and one refers to real Southern barbecue.

1. *A barbecue* is a backyard grill used in suburban America and elsewhere, here and abroad, to cook meats and vegetables over direct heat supplied by gas, charcoal, or wood. These days gas predominates because of its convenience and not because of the bitter flavor it imparts.

2. *To barbecue* is to grill meats and vegetables in this manner. Grilling is probably the oldest human cooking method. Grilled meat is not called barbecue.

3. *A barbecue* can also refer to a party or other social occasion, held outdoors, at which meat is grilled and shared in public, though a festive pig- or calf-roast can surely be called a barbecue.

4. *Barbecue,* however, is a savory and succulent slab of meat that has been cooked in a completely different manner, that is, smoked over charcoal and wood at medium-low temperatures hovering around the boiling point of water in a moist environment for an extended period of time until it is at once perfectly tender and exceedingly juicy and brimming with flavor. The mechanism used to do so is known not as a barbecue but as a pit, a smoker, or a cooker. A party or other social occasion at which barbecue is cooked and consumed is unlikely to be called a barbecue; it will typically have a more graphic and specific name such as a *pig picking, a rib-off,* and so forth. If done on a large scale, it might be called a barbecue cook-off or festival.

It's no wonder that even such a brainy authority on food as Alan Davidson, in his *Oxford Companion to Food,* simply compounds the confusion. The towering achievement known as the *Oxford English Dictionary* dances around the truth but never quite attains it. I have met very few Britons and no foreign speakers who have mastered the meanings of barbecue.

Why is this important? Because barbecue is *very* important, especially pork barbecue.

First off, it is simply the most delectable of all traditional American foods. It is the gaudiest jewel in the crown of the American South, where most of the finest traditional American cooking originated. And as barbecue is one of the few aliments that unaccountably do not trigger our bodies' built-in satiation response, it is impossible to stop eating barbecue once you get started. But even more important, barbecue developed in a particularly American way. You might even call it Creole if you are prepared to argue about that for the next 10 years. There does seem to exist a loose consensus that cooking meat over a smoky pit covered with broad tropical leaves originated in the Caribbean and was mastered by black slaves who brought their knowledge and expertise to the mainland, particularly to the South, where descendants of European white settlers were extremely happy with the results.

Most writing about barbecue, including the present commentary, is a delightful mixture of sentimentality and nostalgia, braggadocio and deep humility, exaggeration and falsehood. Most barbecue stories take place in a rural South that has not existed for 50 years, if it ever did. Mike Mills's book includes so much more. He is fascinated with every minute technical detail in the cooking of barbecue, and he shares many of these with the rest of us. Tips, we learn, are so much more important than recipes, and there's an inside tip on nearly every page. I've never read a barbecue book that includes the information in Chapter 8, for example, the times and internal temperatures for different cuts of meat, and the flavor imparted by a long list of different woods.

But sometimes Mike veers off into territory so fraught with error that I cannot keep myself from exposing it. "Personally," he says, "I've always wondered how white men from

New York City could possibly be experts about barbecue." I can't believe he said that. Let's stop a minute and get the facts straight.

The man who discovered barbecue is a writer for the *New Yorker* magazine named Calvin Trillin—discovered it in the same way that Christopher Columbus discovered America, then discovered cocoa beans. Barbecue, America, and cocoa beans pre-existed both Columbus and Trillin. But they were known only to the natives, what you might call the autochthons, who weren't even literate but only drew cartoons in stone.

Trillin was a flawed Columbus, as was Columbus. He tells Mike, "For me, barbecue is something you eat where the tradition is to eat it," which presumably excludes New York City, where Trillin lives, and San Francisco, and he admits to letting months and even years go by between mouthfuls of succulent smoked pork shoulder. It is as though Columbus, having discovered cocoa beans, refused to enjoy the odd cup of steaming hot cocoa when he returned to Spain, saying, "For me, hot cocoa is something you drink where the tradition is to drink it." (In historical fact, Columbus didn't recognize those cocoa beans for what they could become, apart from their use as currency, and, as he called them "almonds," may not even have brought them back to Spain. But you get the idea.)

You might say that the universe of barbecue appreciation is divided into two galaxies or camps, the contextualists and the gastronomists. Contextualists cannot lose themselves in a plate of barbecue unless they're sitting in a roadside shack somewhere in the South. Gastronomists evaluate food on the microscopic level. If two plates of barbecue are molecularly identical, then eating them in different parts of the world will yield identical pleasure. Location should matter no more than the color of the carpeting at two competing restaurants.

I sit squarely in the gastronomist camp (and not only because we get to eat much more and more often), and I am counting the days until my spanking new pit will arrive. But I am nowhere near as Stalinist and dogmatic as the context junkies, the folklorists. I care about carpeting almost as much as they do. One Sunday in Oxford, Mississippi, after a gathering of the Southern Foodways Alliance, the great Lolis Elie asked me if I had time for a barbecue sandwich on the drive back to the Memphis Airport. (Lolis's *Smokestack Lightning* is one of my three favorite barbecue books. Robb Walsh's *Legends of Texas Barbecue*, and the book you are about to read are the other two.) One of Lolis's heroes, the late Mr. J. C. Hardaway, though getting on in years, was cooking at the Big S Grill in Memphis. I cancelled my flight to New York City and found with great difficulty the Big S Grill in a tumbledown house next to the railroad tracks. There, alone in the tiny kitchen, was Mr. Hardaway. He gave me a tour of his equipment (a small, ancient restaurant stove and in the back yard a rusted old black grill), and though Mr. Hardaway was nearly toothless and spoke with an accent unfamiliar to me, I gathered that he violated every rule of smoking a pork shoulder, starting it on the outdoor grill next to an excessively hot fire, then wrapping the meat in aluminum foil and putting it into the oven, and later, portion by portion, crisping it in a black cast-iron skillet on the stovetop. Judged by any objective standard, my sandwich was very, very good. Whether I would still remember it as the *best pulled pork sandwich I've ever eaten* if I had encountered it at a slick New York restaurant, I cannot say.

Mike loves the competition circuit. "I just enjoy being around people," he writes, "and I like to smell the smoke." He expresses great pride in his acolytes Michael Romano and Kenny Callahan from the New York City restaurant Blue Smoke for taking to competition "like a pig takes to Oreos." For him, barbecue is a way of life, a memory of home and family. But it is also a sport, a business, and an obsession.

Mike and some of his friends on the barbecue circuit joke about their frequent divorces. One pitmaster warns that unless you get your wife involved from the start, you will lose her, as he did. At the same time, these men all talk nostalgically, wistfully about the deep spirit of camaraderie they feel with each other. This is male camaraderie, of course. No, you shouldn't find an innuendo here, an insinuation or oblique hint, a salacious allusion. It's really something else. One of Mike's barbecue friends recalls his own late wife's insight: "She thought a lot of these men were little lost boys who didn't have an opportunity to have a real life. There are a lot of solitary men in this barbecue business."

Maybe so. But aren't all great artists solitary types? The rest of us can only be grateful that these artists sacrificed themselves to create neither paintings nor string quartets, but delicately smoked shoulders and ribs of pork, and gentle briskets of beef—the elements of America's longest and noblest oral tradition.

—JEFFREY STEINGARTEN

BAR
BE
CUE

=
FOOD
+
FAMILY
+
LOVE

My daddy, Leon Mills, smoking some meat over his homemade pit in our backyard. Mama Faye is convinced he invented barbecue.

The strongest memory from my childhood is waking up to the smell of smoke. I'd lie in my bed with my eyes still closed, take a deep breath, and smile. That aroma meant that we'd be having a good supper that night.

Back in the 1940s, long before barbecue was fashionable, my daddy, Leon Mills, had already been up since before daylight, burning wood and making his own charcoal. His pits were nothing more than two holes he had dug in the ground. One hole was simply for prepping the wood. He placed a rock on each side of the second hole and laid a grate over the top. He'd burn down the wood in the first pit and shovel the red-hot coals into the other, where the meat would be smoking.

We weren't the only ones who enjoyed the end results. Daddy was the neighborhood pit boss. Lots of neighbors would bring their meat over, and he'd smoke it for them. He'd cook chickens, pork shoulders, whole hogs—basically any cut or kind of meat they could find or afford at the time. By day, Daddy traveled from town to town, selling cigarettes, candy, and soap products for the Colgate-Palmolive-Peet company. By night, he was the life of the party, tending his pits and holding court with the neighbors and friends who gathered around. I'm fairly sure some liquor was involved, too, but my mama, Faye, would never admit to that. As soon as Daddy's car pulled into the driveway, a steady stream of neighbors would come over to see about their meat.

My mama truly believed that Daddy actually invented barbecue. Never mind that cavemen were smoking meat thousands of years ago. "That wasn't real barbecue," she was always quick to point out, somewhat indignantly. "They may have used smoke, but they had no grates and no sauce."

Sadly, Daddy died when I was nine, so the early years of my parents' marriage became family lore. Mama's often-repeated stories usually centered on barbecue: "We loved to camp as a family," Mama would tell me. "Your daddy would dig a pit and throw a grate over it. Pretty soon the smell of smoke would be filling the air, and the entire campground would show up for the party."

The memory of the scent of that smoked pork has never left me. To this day, when I drive down the road with my window rolled down and I catch a whiff of that sweet, smoky aroma, it takes me right back to childhood. I refer to it now as "essence of pork." And I feel real fortunate to experience that smell every day.

Daddy made a barbecue sauce that family and friends raved about, and his dream was to bottle the sauce and open a barbecue joint. That plan never came to fruition. When he died at the age of 42, he left Mama Faye, as she was called by her grandchildren and half of Murphysboro, with three children to raise: Jeanette (age 11), me (9), and Mary Pat (who was just 15 months old). My older brothers, Landess and Bob, were already grown and married.

Mama Faye was always proud of her heritage and her upbringing; in fact, she considered herself to be somewhat of a blue blood. She came from a well-respected, upper-middle-class family in Southeast Missouri. Her father, Jim Landess, was a landowner, a merchant, and in later years a mortician who owned several funeral homes. She liked to remind us that she went to business college, which was somewhat unusual for a young woman in the 1920s. Mama and Daddy got married in 1925 and lived a fairly comfortable, middle-class life.

When Daddy died, Mama Faye had a little insurance money and three young children still at home. Her beginnings might not have been meager, but she knew how to adapt when she was faced with tough times. She always lived with dignity. I've heard many people ask her how she got through those years after Daddy died, and her answer was always the same. "I viewed it as a challenge," she'd say. Mama Faye took what life handed her and made both a life and a living. Her resourcefulness and resolve made a lasting impression on me.

She had to work very hard. The Fuller Brush company took her on as the first Fuller Brush woman in the country. She also clerked for my brother Landess in his wholesale notions and drug sundries business. And she made gallon after gallon of our locally famous family barbecue sauce to sell to friends and neighbors. She was clever, too. With what little money she had, Mama bought a piece of property with a two-story home and a small, separate garage. She converted the garage into a tiny house. We lived in the "cottage," as we called it, and converted the larger house into two apartments to rent out.

Leon and Faye Mills, circa 1948, posing in front of one of Daddy's smoldering pits

In 1941, when I was five months old, we moved from Cape Girardeau, Missouri, to Murphysboro, Illinois. In the 1940s and '50s, Murphysboro was the small bustling county seat of Jackson County, and it had a variety of small industries, including shoe and glove factories. In Murphysboro, as in most places, there were a whole lot more poor people than there were wealthy people. I guess you could say we were nearer the poor end of the spectrum, but I'm not sure I ever realized that. We always had a warm, tidy home and clean clothes. They may not have been new clothes, but they were clean. And we always ate well, since all of my family are outstanding cooks.

The menus at our family gatherings usually revolved around smoked meats—even in the dead of winter. We didn't call it "comfort" food back then, but that's exactly what it was. After Daddy died, my brothers and I took over smoking the meat. At just nine years old, helping build the fire and tend the pit made me feel grown-up and close to my dad. I suspect my brothers felt the same way, although we never talked about it. Our family suppers and picnics were a way to be together. At a very young age, it became apparent to me that barbecue—and all of the preparation and family time that go along with it—equaled a powerful combination of family, friends, traditions, and, most important, love.

Those memories have stayed with me my entire life. Every time I fire up the pit and cook a meal, whether for family, friends, or guests in my restaurants, I get that same heart-warming feeling that comes from nurturing and connecting with people.

Just after a swim: my sister Jeanette, sister-in-law Joyce Mills holding my baby sister, Mary Pat, and Daddy with his arm around me

Smoked Pork Butt

Daddy used to smoke all kinds of meat. Chicken, pork chops, pork shoulder, and pork butt were our favorites. A smoked pork butt is easy to manage and feeds a crowd. You can serve it sliced or pulled, and a 4- to 6-pound pork butt will take approximately 4 to 5 hours to cook. Don't plan on doing anything else during that time: You're going to need to babysit the meat. Fix yourself a cooler with an ample supply of beer, and get something to read or someone to talk to.

I prefer smoking bone-in pork butts. The bone adds more flavor to the meat, and it allows the heat to follow the bone deep into the meat, making the center of the meat cook faster and more evenly.

You'll need apple wood chips, a disposable aluminum pan, a meat thermometer, a mop (see Chapter 8), and a chimney starter or another small covered grill or bucket to keep additional hot coals.

1 pork butt (4 to 6 pounds), bone-in or boneless

Magic Dust (see page 67)

MOPPING SAUCE

1 quart apple cider vinegar

1 cup water

3 tablespoons vegetable oil

2 tablespoons kosher salt, finely ground

2 tablespoons chili powder

2 tablespoons sugar

1 tablespoon cayenne

Apple City Barbecue Sauce (see page 54)

FOR SERVING

Hamburger buns

Mike's Crunchy Cole Slaw (see page 14)

Tenderize the meat by puncturing it with a fork. Season the pork butt liberally with the Magic Dust. Tenderize again. Return to the refrigerator overnight or for at least 4 hours.

Start a fire following the instructions on page 298.

Soak the apple chips in water for half an hour. Drain.

Remove the grate from the grill and place a disposable aluminum pan in the bottom of the grill or smoker. Arrange the medium-hot coals around the pan. If you're using a grill, it must have a lid. Spread out the wet wood chips on the coals. Replace the rack, close the grill, and check the temperature. It should be between 225 and 250 degrees. If the temperature is too high, open the lid to allow some heat to escape. You'll want to maintain this temperature inside the grill or smoker the entire time you're cooking. Open the lid to lower the temperature, or add more hot coals to raise the temperature as necessary.

Place the meat on the grate, fat side up, and close the lid.

Make the mopping sauce: Place the vinegar, water, oil, salt, chili powder, sugar, and cayenne in a large saucepan. Bring to a boil, stirring constantly to thoroughly dissolve all ingredients. Set aside.

After about 1 to 1½ hours, begin mopping the meat with the sauce every 30 to 45 minutes, or as necessary. Reposition the meat as necessary to avoid hot spots. Turn periodically to keep the meat from burning.

After about 4 hours, insert a meat thermometer into the center of the meat, not near the bone, and check the internal temperature. You'll want to reach an internal temperature of 165 to 170 degrees. This will take approximately 4 to 5 hours. The higher the internal temperature, the more tender the meat will be. If you want to pull the pork, the final internal temp should be 180 to 185 degrees. A temperature of 165 to 170 degrees is better for slicing the meat.

About 15 to 20 minutes before you remove the meat from the pit, mop the butt with the barbecue sauce.

To serve, slice or pull the pork from the bone, removing any big chunks of fat as you go. Shred the meat by hand, using two forks, or coarsely chop with a meat cleaver. You can also slice the pork butt. Eat the meat alone, or pile the shredded or chopped pork on a bun and top with a sprinkle of Magic Dust, some barbecue sauce, and a spoonful of the cole slaw.

Save leftovers for use in the other recipes in the book that call for barbecue. They'll keep in the freezer for about 1 month.

MAKES 15 TO 18 GOOD-SIZED SANDWICHES

ama Faye believed that all children ought to learn to keep a clean house and a neat yard and to cook good, wholesome food. She also recommended we consider those skills when picking a husband or wife. I heeded her advice and chose two wives who were good cooks. Both of those wives are long gone from my life, though, so there must've been some other lesson about choosing that I missed.

Our entire family gets involved in making our favorite Southern-style side dishes for family gatherings. We've experimented with a lot of recipes over the years, and we're always trying new things. But there are certain dishes that make it to every event, and each relative has a few specialties that are always requested. Here are some of our tried-and-true favorites.

Daddy and me in 1942

My Sister Jeanette's Deviled Eggs

Chilled, creamy deviled eggs are truly a treat. The key to great deviled eggs is making sure the filling is very smooth with no lumps. You can do this by using the back of a fork to work out all of the lumps, by mixing the filling in a food processor, or by pushing the yolks through a fine sieve until they're powdered.

Deviled eggs are the first food to disappear at any picnic, family reunion, or church supper. My sister Jeanette and my sister-in-law Judy make the best ones in our family. They're easy to prepare but time-consuming. If you have a family like ours, roughly 40 at any given gathering, that means the person assigned to bring deviled eggs has to make at least 80 so everyone can have 2. Of course, it never fails that at least one person sneaks more than his share.

Deviled eggs are best shown off on china or glass deviled egg plates. All the women in my family have ceramic ones especially made by Mama Faye.

12 large eggs

1½ tablespoons sugar

½ teaspoon kosher salt, finely ground

¼ teaspoon ground black pepper

1 tablespoon apple cider vinegar

1 tablespoon prepared yellow mustard

1 dash hot sauce (such as Tabasco)

¼ cup Miracle Whip salad dressing

1 tablespoon Magic Dust (see page 67) or paprika

Sweet pickles or olives for garnish (optional)

Place the eggs in a large stainless steel saucepan and cover the eggs completely with cold water. Bring the water to a rapid boil and boil for 2 minutes. Cover the pan and remove it from the heat. Allow to stand for 25 to 30 minutes. Drain and cover the eggs with cold water. If you cook your eggs this way, you won't get that dark circle you'll sometimes see around the egg yolk.

Carefully remove the peel from the eggs and slice in half lengthwise. Remove the yolk and place in a medium bowl. Add the sugar, salt, pepper, vinegar, mustard, and hot sauce. Mix with a fork or an electric mixer (or blend in a food processor). Gradually add the Miracle Whip, blending well until smooth and creamy; add a few more tablespoons of Miracle Whip if needed and make sure there are no lumps.

Using a teaspoon, fill the egg whites with the yolk mixture and sprinkle the top with Magic Dust or paprika. Garnish with a sliver of sweet pickle or a slice of olive. Place on a deviled egg plate and refrigerate until chilled.

SERVES 12

John Hudgins's Skillet Cornbread

Jeanette's husband, John Hudgins, comes from a long line of good cooks, too, and he's pretty particular about his food. We welcomed his family recipes—and him, too—right into our own. We especially like his skillet cornbread, and to this day he makes it when we're having barbecue, chili, or the ham and beans we always eat on New Year's Day.

4 tablespoons olive oil	1 teaspoon kosher salt, finely ground
1 ¼ cups coarsely ground yellow cornmeal	1 cup buttermilk or plain yogurt
¾ cup all-purpose flour	1 large egg
2 tablespoons sugar	
2 tablespoons baking powder	

Preheat the oven to 400 degrees.

Coat a 9-inch cast-iron skillet with 1 tablespoon olive oil.

Mix the cornmeal, flour, sugar, baking powder, and salt together in a medium bowl. In a separate bowl, whisk together the buttermilk or yogurt, egg, and the remaining 3 tablespoons olive oil. Combine the wet and dry ingredients until just mixed.

Place the oiled skillet in the oven for about 3 minutes or until hot. Don't allow the oil to smoke or burn. Remove the skillet from the oven and pour in the batter. Bake for 20 to 25 minutes or until a toothpick inserted in the center comes out clean.

Cut into slices and serve with plenty of butter.

SERVES 4 TO 6

VARIATIONS: You can add ½ to 1 cup fried pork cracklings, ½ cup crumbled crisp-fried bacon, ¼ cup drained jalapeño peppers, or ½ cup grated Parmesan or cheddar cheese to the batter.

We often serve sorghum butter with our cornbread for a real taste treat. To make sorghum butter, mix together 4 tablespoons of softened butter and 4 tablespoons of sorghum. Drizzle on warm cornbread.

Bob Mills's Wilted Lettuce

For years, wilted lettuce was my brother Bob's contribution to any family picnic. Sadly, Bob passed in 2003, but he lives on with this salad. Bob used oak leaf and black-seeded Simpson varieties of lettuce straight from his garden and poured a hot, tart bacon-and-vinegar dressing on them just before serving. You can make this dish year-round with lettuces from the supermarket, but it will be its very best if you, too, are lucky enough to be able to harvest fresh greens from your own backyard right before you make it. Lettuce from a farmers' market is a close second.

The trick to making good wilted lettuce: Right after you pour on the dressing, give the lettuce a quick toss and then cover the salad bowl with a plate so it can steam for a minute and wilt the lettuce leaves. I've been known to make a meal out of a giant bowl of this tangy salad.

6 to 8 slices bacon, cut into 2-inch pieces	½ teaspoon celery seed (optional)
½ cup sugar	2 bunches leafy lettuce (Bibb, oak leaf, black-seeded Simpson, red leaf, or field greens), washed and dried
1 cup apple cider vinegar	
⅓ cup water	½ large red onion, very thinly sliced
1 teaspoon kosher salt, finely ground	2 large eggs, hard-cooked, peeled, and sliced
½ teaspoon coarsely ground black pepper	2 or 3 radishes, thinly sliced
¼ teaspoon granulated garlic or 1 clove garlic, minced (optional)	

Brown the bacon in a medium skillet over medium heat until crisp. Remove the bacon from the skillet and set on paper towels to drain. Leave the drippings in the skillet.

Add the sugar, vinegar, water, salt, and pepper—and the garlic and celery seed, if you wish—to the drippings in the skillet. Stir and simmer over medium heat until well blended.

Tear the lettuce leaves into pieces. Don't cut the lettuce, as this causes the edges to darken. Place the lettuce in a large salad bowl and crumble in the bacon. Scatter the thinly sliced red onion rings on top of the lettuce. Pour the hot dressing over the lettuce, toss, and cover the bowl with a plate for a few minutes. Remove the plate, add the eggs and radishes, and toss the salad again. Serve immediately.

SERVES 4 TO 6

VARIATION: You may also add the green tops of scallions to the lettuce.

Mama Faye's Home-Style Potato Salad

There are dozens of different potato salads, but I'm still partial to Mama Faye's. This recipe includes one of our family secrets: pickle juice, straight from the jar. Pickle juice is an easy way to add a little extra zip and flavor. I use the juice from dill pickles, but the liquid from sweet pickles will work, too. Another secret to good potato salad is making it well in advance. The flavors need time to blend, and the salad should be well chilled before you serve it.

3 pounds small red-skinned potatoes, scrubbed

1 cup finely chopped onion

6 large eggs, hard-cooked, peeled, and chopped

1 tablespoon celery seed

2 cups mayonnaise (she used Hellmann's)

1 cup sour cream

2 teaspoons kosher salt, finely ground

1 teaspoon ground white pepper

1 teaspoon dry mustard

1 teaspoon sugar

2 tablespoons pickle juice or pickle relish

Paprika or 2 tablespoons finely chopped scallion tops or chives (optional)

Place the potatoes in a large pot of salted water. Bring to a boil and cook for about 40 minutes or until tender. Test the potatoes by sliding the blade of a sharp knife into a potato. When it slides out clean, the potatoes are done. Don't overcook them or you'll end up with mashed potato salad.

Pour the potatoes into a large colander to drain. When the potatoes are cool enough to handle, cut them into 1/2-inch dice, leaving the skin on. Place in a large bowl and toss the still-warm potatoes with the onion, eggs, and celery seed.

In a separate large bowl, make a dressing by mixing the mayonnaise, sour cream, salt, pepper, mustard, sugar, and pickle juice or pickle relish.

Pour the dressing over the potatoes and mix gently with your clean hands until the potatoes are well coated. Sprinkle the top lightly with paprika or garnish with the scallions or chives, if desired.

Refrigerate 4 to 6 hours before serving.

SERVES 8 TO 12

Mama Faye and me celebrating her 95th birthday in April 1998

Mike's Crunchy Cole Slaw

There are two kinds of cole slaw: creamy and vinegar-based, and both have their merits. At 17th Street Bar & Grill, we use a simple vinegar-based recipe that's always been very popular. When I was young, I looked forward to the annual chicken-and-dumpling dinner held by the Shriners club in Ava, Illinois. Their bright yellow cole slaw was the best I ever tasted. It was an all-you-can-eat event, and I always tried to get my money's worth. I finally figured out how they got that yellow color—they boiled the marinade ingredients with turmeric before pouring it over the cabbage. My slaw has that same great flavor; it's just not yellow.

1 head green cabbage, finely chopped (about 5 cups; see Note on opposite page)

1/4 head red cabbage, finely chopped (about 1 cup; see Note on opposite page)

1 carrot, shredded

DRESSING

2 cups apple cider vinegar

2 cups sugar

1 1/2 tablespoons canola oil or other mild vegetable oil

1/2 cup chopped onion

1/4 cup chopped green bell pepper

3/4 teaspoon celery seed

1/2 teaspoon kosher salt, finely ground

1/2 teaspoon ground black pepper

1/4 teaspoon chopped garlic

Toss the green cabbage, red cabbage, and carrot in a large bowl.

Make the dressing: In another large bowl, mix the dressing ingredients, stirring until the sugar is dissolved.

Use a measuring cup to transfer half of the dressing to the bowl with the cabbage and carrots. Toss with clean hands or a large spatula to combine. Keep adding dressing, 1/4 cup at a time, but be careful not to drench the cabbage. You may not need all of the dressing; any leftovers can be saved, in a covered container in the refrigerator, for up to 5 days and used as a dressing for salad or a marinade for vegetables.

SERVES 10 TO 12

NOTE: Today you can buy your cabbage already shredded. However, chopping it fresh does make a difference in the texture of the slaw. You can use a food processor or a grater to shred the cabbage, but I prefer to prep it by hand. Using a very large, sharp knife, slice the cabbage into ¼-inch slices. Lay the slices flat and finely chop them—first sideways, then up and down.

VARIATION: For a creamy version, mix 1 cup of the dressing with 1 cup of Hellmann's mayonnaise or Miracle Whip salad dressing.

Chow

It's traditional in some parts of the country to serve cole slaw on a barbecue sandwich. Pile chopped or pulled meat on the bun and top the meat with a spoonful of cole slaw, which is also known as "chow" down South. The tart, crunchy cabbage goes perfectly with the smoky flavor of the meat.

Freezer Cole Slaw

Did you know you can freeze cole slaw? Simply boil the dressing and pour it over the cabbage. Let it cool and transfer to large freezer bags or covered plastic containers and freeze. Keeps up to one month.

Marinated Vegetables

Prepare a medley of vegetables—red and green bell pepper slices, carrot sticks, sliced red onion, fresh mushrooms, large black or green olives, broccoli florets, cauliflower florets, or any other vegetables you like. Pour the dressing from Mike's Crunchy Cole Slaw over the vegetables and let marinate for three to four hours or overnight. Serve these vegetables as a side dish or salad alternative.

Judy Mills's From-Scratch Baked Beans

Judy Mills is married to my oldest brother, Landess. She always brings from-scratch baked beans to family picnics, and they are good. She goes on and on about how much better they are because she started with dried beans. When I started working on this book, I asked Landess to watch her make the beans and write out the recipe for me. He laughed and laughed. "She doesn't make those beans from scratch," he said, dashing the story I'd known to be true for more than 50 years.

Judy wrote out the recipe for me, and I've altered it, using dried beans. The color will be lighter since you're starting with white beans, and the texture will be just a little firmer. You'll have to start a day early to soak the beans, but I guarantee the end result will be worth the extra time and effort.

1 pound dried great northern beans	1 cup firmly packed brown sugar
4 to 6 slices bacon	1 tablespoon Worcestershire sauce
½ cup chopped onion	1 tablespoon yellow mustard (I like French's)
1 clove garlic, minced	1 teaspoon chili powder
2 cups ketchup (I like Hunt's)	2 tablespoons Magic Dust (see page 67)
½ cup molasses	

Place the beans in a large saucepan and cover with salted water by 2 to 3 inches. Soak the beans overnight.

The next day, drain and rinse the beans. Return the beans to the saucepan and cover with fresh water by about 4 inches. Bring to a boil, then lower the heat and simmer for 1 to 1½ hours or until the beans are tender but not bursting open.

While the beans are cooking, mix the ketchup, molasses, brown sugar, Worcestershire sauce, mustard, chili powder, and Magic Dust together in a large bowl.

Preheat the oven to 350 degrees.

Cook the bacon in a large skillet over medium heat until crisp. Remove the bacon with a slotted spoon. Drain the bacon on paper towels, crumble it, and set aside. Add the onion and garlic to the bacon drippings and cook over medium heat, stirring constantly, for 2 minutes. The onion should still be a little crunchy.

Drain the beans, reserving 2 cups of the bean water. Pour the beans and bean water into the bowl with the sauce. Add the bacon and onion and stir to combine well. Pour into a 13 × 9-inch baking dish and bake for 1 hour or until bubbly. Will keep, refrigerated, for up to 1 week.

SERVES 8 TO 10

Chris Mills's Chocolate Texas Sheet Cake

Bringing your first attempt at cooking to a family party is a rite of passage in our family. You have to develop a thick skin because your food will be critiqued. When he was a teenager, my son, Chris, proudly made up one of these Texas sheet cakes for Christmas Eve, but he forgot the buttermilk—a key ingredient. The cake didn't rise, and it was as hard as a rock. He knew something was wrong when people ate only one bite, but he's never forgotten that his Uncle Bob tried to make him feel better by eating two large pieces. Chris has mastered the recipe now, and this spongy, chocolatey cake disappears quick. This is a perfect dessert for a large gathering.

CAKE

- 2 cups all-purpose flour
- 2 cups sugar
- 1 cup water
- 8 tablespoons (1 stick) unsalted butter
- ½ cup solid vegetable shortening
- 3½ tablespoons cocoa powder
- ½ cup buttermilk (or ½ cup milk mixed with 2 tablespoons white vinegar)
- 2 large eggs
- 1 teaspoon baking soda
- 1 teaspoon vanilla extract

ICING

- 8 tablespoons (1 stick) unsalted butter
- ⅓ cup milk
- 3½ tablespoons cocoa powder
- 1 box (1 pound) confectioners' sugar
- ¾ cup walnuts, chopped (optional)

Preheat the oven to 400 degrees. Grease an 18 × 12-inch sheet pan.

Make the cake: Combine the flour and sugar in a large bowl.

Combine the water, butter, shortening, and cocoa in a small saucepan and bring to a boil. Pour over the flour mixture.

In a small bowl, whisk the buttermilk, eggs, baking soda, and vanilla together. Add to the batter and blend thoroughly by hand. Don't use an electric mixer. Pour into the baking sheet and bake for 20 minutes or until a cake tester comes out clean.

When the cake has baked for about 15 minutes, make the icing: Combine the butter, milk, and cocoa in a large saucepan. Bring to a boil and stir in the confectioners' sugar and walnuts, if desired. Pour the icing over the cake as soon as it is removed from the oven and spread it out evenly. Let the cake cool completely on a rack before serving from the pan.

SERVES 20

My Sister Jeanette's Fruit Cobbler

When I was a child, most people had a garden, and friends and neighbors shared the harvest. Going to orchards and farms and picking fruit and berries in season was, and still is, a popular seasonal activity. Stopping by with a just-picked bushel of apples or peaches or a right-off-the-bush bucket of fresh berries is a neighborly thing to do in Southern Illinois.

Mama Faye believed that we all needed to learn to make jelly and pickles, can tomatoes, and put up corn, berries, and fruit for the winter. She also thought it was important to learn to make a good pie crust, and Jeanette learned her lesson well. Her crust is so flaky and tender you can eat it all by itself. To this day, she always has a batch of frozen pie crust dough in her freezer just in case a neighbor stops by with some fruit.

Jeanette is the pie and cobbler expert in our family, and she brings a fresh fruit cobbler to all family events. Here are a few of her secrets: First of all, she uses very fresh, local fruit, and she doesn't skimp—she piles it high in the baking dish. She also puts half of the sugar-and-flour mixture on the bottom of the crust before she adds the fruit; then the rest of the mixture goes on top. She often combines several fruits in her cobbler—the very best combination, in my opinion, is peaches, blackberries, and blueberries.

CRUST

- 10 tablespoons ice water
- 2 tablespoons apple cider vinegar
- 2 large eggs
- 4 cups all-purpose flour
- 1 teaspoon baking powder
- 1 teaspoon kosher salt, finely ground
- 2 cups solid vegetable shortening, well chilled

FILLING

- 2 cups sugar
- 6 tablespoons all-purpose flour
- ½ teaspoon ground cinnamon (optional)
- 4 large peaches, peeled and sliced
- 4 cups blueberries
- 4 cups blackberries
- 3 tablespoons unsalted butter, cut into small pieces

FOR SERVING

Ice cream

Make the crust: Whisk the ice water, vinegar, and eggs together in a small bowl. Set aside.

Combine the flour, baking powder, and salt in a medium bowl. Mix well. Use a pastry blender or two knives to cut in the shortening until the mixture resembles coarse meal. (Or use a food processor and pulse to cut in the shortening. Do not overprocess.)

Sprinkle the flour mixture with the liquid mixture, 1 tablespoon at a time. Toss with a fork after each addition of liquid until the flour is all moistened and the dough cleans the side of the bowl. Shape the dough into a ball. (If you're using a food processor, pour the liquid, 1 tablespoon at a time, down the feed tube and pulse to combine after each tablespoon of liquid is added. Stop when the dough forms a ball.)

Divide the dough into one-third and two-third portions. Shape each portion into a flat disk and wrap in plastic wrap. Refrigerate for at least 1 hour.

Preheat the oven to 350 degrees.

Make the filling: Combine the sugar, flour, and cinnamon (if desired) in a small bowl.

Roll out the larger portion of dough on a floured surface to a thickness of $\frac{1}{4}$ inch and large enough to fit a 13 × 9-inch baking dish. Lift carefully into the baking dish. Sprinkle half of the sugar-and-flour mixture on the bottom of the dough. Add the fruit. Sprinkle the other half of the mixture on top of the fruit. Dot with the butter.

Roll out the remaining dough; carefully lift and place on top of the fruit. Crimp the edges together to form a seal. With a knife blade, slit the top of the dough in several places.

Bake for 45 minutes to 1 hour. The pastry should be browned and the fruit bubbling. Serve warm, with a scoop of ice cream.

SERVES 10 TO 12

Jeanette and me, circa 1948

ost people are a little confused when they learn Southern Illinois is a barbecue mecca. Illinois is a pretty long state, though, and Murphysboro, located near the tip, is farther south than Louisville, Kentucky. Murphysboro is 365 miles southwest of Chicago and only 200 miles north of Memphis, so many claim it's below the Mason-Dixon line. The area is also known as Little Egypt. There are several theories as to this nickname, the most popular being that in the early 1800s, when the northern counties of Illinois were suffering from a drought, crops were flourishing in Southern Illinois. People from the north came to buy corn and wheat, just as they flocked to Egypt in biblical times. Cairo, Illinois—as in Cairo, Egypt, but pronounced KAY-row, like the syrup—is another Southern Illinois town known for barbecue. Southern Illinois is beautiful country, characterized by hundreds of family farms and dozens of small towns. The Mississippi River runs the length of one side of the state, and the nearest big city is St. Louis, about 100 miles away.

I grew up in the 1950s, before the civil rights movement. Whites and blacks coexisted peacefully in Murphysboro, but as in many small rural communities, most blacks lived near one another in one part of town. In Murphysboro, this part of town was known as "the Flats." On the edge of the Flats was a barbecue joint called Whitt's. For years, Whitt's had only curb service and takeout. You'd just pull up outside and honk, and somebody would come out to take your order. Later on, Mr. Whitt added a few tables and booths. From this humble shack, Mr. Whitt graciously served, to blacks and whites and the rich and the poor, the most delicious barbecue I've ever tasted.

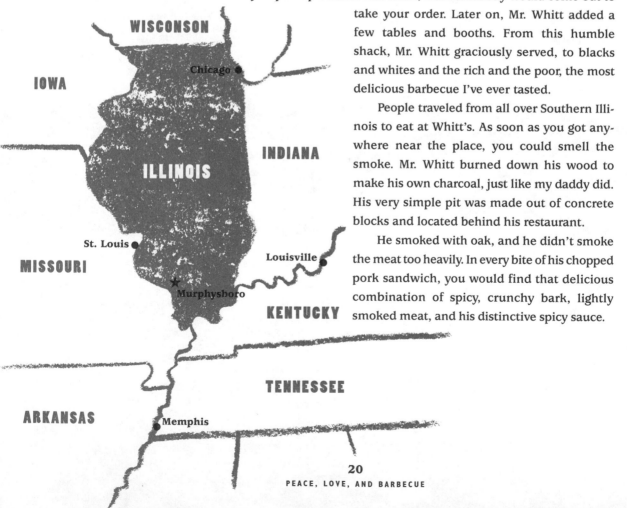

People traveled from all over Southern Illinois to eat at Whitt's. As soon as you got anywhere near the place, you could smell the smoke. Mr. Whitt burned down his wood to make his own charcoal, just like my daddy did. His very simple pit was made out of concrete blocks and located behind his restaurant.

He smoked with oak, and he didn't smoke the meat too heavily. In every bite of his chopped pork sandwich, you would find that delicious combination of spicy, crunchy bark, lightly smoked meat, and his distinctive spicy sauce.

Whitt's Corner drew customers from all over Southern Illinois for years.

Mr. Whitt was known for three things: his barbecue sauce, his french fries, and his salad. Whitt's sauce had a bite. People would order "easy on the sauce" or "no sauce" if they couldn't handle the heat. It was semiclear with a reddish tint, and you could see flecks of pepper and spices suspended in it. It was tangy, not at all sweet, and heavy on the vinegar.

His french fries were made from scratch and cut more on the thin side. He fried them in the same grease he used to fry fish, so they had a unique taste. Mr. Whitt made his french fries in a deep pot on the stove. Like everything he served, they were cooked to order. This wasn't like McDonald's; there was no fancy fryer with a timer. The fries just floated loose in the oil. Mr. Whitt kept one eye on them, and when he felt they were ready, he scooped them out with a slotted spoon right onto the plate—no draining—and then he'd give them a quick shake of salt. They were greasy and they were good. And the orders were enormous and made for sharing.

The green salad was very simple: just iceberg lettuce served in a plastic soup bowl. The tart dressing is what made it special. It was nothing more than a mixture of vinegar, oil, water, and sugar, but it was refreshing and delicious.

In high school, if you really liked a girl, taking her for barbecue at Whitt's was about the best way to show it. If you were really flush, you would each get a sandwich and a salad and share a plate of those fries, too. And you'd each get a drink, either a Coke, a root beer, or an orange, grape, or cream soda, icy cold, in a small glass bottle with a straw. A sandwich was $1.25, and the whole meal, for two, would set you back about five dollars.

I couldn't afford to pay to eat there, so I'd trade fish and game I caught for barbecue. I was about 14 at the time, and one or two buddies and I would ride our bicycles down to Whitt's, our baskets filled with fish, rabbit, squirrel, duck, or geese. Sometimes I'd bring in two geese, and Mr. Whitt would smoke one for me to take home. Pound for pound, Mr. Whitt got the better end of the deal. But I certainly never complained. I savored every bite of his barbecue.

Mr. Whitt's son, Lionel, was my age. Sometimes, if Lionel was working, I'd go in empty-handed. He'd make me a barbecue, and he'd add a lot of hot sauce. If I could handle the heat, he wouldn't charge me. But if I couldn't eat it, I had to pay. I learned to tolerate it.

I'll never forget sitting at the counter and watching Mr. Whitt prepare those sandwiches. Mr. Whitt did everything the old-fashioned way, which fascinated me. He stored the smoked meat in a large roasting pan that sat inside an old household oven with the door always open, and he had a pot of sauce warming on the stove. Each sandwich was prepared to order. First he'd lay out two slices of white bread. Then he'd reach into the oven with his knife and slice off a hunk of meat and set it on the counter. He'd dip his mop—a stick with a rag tied to one end—in the sauce and dab it on the hunk of meat and on one slice of the bread. Then he'd give the meat four or five quick chops. He'd pile the meat on one slice of bread, top it with the other slice, and wrap the sandwich up in waxed paper. You could eat it outside or take it home.

Mr. Whitt took a liking to me as a youngster, and he taught me a number of his tricks of the trade. I'd sit at the counter and we'd chew the fat a little. I'd watch his every move. Little did he (or I) know I'd one day be a pitmaster, carrying on the legacy of barbecue in Murphysboro.

One of Mr. Whitt's secrets was freezing his meat. He felt it was always better after thawing, that the smoke flavor had mellowed out. That sounds pretty simple, but freezing and thawing all that meat took time and space. His small, bare-bones building had no professional equipment; he used three circa 1950 household refrigerator/freezer units to keep his meats and a standard household range with an oven to heat them.

Consistency was another of his secrets. Mr. Whitt served barbecue for 40 years, and over the years I ate there, nothing changed—it was always the same smell, same sauce, same white bread, same waxed paper. There's something comforting about that. Lionel tried to make a go of it when his dad passed away. Sadly, the magic seemed to die with Mr. Whitt.

I always thought that some day I'd locate his widow and offer to buy the recipe for that barbecue sauce. I wasn't at all happy when I learned someone sweet-talked her out of it before I could track her down. Today if you want some of Whitt's authentic sauce, you can get it at the Lodge in the Giant City State Park, just south of Carbondale, Illinois. Tell my friend Richard Kelly that Mike sent you. And see if he won't give up some of the ingredients.

Close to Mr. Whitt's Barbecue Sauce

Over the years, I've tried to replicate Mr. Whitt's sauce, and I came up with a pretty close rendition. This recipe tastes almost exactly like the sauce I remember.

This is a finishing sauce to use at the table. It is exceptionally good on pulled pork sandwiches, ribs, and chicken.

1 cup light corn syrup (such as Karo)	1½ teaspoons pectin (such as Sure-Jell)
1 cup white vinegar	2 teaspoons prepared yellow mustard
½ cup water	1 teaspoon noniodized salt
3 tablespoons ketchup (I like Hunt's)	1½ teaspoons ground black pepper
2 tablespoons sugar	1½ teaspoons red pepper flakes
1 tablespoon unsulfured molasses	½ teaspoon paprika

Blend all the ingredients together in a medium saucepan over medium-low heat. Slowly bring to a boil, stirring continually. Remove from the heat, cool, and transfer to airtight containers. Store in the refrigerator.

MAKES ABOUT 3 CUPS

You could say cooking with smoke is in my genes, but I entered the professional barbecue arena in a roundabout way. You see, since 1962 I had been a dental technician, supplying area dentists with prosthetics, which is a fancy name for dentures and bridges. My brother-in-law John was a dentist, and he owned a small building in downtown Murphysboro. His dental practice was on the first floor, and my lab was on the second. In the 1960s and '70s, two or three times a week during the season, we'd get up before dawn and hunt and fish whatever was in season—deer, pheasant, quail, rabbit, squirrel, and geese; crappy, bluegill, bass, and catfish. These hunting trips weren't all-day affairs. We'd leave about five in the morning, and we had to be back and have the game cleaned and packaged by eight o'clock, when our workdays started. We'd use the boil-out tanks in the dental lab to scald the game, and we'd clean the fish at the back end of the parking lot. We always had a big roll of butcher paper in the lab, and we'd clear off a table and wrap up the meat, label it with a china marker, and store it in the big deep freezer I kept along one wall. The health department would've had a field day.

I was always cooking at work. In my laboratory, right alongside vats of wax and boiling dentures, I'd have big pots of soup, balanced precariously over Bunsen burners. I also had a hot plate, and I cooked all kinds of meals—chicken and dumplings, navy beans with squirrel (or rabbit or ham), soups, beef and noodles, Italian beef—anything that could be made in a pot. Sometimes I'd fry up some fish and hush puppies. Family and friends regularly stopped by during lunch hour. Even the UPS man timed his deliveries around lunchtime. Chili was one of my signature lunches.

I won a number of chili cook-offs before I ever entered a barbecue contest. Today, chili is a popular menu item at all of my restaurants. Once a woman from Cincinnati called one of the Las Vegas restaurants and ordered 30 gallons of chili for the following week. "I'm coming out there for a chili cook-off, and I'm going to use your chili. It's the best I ever had," she said, very matter-of-factly. She wasn't embarrassed at all and didn't even try to hide what she was doing. "I just want to make sure you'll have enough on the day I need it." She called back later to let us know that she won second place.

A scene from the good life:
the Mills family fishing at Lake
Murphysboro, circa 1945

BARBECUE = FOOD + FAMILY + LOVE

Mike's Steamy, Spicy Chili

Chili has always been a Mills family favorite. When the first cool breeze of fall was in the air, Mama Faye would start making chili, and it seemed as though a pot simmered on the stove all winter. I loved coming home after school to the delicious smell of browned hamburger, onions, garlic, chili powder, and tomato. I polished off bowl after bowl, along with a sleeve of saltine crackers and slices of yellow American cheese.

2 pounds ground beef (chuck or hamburger)

1 cup chopped onion

¼ cup chili powder

1 tablespoon beef baste or 2 beef bouillon cubes

½ tablespoon granulated garlic or 1 clove garlic, minced

½ tablespoon kosher salt, finely ground

½ tablespoon ground cumin

½ teaspoon ground black pepper

½ to ¾ tablespoon sugar

1 bottle (12 ounces) V-8 juice

1 can (46 ounces) tomato juice

1 can (24 ounces) diced tomatoes

¼ cup pickle juice

1 can (15 ounces) kidney beans, drained and rinsed

3 cans (15½ ounces each) hot chili beans (such as Bush's or Brooks)

Brown the ground beef and onion in a large pot over medium heat. Do not drain. Stir in the chili powder, beef baste or bouillon cubes, garlic, salt, cumin, pepper, and sugar. Add the V-8 juice, tomato juice, diced tomatoes, and pickle juice. Simmer for 20 minutes. Stir in the kidney beans and chili beans and simmer until hot.

Freezes well.

SERVES 10

Smoked Stuffed Green Peppers on the Pit

We ate stuffed green peppers at least once a week for years when I was growing up. They were, and still are, economical, easy, and delicious—especially when you can pick the green peppers right out of your own garden. Cooking them on the pit instead of in the oven elevates the taste to a whole new level.

1 pound ground beef (chuck or hamburger)	6 green bell peppers, tops cut off and peppers seeded
½ medium onion, diced	½ cup bread crumbs
1 teaspoon Magic Dust (see page 67)	2 cups ketchup (I use Hunt's)
1½ cups cooked white rice	½ cup packed brown sugar
1 can (15 ounces) diced tomatoes, drained	

Brown the beef and onion in a medium skillet over medium heat. Stir in the **Magic Dust** while you're cooking. Remove from the heat and pour the meat into a sieve to drain the grease. Transfer the meat to a medium bowl and stir in the rice and tomatoes. Arrange the green peppers upright in a baking dish. Spoon the hamburger mixture into the peppers and top with the bread crumbs.

Smoke on the pit for 1½ hours at 210 degrees.

Meanwhile, combine the ketchup and brown sugar in a small saucepan and cook over medium heat until the sugar dissolves and the sauce is warm. Spoon the sauce over the peppers during the last 10 minutes of smoking.

SERVES 6

17th Street Bar & Grill

Back in 1985, I bought a local bar and grill known for its beverages but also for its hamburgers and barbecue. I slowly started adding the homey, comforting dishes my family and friends loved—including smoked meats and ribs one or two days a week as a special. I called my place 17th Street Bar & Grill, and before long it became better known as an eatery than a place to drink. I still worked in the dental laboratory full-time during the day, but I got to 17th Street about six every morning to open up. I'd come back again and spend all evening, visiting tables and holding court at one end of the bar. 17th Street is a down-home joint and pretty nondescript. The one thing that makes a statement, and everyone remarks on this, is the bar. It's about 25 feet long and made of solid oak; it came out of a speakeasy in Chicago. The surface is wavy and worn, marked by years of use. My favorite bar stool is at the very end, by the door, where I can talk to guests as they come and go.

In 1988, a group of friends and I decided that starting a barbecue contest in Murphysboro would be a good thing for the city, both economically and socially. We figured the contest would draw hundreds of out-of-town barbecuers, judges, and aficionados to the area. We traveled around and visited other cook-offs, but we ran that first Murphysboro Barbecue Cook-Off without ever having competed ourselves. We saw how much fun those barbecue teams were having, though, so in 1989 we formed our own team, "Apple City Barbecue," playing off of our town's CB radio handle and the area's abundant apple orchards.

Apples take them to world fame

By P. Wiseman

Recorded throughout the history of man's culinary skills, is the combination of the roast hog served with an apple in its mouth. The tradition of carrying a suckling pig in on a giant platter surrounded with fruit and a red apple in its mouth can be traced to the times of the Roman empire.

Now the combination of apples and pork has taken the local Murphysboro Apple City Barbecue team to the number one spot in the world championships of barbecue fame, placing them in the annals of history for years to come.

They left Murphysboro a week ago in a convoy of a packed truck, trailer and van, and arrived in rain-soaked Memphis. After months of careful plotting and planning the team had hoped to at least leave there and come back home with a second or third place in ribs, the category they cooked in.

They came home first in ribs, and first in the overall championship, beating out 174 other teams for the title, many from foreign countries. And, for the record, it was only the second time ribs won in the history of _____ championship. Ribs won

They set up their display area to resemble a village cafe from the French province of Normandy, since this year's theme was honoring France.

On Wednesday night Memphis had strong winds which helped dry up the Tom Lee Park where the cookoff was held. The Apple City team started early Thursday morning setting up their booth and making sure it was ready and visiting with other teams. They had to make sure the Red-Eyed Water Hogs from Blythesville, Arkansas were doing ok, because the Red-Eyes (formerly Terra Water Hogs) won in Murphysboro last year and were sponsored by the Murphy championships. Then there was a lot of visiting and recruiting of other teams, trying to lure them to Murphy for this fall's contest.

Cooking really didn't get underway until Saturday at 5:30 a.m. They cooked 60 sides of ribs total during the contest.

The team was a little tired because they had stayed up until 2:30 a.m. the night before waiting to greet the chartered bus of fellow Murphyities coming down to cheer them on. The bus, due in at Memphis at 11:30 p.m. had a long delay. The team was _____ until they learned the bus _____ 50 miles outside _____

Don Stanton, (world trophy) Mike Mills, Mary _____ row - Pat Burke, Dale Pierson _____ present for the

Yanks reign supreme in South's backyard

By Deborah D. Douglas
The Commercial Appeal

What's the world coming to when the Yankees beat us at our own game?

A team from Illinois won the grand prize in the 13th annual Memphis in May World Championship Barbecue Cooking Contest in Tom Lee Park Saturday night.

"This is the first time in the contest's history that we've had a winner from the North," said Deanie Parker, Memphis in May marketing director.

About 150 teams from 20 states and five foreign countries participated in the soggy three-day event that ended Saturday night. Rain fell during much of the contest, diminishing crowds if not dampening the enthusiasm of the participants.

MIM officials expect to have attendance figures for the event later this week.

This year's grand prize winners, who will take home a trophy and a $5,000 cash prize, were the Apple City Barbeque team from Murphysboro, Ill. The team from the southwestern Illinois town of 10,000 also won the competition in the ribs category.

"In no way did we expect to be grand champions," said Mike Mills, an Apple City team member. This was the team's first time in the Memphis contest.

Besides ribs, winners also were named in the pork shoulder and whole hog categories, as well as the "anything but" competition for other kinds of meat. Prizes also were awarded for showmanship and hog calling.

The Pepto Porkers of Memphis won first place in the shoulder category and Willingham's Riv-

Local and regional barbecue competitions have three categories: ribs, shoulder, and whole hog. A team can enter and win in any or all of those categories. Apple City Barbecue first competed in Caruthersville, Missouri, and we won third place in ribs in that contest. We got lots of compliments and a real nice trophy, and we made lots of new friends. We got bit hard by the barbecue bug. In our fifth contest, in Demopolis, Alabama, we placed first in ribs and second in shoulder, and we won overall grand champion of that contest. You have to be the grand champion of a local or regional sanctioned cook-off to cook at Memphis in May—the Super Bowl of Swine—and that win qualified us to compete in May of 1990.

Having cooked in only six contests, we weren't sure we were ready to compete with the big boys just yet. But we talked it over as a team and came to a decision: If we could place in at least the top 25 of the 180 teams, then that wouldn't be too embarrassing.

You can imagine our surprise when we won World Champion in ribs and overall Grand World Champion of the entire contest. Then we learned that we had received the first perfect score ever in the history of Memphis in May. The next morning, the headline of the Memphis *Commercial Appeal* read, "Yanks Reign Supreme in South's Backyard: What's the world coming to when the Yankees beat us at our own game?"

The barbecue gods did not smile on us at Memphis in May in 1991. But in 1992, we came back with a vengeance and again won World Champion in ribs as well as overall Grand World Champion. That year, a man, wearing blue jeans and the only navy blazer I have ever seen at a cook-off, strolled into our booth and introduced himself as Jeffrey Steingarten, food writer for *Vogue* magazine. He asked me some questions for an article he was writing. No man I know reads *Vogue*, especially not in Murphysboro, and I really wasn't sure how a story about barbecue would fit into a highfalutin fashion magazine. But I would soon find out.

The winning Apple City team, waving for the camera
as we were filmed for Good Morning America.
Front row: Mary Ann Stanton, Aliene Burke, me, and Susie Mills
Back row: Jim Tweedy, Jean Tweedy, Dale Pierson, Donny
Stanton, Rob Williams, Mary Jane Williams, and Pat Burke

Jeffrey had heard the buzz about Apple City Barbecue in the judging tent, and he wanted to sample some ribs. Finals judging was starting at that time, so I didn't have any ribs to share with him. He came back four or five times that afternoon, and each time I had to turn him away because the ribs would get eaten after each set of finals judges finished. Bright and early the next Monday morning, he called me at 17th Street. He had judged three teams, thought each had outstanding entries, and couldn't believe that none of them placed in the contest. He wanted to taste our ribs to see just what was so special. So I sent him some ribs, and the next morning he called. "Now I understand," he said. In the September 1992 *Vogue,* he wrote about Memphis in May and said some real nice things about the ribs we shipped him that day. That was our first national recognition, and it changed our lives forever.

I found out that the article had been printed when a man called at about 6:30 one morning in August of 1992, and said, "My name is George Wendt, and I'm reading about you in *Vogue.* I want to know how I can get some of your ribs."

He read the whole thing to me over the phone. Well, every August we run a concession stand at the Du Quoin State Fair, and I needed all the ribs I had cooked at that time to sell at the fair. So I had to tell this man, "I don't have any to send you right now, but if you'll call me back in a couple of days, I'll see what I can do."

It was obvious I had no clue who this man was, so George gave me a helpful hint: "Let me give you my name again. This is George Wendt, and I'm Norm on *Cheers.*"

"No shit," I laughed, putting a face to the name.

"Yeah, no shit," he said.

George took to calling back every day, at all hours. One night he called at about eleven-thirty, and the bartender handed me the phone and said, "Please talk to this guy; he's driving us bananas!"

"Okay, George," I told him. "I'm cooking tomorrow, and I'll send you out some ribs."

A few days later, again late at night, the phone rang and it was George. There was lots of noise in the background, and he said, "I'm having a party and we're eating your ribs and they are fabulous!" And then everyone at the party screamed out how much they liked them.

George handed the phone to Rick Beren, one of the *Cheers* directors. He introduced himself and asked, "How can *I* get some of those ribs?" I'm still sending him ribs to this day.

Because of the *Vogue* article, people from all over the country were calling to order ribs. At the time, I still only smoked at 17th Street one or two days a week. Even after our Grand World Championships, we were not yet totally devoted to barbecue—and certainly not the mail-order business. Bartenders and waitresses took calls and scribbled down the information on napkins. Every time someone called with an order, we'd have to scramble and smoke up some ribs and then try to find a box to send them out in.

As we began to get more and more publicity for our competition success, people from all over the four-state region began to flock to 17th Street to see what all the fuss was about. In 1994, after we retired from the circuit, I revamped the menu again and started serving barbecue every day.

We've become a destination; most people in serious search of good barbecue will make the trip to find us. My buddy and barbecue aficionado, Jim Tabb, used to be a captain for TWA. He would routinely schedule his flights so that he had enough time to rent a car in St. Louis, drive two hours to Murphysboro to eat, then drive two hours back to St. Louis to continue on his way. On any given night, well over half the people in the restaurant are from out of town.

Carlene Phelps, editor of the *National Barbecue News,* once said to me, "I think 17th Street and Big Bob Gibson are the two finest barbecue restaurants in America." That is some high praise from someone who's eaten a lot of barbecue. I'm proud to be mentioned in the same breath as Big Bob Gibson, and I relayed the compliment to the owner, Don McLemore. He puffed right up, too. "Man," he said. "Now that's a compliment."

In my humble opinion, 17th Street serves real good food, and our award-winning Apple City Barbecue ribs rarely disappoint. One of my favorite compliments came from Jim Tabb, who wrote in the *National Barbecue News*: "Leaving the Kansas City Royal for North Carolina, my wife and I headed south out of St. Louis along the Mississippi River to Murphysboro. . . . In K.C., I judged ribs, and I'll have to say that the ribs I ate at 17th Street would've held their own or beat the six teams I judged at my table. It's difficult for a restaurant to serve competition barbecue; maybe these had just come out of the cooker and had just the right time and temp on them; at any rate, my wife almost ate a whole slab." These ribs are a labor of love.

The bar at 17th Street came out of a speakeasy in Chicago.

Apple City Barbecue
Grand World Champion Ribs

People are mystified about how to cook ribs properly. I'm going to walk you through every step of the way as though you're using a basic charcoal grill. Obviously if you have different or more high-tech equipment, you'll need to modify these procedures. If you're setting up your backyard charcoal grill for indirect cooking, you'll want to use a disposable aluminum pan to capture the grease as the fat renders while cooking. Some people add water to this pan to add moisture to the cooking environment, as discussed on page 306.

Let me caution you right up front to mop the ribs with sauce no more than 10 minutes before you take them off the grill. Saucing the meat too early is a mistake many people make when smoking or grilling. Virtually all barbecue sauce contains sugar, and your meat will have a burned crust around the outside if you use sauce too soon in the process.

Ribs are readily available in most grocery stores. A full description of the four types of ribs (spareribs, St. Louis–style, baby back, and loin back) is in Chapter 8; read it before you start this recipe. When selecting ribs, try not to buy ones that weigh less than 2 pounds. A true baby back rib weighs about 1 1/4 to 1 1/2 pounds; they are very fragile and dry out quickly. This recipe calls for a meatier rib. A loin back rib is preferable; they're easier to cook, less fragile, and have more meat.

Be sure to read the smoking secrets and tips in Chapter 8 before you fire up your smoker.

Once you start smoking ribs, you can't leave the smoker unattended for any more than about 20 minutes. You'll need to continually check that the temperature in the grill remains between 200 and 210 degrees at all times. If it gets too hot, open the lid and allow some of the heat to escape. Coals that appear to be glowing red will cause a hot spot. Don't cook the ribs directly over the hot spot; move the ribs to a different, cooler part of the grill. If the temperature dips below 200 degrees, move the ribs to a hot spot for a while. If the temperature gets too low, add some more coals.

You'll need about 4 cups of apple wood chips to be authentic; you can use hickory, pecan, sweet maple, or cherry, but the ribs won't taste as sweet. You'll also need a chimney starter or another small covered grill or bucket to keep extra hot coals.

4 racks of ribs (about 2 pounds each)	4 cups apple juice in a spray bottle
Magic Dust (see page 67)	Apple City Barbecue Sauce (see page 54)

Follow the instructions on page 302 to prep your ribs.

Sprinkle the ribs liberally with Magic Dust, coating both sides. Put them in a shallow pan or on a cookie sheet and cover them with clear plastic wrap or a lid. Refrigerate them until you're ready to use them. I recommend letting them marinate for at least an hour. At the restaurant, we dust the ribs up to a day in advance.

Start your fire per the instructions on page 298.

Soak the apple wood chips in water for half an hour. Drain.

Remove the grate and arrange the medium-hot coals in a grill or smoker. If you are using a grill, it must have a lid. Set an aluminum pan next to the coals as a drip pan. Spread out the wet wood chips on the coals. Replace the rack, close the grill, and check the temperature. It should be between 200 and 210 degrees. If the temperature is too high, open the lid to allow some heat to escape.

Notice that the meat on a rack of ribs is on the top. The bottom, where you removed the membrane, is called the "bone side." Once the temperature is steady, place the ribs on the rack, bone side down. You want to cook them bone side down as much as possible. Turning them dries out the meat. If necessary, you can cut the racks of ribs in half to comfortably fit your grill.

Cover and smoke the ribs for about 6 hours or until the ribs are done and tender. Do all your homework and read the characteristics of a perfectly cooked rib in Chapter 8.

You'll want to check the ribs every 20 minutes or so. Examine them to see if the surface of the meat looks dry or moist. Ribs "sweat" about three times during the smoking process. The pores of the meat open, and this allows moisture to escape. This is when the seasoning from the dry rub and the smoke itself are reabsorbed into the meat. When they're sweating, mop or mist them with some apple juice and sprinkle them with a little more Magic Dust. Opening the lid will lower the temperature; add more coals and wood chips as needed to maintain the temperature.

About 10 minutes before you remove the ribs from the pit, mop them with the sauce. When you take them off the pit, mop again with sauce and sprinkle some more Magic Dust on them. Serve immediately.

SERVES 4, OR YOU CAN CUT THE RACKS IN HALF TO SERVE 8

"Life is too short for a half-rack."
—MIKE MILLS

nterestingly, barbecue has been served at this establishment (under various names) for more than 85 years. It was opened as Ellis Tavern during World War I—unescorted women were not permitted and no woman could sit at the bar. The place was known as Al & Ray's when I bought it in 1985, and although it was better known as a place to drink, its hamburgers and barbecue were also popular. There was a drive-through window so church people and families could pick up food to enjoy at home.

We've expanded once, and the place now seats 96, but it's a wonder we're still standing. I've had 13 robberies, three fires, and not too long ago a woman accidentally hit the gas while in reverse instead of drive, and she came barreling through the drive-through window and into a walk-in cooler. But other than that, we're holding up pretty well.

My worst catastrophe was back in 1997. I owned an old wooden railroad depot across the street. My plan was to make a barbecue museum out of it someday. But in the meantime, I had an enormous freezer in there, and one day I got a really good deal on some pork. I borrowed $29,000 to make the buy, and I filled up that freezer. A few days later, some local kids came by and set the depot on fire. That old, dry wooden building was blazing hot and covered in flames very quickly, and that very, very cold freezer blew up under the pressure, sending hundreds of sides of frozen ribs and hundreds of frozen pork butts flying into the air, just like a popcorn popper. The firemen were trying to hold their hoses with one hand while shielding their heads with the other. They were running all around the building, dodging and ducking the pork "missiles."

Of course, all this meat thawed and began rotting the next day. Pat Burke, my friend and Apple City Barbecue Team cocaptain, has a bulldozer. He came over and helped me clean up the property, and the town dump opened on a Sunday so we could properly dispose of the meat. Most people can't help but laugh when they hear this story. It's only moderately funny to me. I'm not quite over it yet.

Across the street from the restaurant, I've renovated an old brick warehouse where my brother Landess used to have a store. We have three real nice function rooms there, a catering kitchen, a USDA kitchen, and our corporate offices. People come from all over the area to have weddings, reunions, meetings, and all sorts of parties.

In 2004 we opened a 17th Street restaurant in Marion, Illinois, about 20 miles from Murphysboro. This newly constructed restaurant seats about 250 people, and while the atmosphere is more upscale than in Murphysboro, it still has the personal feel of a family-owned establishment. The building sits right off Interstate 57, the highway that runs from Chicago to Memphis, so we get lots of travelers, too.

Here are recipes for some of our most-loved menu items. You'll notice many of our recipes call for Magic Dust, our special dry rub blend. I'll talk more about dry rubs and their use in Chapter 2.

17th Street's Tangy Pit Beans

These baked beans are the most popular side dish in my restaurants. Their sweet, smoky flavor is an excellent complement to barbecue. We also use them to make Barbecue Nachos (see page 39), one of our best-selling appetizers.

Each type of bean has a different texture, so the different varieties used in this recipe make these beans a bit more interesting. At 17th Street and my Memphis Championship Barbecue restaurants, I use pulled pork instead of bacon to achieve a bit of a smoky taste. You could also bake them with a few already-smoked ribs. Just take four or five already-smoked rib bones, with the meat still attached, and lay them across the top of the beans. Or you can push them down into the beans so they're covered. After baking, pull the meat off the bones, discard the bones, and gently mix the meat back into the beans.

2 tablespoons prepared yellow mustard (I like French's)

3 cups ketchup (I like Hunt's)

1 cup diced onion

1 green or red bell pepper, seeded and diced

1½ cups packed brown sugar

½ cup sorghum or honey

1 to 1½ tablespoons Magic Dust (see page 67)

1 large can (28 ounces) pork and beans (such as Campbell's or Showboat)

1 can (19 ounces) large red kidney beans, drained and rinsed

1 can (15½ ounces) chili beans (such as Bush's Chili Starter)

1 can (15½ ounces) large butter beans, drained and rinsed

1 can (15½ ounces) of a fifth bean, your choice, drained and rinsed

4 or 5 slices bacon or a few cooked ribs or some barbecued pulled pork

Preheat the oven to 350 degrees.

Mix the mustard, ketchup, onion, bell pepper, brown sugar, sorghum or honey, and Magic Dust together in a large bowl. Be sure to work out all of the lumps of brown sugar. Add the beans, stirring gently with clean hands or a big spoon, just enough to evenly distribute the mixture. Overmixing will cause the skins of the beans to burst and the consistency will become mushy, more like refried beans, which you don't want.

Pour into a 13 × 9-inch baking dish. Lay the bacon strips, ribs, or pork across the top. Cover with aluminum foil and bake for 45 minutes. Remove the foil and bake for an additional 15 minutes or until bubbly.

These beans reheat well. Will keep in the refrigerator for up to 1 week. May also be frozen for up to 1 month.

SERVES 10 TO 15

BARBECUE = FOOD + FAMILY + LOVE

17th Street Barbecue Salad

Even the heartiest of meat eaters need something green every now and then. This simple fresh salad fits the bill. Many restaurants have a barbecue salad, but I've never tasted one quite like this. One of the secrets is to lightly toss the lettuce with the dressing before adding the other ingredients so that all of the lettuce is coated.

I head iceberg or romaine lettuce, torn into bite-size pieces

1½ cups grated Parmesan cheese

I cup croutons, preferably homemade (see opposite page)

½ cup creamy Italian salad dressing or 17th Street Special All-Purpose Dressing (see below)

2 large eggs, hard-cooked, peeled, and chopped

I medium tomato, diced

½ cup shredded cheddar cheese

2 cups shredded barbecued pork, chicken, or beef brisket

I red onion, sliced into rings

Magic Dust (see page 67)

Put the lettuce into a large bowl with I cup Parmesan cheese and the croutons. Pour on the salad dressing and gently toss until all the lettuce is coated. Add more dressing if necessary, but don't drench the lettuce. Add the eggs, tomato, and cheddar cheese and toss again. Divide among 8 salad plates and top each with ¼ cup shredded meat. Top each salad with a few onion rings and sprinkle with Magic Dust and a little more Parmesan cheese.

SERVES 8

17th Street Special All-Purpose Dressing

They call this dressing "pickle sauce" in the 17th Street kitchen because we serve it as a dip for the fried dill pickles and some other appetizers. It's not listed on the menu, but some regulars ask for it on their salads. As my daughter Amy says, it's really good.

½ cup Apple City Barbecue Sauce (see page 54)

½ cup ranch-style dressing

Mix the sauce and dressing well in a medium bowl and store in the refrigerator in a covered bottle or container.

MAKES I CUP

17th Street Homemade Croutons

These crunchy, lightly seasoned croutons add a special touch to our salads. Some customers buy them by the bagful. Once you've tried these, you'll never use a store-bought version again.

1 cup vegetable oil

2 teaspoons dried Italian seasoning

1½ teaspoons lemon pepper

1½ teaspoons ground black pepper

¼ teaspoon dried oregano, crumbled

10 slices (½ loaf) white bread, cut into 1-inch squares

Garlic salt

Preheat the oven to 350 degrees.

Combine the oil, Italian seasoning, lemon pepper, black pepper, and oregano in a squeeze bottle and shake well.

Place the bread on a baking sheet and season lightly with garlic salt. Squeeze on some of the seasoned oil and toss. Bake for 15 to 20 minutes or until the bread starts to turn lightly golden. Remove from the oven, toss the bread, and squeeze on a little more oil if you think it needs it. Return to the oven and continue baking until the croutons are dry and golden. Let cool completely and store in an airtight container. The croutons can be frozen. Any leftover seasoned oil can be kept around for your next batch of croutons.

MAKES ABOUT 7 CUPS

17th Street Barbecue Nachos

This is a 17th Street original and that's no lie. I've eaten hundreds of plates of nachos at all kinds of restaurants, so I decided to try making some nachos with a barbecue flair. These are great at a party, so this recipe will serve a crowd.

1 bag (13½ ounces) tortilla chips

2 cups pulled pork, chicken, or beef, heated

2 cups baked beans, heated

2 cups chili, heated

1½ to 2 cups shredded cheddar cheese

1 container (8 ounces) sour cream

Magic Dust (see page 67)

Spread the tortilla chips on a large tray or serving platter. Spoon on even layers of the following ingredients in this order: meat, baked beans, chili, and cheese. Finish with a layer of sour cream and sprinkle lightly with Magic Dust.

SERVES A CROWD

Becky's Deep-Dish Barbecue Pie

I'm fortunate to work with some excellent home cooks at the 17th Street kitchen. Becky Streuter and Dana Ritcheson are among the best I know. They are my right and left arms. These two ladies are always trying to fatten me up, and as you can see by my more recent pictures, they are succeeding. Becky created this unique dish, and it's one of our customers' favorite specials. Pulled pork and baked beans are layered and topped with a cornbread crust—a perfect way to use leftovers. Toss together a crisp green salad and you've got a perfect meal.

This dish is best prepared with 17th Street Tangy Pit Beans. We made several test batches using other baked bean recipes, and they just don't quite measure up. Trust us.

2 pounds chopped or pulled pork

6 tablespoons barbecue sauce, preferably Apple City Barbecue Sauce (see page 54)

2 teaspoons Magic Dust (see page 67)

4 cups 17th Street Tangy Pit Beans (see page 37)

2 cans (15 ounces each) diced tomatoes

1 can (4 ounces) chopped jalapeño peppers

2 tablespoons instant tapioca

2 boxes Jiffy corn muffin mix (or use your favorite) and the ingredients listed on the box

2 tablespoons sugar

Preheat the oven to 350 degrees.

Lightly coat a 13 × 9-inch baking dish with nonstick cooking spray. Spread the pulled pork in an even layer on the bottom of the dish. Drizzle the barbecue sauce over the pork and sprinkle with the Magic Dust.

Stir the beans together with the diced tomatoes and their juice, the jalapeños, and the tapioca. Spread the bean mixture evenly over the meat.

Stir the cornbread mix and sugar together in a large bowl. Prepare the cornbread according to the instructions on the box. Spread the cornbread batter in an even layer on top of the baked beans.

Bake for 35 to 40 minutes or until a toothpick inserted into the cornbread comes out clean. Let set for 5 minutes or so and cut into slices to serve.

SERVES 8 TO 10

Dana's Apple Dumplings

Dana knows how dearly I love dessert, and she conceived this apple dumpling for me, taking advantage of the plentiful apple harvest season. The tangy and sweet orange-scented sauce clings to these little pockets of goodness, each filled with a surprise bite of cream cheese.

1 package puff pastry (found in the frozen foods section), thawed

2 large Granny Smith apples, peeled, cored, and quartered

1 package (8 ounces) cream cheese, cut into 8 pieces

1 cup orange juice

⅔ cup plus 2 tablespoons sugar

8 tablespoons (1 stick) butter

1 teaspoon ground cinnamon

Preheat the oven to 350 degrees. Grease a 13 × 9-inch baking dish.

With a sharp knife, cut the pastry sheets into 5-inch squares. Place each apple wedge on a piece of puff pastry and top with a piece of cream cheese. Wrap the puff pastry sheet around the apple and cream cheese and crimp the edges to seal. Place the apple dumplings in the baking dish.

Bring the orange juice, ⅔ cup sugar, and butter to a boil in a small saucepan. Pour over the dumplings.

Sift together the remaining 2 tablespoons sugar and the cinnamon and sprinkle over the dumplings. Bake for 25 minutes or until golden and bubbly.

SERVES 8

Michael Romano and Kenny Callaghan pose with me under the marquee at the opening of my third Las Vegas location.

Memphis Championship Barbecue

When I retired from the barbecue circuit in 1994, I went back to Murphysboro and got back to work. I was still running Murphysboro Dental Laboratory, but I was spending more and more time at 17th Street because I had finally converted the menu over to barbecue. I was completely surprised to get a call from a businessman in Las Vegas who wanted me to help him open some barbecue restaurants out there. "You have the know-how, and I have the money," he told me.

The idea was intriguing, but I really didn't think it would come to fruition. I flew out to meet with him, though, and he convinced me to give it a go. At first I wondered if going to the big city was somehow selling out. Would people view this differently or think it wasn't authentic or pure? Ultimately, I decided that it was the best way for me to share my barbecue with thousands of other people. Only the diehards make the trek to Southern Illinois, but hundreds of thousands of people visit Las Vegas. Those who know about barbecue find their way directly to our door.

We thought the name "Memphis Championship Barbecue" would be good for this venture. "Memphis" denotes the style of barbecue that I cook, and I felt I could claim it was championship quality. Little did I know at that time that there were other restaurants with similar names. And I never dreamed that I would become well-known enough to have to explain why I have two different operations with two entirely different names. Explaining all of this is a little confusing, but it's a good problem to have.

As of 2004, we have four restaurants in the greater Las Vegas area, and they are going like gangbusters. Our customer base is mainly local, although in Las Vegas most everyone's a transplant, and our locations are in neighborhoods, not on the Strip. Of course, we do get some tourists who simply love barbecue. Even though we have levels of management and computerized systems, it feels like a locally owned neighborhood joint. "High tech, low touch," we like to say. Customers feel at home here; we have lots of regulars, and everyone knows their names.

There are some differences in taste out in Las Vegas. First of all, those people are into healthy. They think fat is bad. Visible fat on a sandwich will get it sent right back to the kitchen. I've just about given up trying to explain that fat is flavor.

These customers come from many different barbecue traditions, too. Almost everyone from North Carolina asks to see the barbecue before they order it. They want to see that the meat is chopped and pulled, not "Crockpot barbecue" that's some kind of meat mixed with sauce. Brisket was always on the menu, but the Texas crowd forced me to put beef ribs on the menu in Vegas. Now they're popular in Southern Illinois as well.

These people out here are also squeamish about the pictures on the walls. I had some real artistic photographs of pigs being prepared for barbecue. In fact, I've used some of them in this book. Some were dead pigs, just lying there. Others were of the pigs getting their feet sawed off. People complained so about those pictures that I finally took them down. They must never have been around a farm when they were growing up. And how do they think those animals get from the farm to their plates, anyway?

Despite these differences, people are people, and most people love good barbecue. The menu is basically the same as it is in Murphysboro. Here are some of the favorites in Las Vegas.

Fried Green Tomatoes

This distinctly southern side dish goes perfectly with barbecue. Many people in Las Vegas didn't grow up with fried green tomatoes and are amazed at how good they are. Panko, Japanese bread crumbs available in specialty stores, make them lighter and tastier than regular bread crumbs would.

1½ cups panko bread crumbs

1 teaspoon Magic Dust (see page 67)

2 medium green tomatoes, sliced ¼ inch thick (don't use the top slice, with the core in it)

2 large eggs, beaten

Vegetable oil for frying

Combine the bread crumbs and Magic Dust in a small bowl, then pour onto a flat plate. Dip the tomato slices in the beaten eggs and dredge through the bread crumbs. Coat well. Deep-fry or pan-fry for a few minutes on each side until brown. You want to cook only the breading, not the tomato. Serve immediately.

SERVES 4

Fried Dill Pickles

I can't claim to have invented fried dill pickles, but I do claim to be the first to serve them in Southern Illinois and Las Vegas. We serve these with 17th Street Special All-Purpose Dressing as a dipping sauce.

Peanut or vegetable oil for frying

2 cups all-purpose flour

½ cup yellow or white cornmeal

¼ cup Magic Dust (see page 67)

1 teaspoon cayenne

1 teaspoon granulated garlic

1 jar (8 ounces) wafer-cut dill pickles (sometimes called hamburger chips), drained

17th Street Special All-Purpose Dressing (see page 38)

Heat at least 3 inches of oil in a deep saucepan to 325 to 350 degrees.

Stir the flour, cornmeal, Magic Dust, cayenne, and garlic together. Put the pickles in a large bowl, pour the dry mix over them, and toss to coat the pickles well.

Deep-fry the pickles, in batches so you don't crowd them, until the coating is crispy, about 3 to 4 minutes. Don't stir while you're frying. If you take them out too soon, the pickles will be soggy; but you don't want them too crispy or burnt, either. Drain on paper towels.

Serve the salad dressing as a dipping sauce.

SERVES 4 TO 6

Barbecue-Stuffed Baked Potatoes

This is a barbecue twist on an old standard. These stuffed potatoes are a lunchtime bestseller. Add vegetables and you've got all your food groups covered.

4 large baking (russet) potatoes

1 cup barbecue (pulled pork, chicken, or beef), heated

1 cup steamed broccoli, cauliflower, carrots, or other vegetables, heated

Magic Dust (see page 67)

1 cup shredded cheddar cheese

Chives, for garnish

Sour cream (optional)

17th Street Special All-Purpose Dressing (see page 38), optional

Bake the potatoes as you usually would and split them in half lengthwise.

Divide the meat and vegetables among the potatoes, piling them onto each half. Sprinkle with Magic Dust and top with cheddar cheese. Garnish with chives.

Serve with sour cream or dressing on the side, if desired.

SERVES 8 AS A SIDE DISH OR 4 AS A MAIN COURSE

Baked Sweet Potatoes

Every dish on our menu is there because I like it and I think other people will, too. I also like to have items you don't see frequently on other menus. These baked sweet potatoes are one of our most popular side dishes. They're so very simple and so very good.

3 large or 6 small sweet potatoes

Vegetable oil

8 tablespoons (1 stick) butter, softened

1 cup packed brown sugar

¼ teaspoon ground cinnamon

Preheat the oven to 350 degrees.

Rub the skins of the potatoes with vegetable oil to keep the skin soft. Bake for about 45 minutes or until a toothpick or a knife tip will slide in easily.

Combine the butter, brown sugar, and cinnamon in a bowl and work with your fingers or a fork to combine well.

Cut the potatoes in half lengthwise and spoon the brown sugar mixture liberally on each half.

SERVES 6

I Check Out Okay

When Bill Clinton was president, he spoke at Southern Illinois University, and he was on his way to 17th Street for dinner when he got called back to Washington because of an international emergency. His people called and asked if we could meet them at the airport instead. We packed up everything and drove out there. He invited me right onto Air Force One, and that was a thrill.

"How do you know I'm okay to have on board?" I asked. After all, this was an impromptu visit.

"Don't worry," a Secret Service agent told me, "we've already checked you out. You have Top Secret Security Clearance for these few minutes."

Unbeknownst to me, Clinton's advance team had eaten in my restaurant several times in the previous weeks. And one of the Secret Service agents liked the food so much he called back a few months later to mail-order ribs and apple cheesecakes for his wedding rehearsal dinner.

What a Life

Today, after dozens of awards and accolades, I feel I'm the luckiest man in the world. I get to barbecue every day at one of my six barbecue joints, and I am honored to be the barbecue guru and a partner in Blue Smoke, which you'll read more about in Chapter 6. I've served barbecue to the rich, to the poor, to everyone in between, and to people of practically every nationality under the sun. Broadway producers, movie stars, famous musicians, politicians, members of the Secret Service, and even a United States President have eaten my barbecue. In fact, I'm the only pitmaster in the country who has had security clearance to board Air Force One. Meeting famous people has been enjoyable. But the people I want to impress most are those everyday people who come into my restaurants to simply enjoy good food.

One of the greatest rewards of immersing myself in the barbecue world has been meeting people from all over who share my passion for barbecue. Some are competitors, some own barbecue joints, others just flat out love barbecue. You'll get to meet a number of these people in the pages that follow.

As you read this book, don't forget how time and retelling color memories. Simple stories just seem to change and grow. Sometimes people think you're tellin' 'em a fib when all you're really doing is making the story a bit more interesting. I may exaggerate now and then, and I know for sure a lot of my friends and colleagues are outright liars. But these are our stories. And we're sticking to 'em.

Chapter Two

CAN YOU SEE

KEEP A RET.?

et's make some things clear about real barbecue. First of all, real barbecue is not burning weenies on the backyard grill. Real barbecue is about smoke, seasoning, patience, and perseverance—along with a few secrets, of course. And maybe some tall tales and outright lies.

The history and lore surrounding a restaurant develop naturally over the years. But when you put together a barbecue team, you have to come up with some stories right off the bat—something interesting that will set you apart, something the judges will remember. These stories might be true or based on the truth, but it's often hard to tell. The idea is that your story, along with your food, of course, will make you memorable. Our team, Apple City Barbecue, almost always told the truth, but I've heard some whoppers in my days.

If you're fortunate enough to win some trophies, though, people will be more interested in your recipes than your stories. They start asking you about your secrets—everything from the wood you use and the way you prep your meat to the ingredients in the rub and sauce itself.

State Secrets

When *Vogue* food writer Jeffrey Steingarten asked me for some of my classified barbecue secrets, I jokingly told him, "I'll tell you, but then I'll have to shoot you." That's not far from the truth. Barbecuers love to talk to their customers and are usually tickled to death when someone asks how something is made. Often they'll tell you; sometimes they won't.

Barbecuers do hold their secrets close. Even my competition teammates didn't know all of my methods. Since competitive barbecue teams have to have some good stories to tell the contest judges, we used to say that each Apple City team member knew only three spices in our Magic Dust and we each added our spices to the bowl separately. I'll admit that was a lie. In truth, I always blended the Magic Dust and cooked the barbecue sauce at home—and alone. I'll admit that there's just something about being indispensable that appeals to me.

One reason to keep recipes a secret is wanting to serve food that's unique to you. Part of the fun at a barbecue cook-off is knowing that on Friday night, when all of the teams prepare special meals for their friends, you can count on homemade pies at Big Bob Gibson's, Canadian loin back sausage at Apple City Barbecue, and the Perfect Sandwich at Ubon's.

I know that imitation is supposed to be the sincerest form of flattery, but if somebody copies your food, it can be pretty annoying. I know one woman who keeps new recipes to herself for a year or so. She doesn't want to go to someone else's house and see her food served. If you ask her for a recipe, she'll nicely tell you, "I don't give out that recipe just yet." People respect that. But she's getting to where it's harder to do all her prep work alone, so she hired a woman who caters to come and help her. Next thing she knew, that catering woman was serving her special recipes at parties all over town!

> ## Family Secrets
>
> Mama Faye taught each of her five children how to make our secret family barbecue sauce. She was determined to bottle that sauce someday, so she made us promise not to give the recipe to anyone, including our spouses. I never told either of my wives the recipe. Let me tell you, this didn't set too well with either one of them. I have it in my head, so it isn't written down anywhere. It's not as though they could've found it in the recipe box.
>
> My first marriage lasted only seven years, so keeping a secret wasn't too much of a problem, although Wife #1 wasn't amused. Marriage to Wife #2 lasted for only 27 years, so she didn't make the cut either. Now if we'd made it to 30 years, I might've broken down and spilled my guts. But she would've had to change her ways.

How to Be a Good Home Cook

Mama Faye was tickled to death once when someone asked her for the recipe for her Thanksgiving dressing. She sat right down and very carefully wrote it out. It began, "Take as much bread as you think you're going to need for the number of people you think you're going to serve . . ."

That's the way people used to cook. It was all by feel and taste and common sense. They learned by watching their own mothers and grandmothers. And when they went from watching to doing, they developed confidence. Confidence is important. Once you master a recipe, you'll start altering it, adding more of one ingredient and less of another, all according to your own taste. To me, one of the best things about barbecue is how gratifying it is to make your own sauces and dry rubs. Use the recipes we've provided as a starting point, and then experiment until you come up with a flavor that's unique to you—and you'll be on your way to being a good home cook.

Developing recipes was the most difficult part of writing this book. Only the professional chefs had a real recipe written down. Seems most of the rest of us don't cook with recipes. We had to sit down and put measurements to "a handful of cornmeal," "a dash of dry rub," and "a scoop of brown sugar." I have a stack of recipes from all over the country written on paper towels, the backs of menus, and paper bags.

Desiree Robinson of the Cozy Corner in Memphis has a real good point about recipes. "You got your recipe, and you got your tips. The tips are just as important as the recipe. People don't listen to the tips, don't matter what recipe they got."

By tips, Desiree means the techniques or the special things you do that aren't necessarily written down. She's right. Some people are so intent on getting the ingredients that they don't listen to the methods that make all the difference in the outcome. For example, Mama Faye always told me to add a pinch of sugar to vegetables to take away some of the bitterness and tartness. But that's something she would never have written down in a recipe. Another example is me saying not to turn your meat too often when you're smoking it (something you'll find in Chapter 8). It might not be in the recipe, but it's in the book. Good cooks look and listen for tips—even if they can't get actual recipes.

Desiree is teaching her granddaughter to cook, and she told her first thing, "These are family recipes, and they stay in the family. Don't be giving out the family secrets." Desiree has been running Cozy Corner with her son and daughter, Ray Jr. and Val, since her husband, Ray, passed in 2000. "By agreement with my husband, the sauce recipe is still a secret. I mix it up at home on the days we're closed. I'm not ready to pass it on yet. If I get amnesia, it goes with me."

One thing that differentiates barbecue restaurants from other restaurants is the emphasis on home-style cooking. The vast majority of barbecue joints are family affairs, and the way that particular family cooks is what makes each one special. And these are also places where the staff becomes part of the family. At Big Bob Gibson Bar-B-Q in Decatur, Alabama, for example, Betty Knighten and Evelyn Harvel have made the restaurant's much-loved pies five days a week for over 40 years. When I bought 17th Street, it came with Betty Spurgeon, who has made our signature hamburgers for 25 years.

Mama Faye was giving cooking directions until the day she died on Christmas day in 2001, at 98 years old. She lived in an assisted-living facility for the last three years of her life, and the food was not at all to her liking. I had someone deliver lunch from 17th Street to Mama Faye every day, but in an effort to be social, she did eat dinner in the community dining room. When we were going through her effects after she died, we found a survey she had just written out for the cook. She had lots of tips for the kitchen staff. Here were her suggestions.

1. Pancakes, please.
2. Improve on the items you are now cooking.
3. When serving lima beans, put a little extra broth on them.
4. When serving Italian beef sandwiches, always serve some of the liquid or broth to dip them in. Use a little more Italian seasonings. A can of beer improves the taste of meat when you're making this.
5. Don't serve meat or any food that has been overcooked or burned black.
6. Don't swim the cole slaw in too much mayonnaise. Simply coat the cabbage.
7. Use garlic in your seasonings—good for us!
8. When serving spaghetti and sauce, be sure all water has been drained off spaghetti.
9. Use more hamburger meat in the chili and not too many beans. Use tomato juice for liquid. Simmer until thick. No vegetables, please.
10. Be sure you have a good cook.

The Barbecue Kitchen Cupboard

Let me tell you a couple of things about the ingredients required for the recipes in this book. Barbecue joints are about as down home as you can get. Based on tradition and often in rural locations, they use pretty simple ingredients—things you can buy at the local supermarket if you run out. Unless otherwise specified, when a recipe calls for vinegar, it means apple cider vinegar, mustard means cheap and yellow, and ketchup is Hunt's because I think it has the best flavor. I've switched over to kosher salt, and I use two kinds of pepper—finely ground for dry rubs, and coarsely ground for other types of cooking. I buy my spices and herbs in bulk, and they're dried, not fresh. Dried spices lose their flavor in a few months, so make sure you replace your spices frequently, as I do. For best results, always use real butter, not margarine or any type of butter substitute. Life is just too short to use fake butter. Use whole milk, not 2 percent or skim. I never have understood why anyone would bother with skim milk, but that's another subject.

As a general rule, I avoid any recipe that calls for liquid smoke. I can tell right away if a dish contains it; the taste just kind of hangs in my mouth. I just don't understand why anyone would spend the time and effort it takes to make good barbecue and then use liquid smoke on it. The label says it's a "natural" product. You and I both know better than that. There is no substitute for real, authentic smoke flavor, so don't try to fake it.

If a recipe calls for Miracle Whip, don't turn up your nose and use mayonnaise instead. Miracle Whip is a staple in the Midwest and the South, and it gives dishes a very distinct taste. I'm not sure why it gets such a bum rap. Some of my gourmet friends swear they'd never buy it, much less use it. If you're really that concerned about what your friends will think, seems to me you might be running with the wrong crowd.

Later on in the book, you'll hear from executive chef and pitmaster Kenny Callaghan and chef/partner Michael Romano, both of Blue Smoke in New York City. They give their side dishes a more upscale twist at Blue Smoke than you'll find in most barbecue joints, which you'll see by the ingredients they use in their recipes. When Michael and Kenny came to cook in the 17th Street kitchen, they were surprised by the humble nature of our ingredients. They were used to fancier stuff. We made a number of trips to the store for gourmet goods, some of which were simply not available. For example, if you live in Southern Illinois, you'll know that juniper berries are just not to be found. If you need them, however, you can substitute a healthy splash of gin.

As you're making any recipe in this book, feel free to use Dijon mustard, infused vinegars, fresh herbs, fresh ground pepper, and other specialty ingredients to come up with your own unique dishes. After all, a good cook will adapt recipes and add a personal touch.

The Gospel on Sauce

When I bought 17th Street Bar & Grill in 1985, Mama Faye was 82 years old and in excellent health. For several years, she made gallons of our family's barbecue sauce each week, but once the place got going, the amount I needed for the restaurant and for competition quickly got to be overwhelming. I had to cook hundreds of batches myself.

To Mama Faye's dismay, I did alter our recipe ever so slightly. I only added some apple juice and a few different spices, but she never let me forget it. "This isn't the original sauce," she'd tell anyone who'd listen. "Mike *veered* off the recipe."

She was awfully proud, however, when the sauce won the Grand Sauce Award at the Jack Daniel's World Championship International Barbecue Cook-Off in 1992.

Apple City Barbecue Sauce

This award-winning sauce enhances just about any barbecue. Some barbecue sauce is very thick and just sits on top of the meat. This sauce is smooth and on the thin side, and it seeps down into the meat.

1 cup ketchup (I use Hunt's)	¾ teaspoon garlic powder
⅔ cup seasoned rice vinegar	¼ teaspoon ground white pepper
½ cup apple juice or cider	¼ teaspoon cayenne
¼ cup apple cider vinegar	⅓ cup bacon bits, ground in a spice grinder
½ cup packed brown sugar	⅓ cup peeled and grated apple
¼ cup soy sauce or Worcestershire sauce	⅓ cup grated onion
2 teaspoons prepared yellow mustard	2 teaspoons grated green bell pepper

Combine the ketchup, rice vinegar, apple juice or cider, cider vinegar, brown sugar, soy sauce or Worcestershire sauce, mustard, garlic powder, white pepper, cayenne, and bacon bits in a large saucepan. Bring to a boil over medium-high heat. Stir in the apple, onion, and bell pepper. Reduce the heat and simmer, uncovered, 10 to 15 minutes or until it thickens slightly. Stir it often. Allow to cool, then pour into sterilized glass bottles. A glass jar that used to contain mayonnaise or juice works real well. Refrigerate for up to 2 weeks.

MAKES 3 CUPS

VARIATION: To make this sauce a little hotter, add more cayenne pepper to taste, approximately another ¼ to ½ teaspoon. Be careful; a little cayenne goes a long way.

Big Bob Gibson's White Sauce

My friend and colleague Don McLemore and his son-in-law Chris Lilly run Big Bob Gibson Bar-B-Q in Decatur, Alabama. Don's granddaddy started Big Bob's in 1925, and he's famous for having invented the white barbecue sauce they use on chicken and turkey. Sadly, the original recipe isn't much of a secret anymore. His grandfather shared the recipe freely, and several family members and former employees left and started up their own establishments using that recipe. Nobody moved too far away. To this day, white sauce is indigenous to Northern Alabama; I've never seen it anywhere else. Don and Chris graciously share the family's secret white sauce recipe here. You'll read more about these guys in Chapter 3.

1 cup mayonnaise	1/2 teaspoon kosher salt, finely ground
1 cup apple cider vinegar	1/4 teaspoon cayenne
1 tablespoon lemon juice	
1 1/2 tablespoons cracked black pepper	

Combine all the ingredients in a large bowl and mix thoroughly. Place in an airtight container or bottle and refrigerate until you're ready to use. Keeps up to 4 days.

MAKES 1 1/2 CUPS

> "Sauce preferences are partly regional. People in Texas are sort of militantly anti-sauce. They eschew sauce. You don't hear 'em use that word very much, but they're against it. I once met my nephew at Kreuz Market in Lockhart. He lived in Kansas City all his life and then moved to San Antonio. When he got out of the car, I noticed he had a little ice pack on his belt and I asked, 'What's that?' He said, 'A bottle of Gates and a bottle of Bryant's.' He brought his own sauce because he was suspicious of not eating barbecue with sauce."
>
> —Calvin Trillin

Big Bob Gibson's Hickory-Smoked Chicken

Big Bob's chicken is among the best I've ever eaten. The birds are simply seasoned with lots of salt and black pepper and smoked with hickory wood at a temperature higher than I usually suggest. Then they pull 'em off the pit and dunk 'em in a 5-gallon bucket of white sauce, leaving the crispy, smoky skin with a thin coating of the tangy sauce. The flavor is just awesome.

1 whole chicken, cut in half	½ cup vegetable oil
Finely ground kosher salt and ground black pepper	Big Bob Gibson's White Sauce (recipe on page 55)

Wash the chicken and season it liberally with salt and pepper. Smoke over hot coals and hickory wood at 300 to 350 degrees for 3 to 4 hours or until the internal temperature reaches 170 degrees. Halfway through the smoking process, baste the chicken with oil and sprinkle with salt and pepper once more.

After you take the chicken off the pit, immediately place it in the bowl of white sauce, turning the chicken to coat evenly. Place the chicken on a cake rack and allow it to rest for a few minutes prior to serving. Discard any sauce that you've used for coating chicken.

SERVES 2 TO 4

Here's Don McLemore teaching me how to make his world-famous chicken at Big Bob Gibson.

Hybrid Barbecue

Barbecue sauce typically has one of four bases: vinegar, tomato, ketchup, or mustard. Many sauces contain all of these ingredients, but one will be prominent. Tomato-based can mean several different things: tomato paste, puree, sauce, soup, or chili sauce. Of course, chili sauce and ketchup contain other seasonings that add to the flavor of the sauce.

Memphis is known for dry-rubbed ribs. The sauce used to be a vinegar sauce, but I'm noticing more ketchup down there these days. Memphis is also the birthplace of barbecue oddities like barbecue spaghetti and smoked bologna.

The ribs in Kansas City are wet, and the sauce is traditionally sweet and tomato-based—although the sauces from Gates and Arthur Bryant's, two Kansas City shrines, are not very sweet. Due to the proximity to the stockyards, brisket is also popular in Kansas City, and one of the favorites is burnt ends, little end pieces of the brisket that get over-done because they're so thin.

Beef brisket and shoulder clod reign in Texas, as does sausage made in the Czech and German traditions. The sauce situation varies. Some places don't serve it at all; others offer some sort of spicy ketchup-based sauce or perhaps just a bottle of hot sauce.

Alabama has some vinegar and ketchup-based sauces, but their most unusual sauce is a white sauce used on poultry. Alabamans serve parts of the pig like pork shoulder and ribs.

Styrofoam containers of homemade sauce at Gonzales Market in Gonzales, Texas

Eastern North Carolina pig sandwiches use the whole hog and a thin vinegar mop or dip just to add moisture and complement the delicate flavor of the pork. Western North Carolina is known for smoked pork shoulder, chopped or sliced, and they use a vinegar sauce with a little ketchup in it.

Chuck Kovacik, a professor of geography at the University of South Carolina, charted his state's diverse array of sauce regions. He found that vinegar and pepper sauces are popular in the northeastern corner of the state. The northwestern region that borders North Carolina favors a tomato-based sauce while the western region bordering Georgia prefers ketchup-like sauces. Mustard sauces are popular smack dab in the middle of the state. Pork, again, is the meat of choice.

Chuck and a colleague wrote a book about South Carolina, and they used barbecue to illustrate the concept of regions, showing that you can regionalize or chart anything.

"The book didn't get that much attention, but the map sure did," Chuck laughs. "The map was excerpted in a little section in the *Wall Street Journal* in 1989, and my phone rang constantly for two weeks. People would say, 'If you didn't eat barbecue at this place or that place, then you don't know what you're talking about!' That's when I really understood how important barbecue is."

"Every place has an identity and in the South, dialect, religion, and food give a place its identity. As you know, you can't go too far in this state or many southern states without bumping into barbecue," Chuck tells me.

All these regional differences have blurred a bit due to today's transient society and the way that barbecue has spread way beyond its traditional home ground. Old-timers may still be true to their regions, but the new breed of barbecuers is openly combining different styles. For example, Jake Jacobs grew up in Massachusetts and fell in love with barbecue while living in Texas. At Jake's Boss Barbecue in Jamaica Plain, Massachusetts, he serves a sort of Texas-style barbecue but with his own twist. His ribs, however, are more of a Memphis style.

I've seen lots of new restaurants that try to offer a little bit of all types of sauces to their guests—six-pack beer cartons filled with different types of sauce. You'll never see that in my restaurants for one specific reason: The first thing a person does is to start testing and rating those sauces and talking about what he doesn't iike. I prefer to offer the one sauce I believe in, the one that specifically complements the meat I serve.

Lexington Barbecue
North Carolina–Style Kitchen Dip

I ask Wayne Monk, of Lexington Barbecue in North Carolina, if he has a sauce recipe, or some semblance of a recipe, he could share.

"We tell the ingredients on some of our things, but we don't give out the proportions. I don't have but two or three recipes. That's all I got. But here's what I'll give you: the barbecue sauce we use in the kitchen. You ready?"

I grab my pencil and paper. "Ready."

"Pepper, a little vinegar, tomato ketchup, and water. About two-thirds water. The rest of it, you're on your own," he says with a grin.

He gave me a cup of the sauce to take home. I experimented and decided it tastes best with a little salt and sugar. Oh, and I think he lied to me about the amount of water. You'll read more about Wayne Monk and Lexington Barbecue in Chapter 3.

¼ cup water

¾ cup ketchup

¾ cup white vinegar

1 teaspoon sugar (optional)

Ground black pepper (to taste)

Finely ground kosher salt (optional)

Combine all the ingredients in a small saucepan and bring to a simmer. Cook, stirring often, for about 5 minutes. Cool and store in an airtight container or jar. Shake before using. Serve with pork shoulder.

MAKES ABOUT 2 CUPS

"You go to these cook-offs and those boys tell you, 'I've got 600 to 700 ingredients in my sauce and it's top secret.' My sauce just has three ingredients: vinegar, pepper, and sugar."
—ED MITCHELL, WILSON, NORTH CAROLINA

Gates Family
Kansas City Barbecue Sauce

Now, I know I've preached to you about the evils of liquid smoke, but along comes Ollie Gates with a lip-smacking sauce that has liquid smoke as one of its ingredients. Ollie is a second-generation barbecue legend. You'll read more about him in Chapter 3. Gates's sauce recipe has been requested so often that he has it written down. "Is this the recipe you use in the restaurant?" I ask. I never did get a straight answer, but it doesn't matter. This tasty sauce's popularity reaches far beyond Kansas City.

1 cup sugar	2 tablespoons chili powder
¼ cup kosher salt, finely ground	2 quarts ketchup
2 tablespoons celery seed	2 cups apple cider vinegar
2 tablespoons ground cumin	1½ teaspoons liquid smoke
2 tablespoons cayenne	1 teaspoon lemon juice
2 tablespoons garlic powder	

Mix the sugar, salt, celery seed, cumin, cayenne, garlic powder, and chili powder together in a small bowl. Combine the ketchup, vinegar, liquid smoke, and lemon juice in a large bowl. Add the dry ingredients and mix until very well blended.

Sauce may be stored in an airtight container in the refrigerator for 2 to 3 weeks or in the freezer up to 6 months.

MAKES ABOUT 3 QUARTS

One Way to Develop Barbecue Sauce

Many people start with a bottled sauce and doctor it up. You can cut the thickness (bottled sauces are usually too thick) and boost the spice fairly easily. My favorite bottled sauce is Maull's, out of St. Louis, and here are some ideas on how to doctor it. Start by simmering a bottle of sauce over low heat. Add $\frac{1}{4}$ to $\frac{1}{3}$ cup of cider vinegar or rice vinegar. Or put in the same amount of beer. A lot of people use Pepsi, which gives a sweet, caramel flavor. Add a tablespoon of granulated or fresh garlic. Throw in a little chili powder for an outdoorsy quality. Maybe add a tablespoon of Worcestershire sauce. A tablespoon of butter or prepared mustard tastes good, too. And you'd be surprised by how many sauces have a little chocolate in them.

Woody Wood and his wife, Cecelia, out of Waldenburg, Arkansas, came up with their barbecue sauce years ago using Wicker's as a base.

"Whatever did happen to Wicker's?" I wonder. "They used to be going like a house afire. There was a time that all winning barbecue teams used Wicker's. Let me put it to you this way: If they didn't use Wicker's, they didn't win."

"I used to buy it in 55-gallon drums." Woody tells me. "Well, the old boy who run it, the manager, me and him had a real close working relationship. He ended up quittin', and when he did, I thought, 'Man, this is not good.' They could have me over a barrel and raise the price of that to where I can't afford to buy it. Or they could say, 'Hey, we're not gonna sell you any more of this.'"

"That could be a problem," I agree.

"I had tried and tried and tried to make it. This here on the bottle says 'vinegar, salt, and spices.' That covers a lot of territory."

"You bet it does," I laugh. "Actually, I think I have a recipe for Wicker's; someone gave it to me a long time ago."

"Yeah, that old man who started Wicker's a long time ago, he was very loose-tongued with his recipe. But the only thing about it, he never told the same thing twice. I can't tell you how many people over the years that I've run into would say, 'Well, I know what's in that! Me and that old man used to go to barbecue cook-offs and we used to make that stuff.'

"So I'd say, 'What's in it?' And he'd say, 'Well you've got this and this and this.' So I'd try it and then pour it out. Then I'd run into somebody else and get another recipe. And none of 'em was ever the same. I even got a recipe for Wicker's off the CB radio going down the interstate!

"I worked on this recipe on and off for 10 years. Finally, I sat down and took all of these recipes that people have give me and I said, 'Well, I know that's not in there.' I kept working back and forth and finally, one day, I come up with it. Now we sell it as our Marinade and Baste." You'll read more about Woody in Chapter 4.

A Dry Rub Primer

Just about every barbecue champion has a secret dry rub recipe. A dry rub is essentially a dry marinade. You sprinkle it liberally on the meat and let it marinate for at least six hours and as long as overnight. The dry rub will season the meat and give great flavor to the "bark" on the surface. Bark is that highly seasoned crust that forms on the outside of the meat, and it's what keeps the moisture inside.

What you don't want to do is literally "rub" the dry rub into the meat. Rubbing it in will clog the pores of the meat, and the smoke won't penetrate. Clogged pores will also hinder what's called the "sweating." All smoked meats sweat during the cooking process. The pores of the meat literally open up and release moisture. When this happens, the smoke and dry rub seasoning are absorbed into the meat. This forms

Certain Flavors Don't Belong in Barbecue

I was talking to this guy once about a very intent and very serious barbecue team. They really put forth time and effort, and they consistently end up at the bottom end of every contest.

"I just don't understand it. They work so hard, they make up their own sauce and dry rub," the fellow said. "What do you think they're doing wrong?"

I'd watched this team and I'd often wondered the same myself. Then I tasted their ribs. "What all you got in this rub?" I asked one of the team members.

"One of our secret ingredients is apple pie spice," he said proudly.

"Oh," I thought to myself. "*That's* the problem."

If he'd asked my opinion, I would've told him that apple pie spice belongs in apple pies or in baked goods. But he didn't ask. You can get creative, but there is such a thing as being too creative. In my opinion, mint goes in juleps, bay goes in soup, and caraway seeds go in rye bread. I've tasted dry rubs with anise in them. Now, if I wanted to taste licorice, I'd go buy myself a Twizzler stick. All the time and care in the world won't give you prize-winning results if you're using ingredients that just don't belong in barbecue.

that dark, caramelized, spicy outer bark. If the pores are clogged, the meat can't sweat, the bark doesn't form, and the meat will be mushy and not nearly as flavorful.

I'm going to give you several recipes for dry rubs, but really, you'll want to learn to mix your own. First of all, buy yourself a little notebook and take good notes when you're mixing up batches of barbecue sauce and dry rub. You'll be able to write down your successes and your mistakes—and you will make some mistakes. When you finally come up with the mixture that tastes best to you, you want to be sure you can replicate it again and again. You won't remember if you don't write it down. I speak from experience.

Coming up with a rub recipe of your own might take awhile. Keep in mind that I spent over a year making batch after batch of dry rubs before I came up with my final Magic Dust blend.

Getting Started

First of all, go through your spice cabinet and discard any spices that are over six months old. For the best results, buy all new tins or jars of the spices you plan to use in your dry rub. If you're planning to make large quantities, you might want to think about buying spices in bulk. (See page 315 for my favorite mail-order source. They have excellent quality and prices.) Next, gather the following equipment and ingredients:

- Large nonaluminum mixing bowl

- Spice mill or grinder (Buy an electric coffee mill and dedicate it to spices.)

- Sifter

- Zippered plastic bags or storage containers with airtight lids

- Funnel

- Empty shaker with an airtight lid

- Paprika

- Sugar

- Pepper

- Salt

- Chili powder

- Assorted dried herbs and spices

Now, there are some excellent books out there about dry rubs, and each will tell you a slightly different method. But this is my book, so I'm going to teach you my way. The basic process is to start with a carrier, then add salt, sugar, chili powder, pepper, and other herbs and spices. I keep experimenting until I get the flavor I want. Something that has a pleasant taste to it straight on the tongue.

PAPRIKA I always start with 1 cup of paprika as the carrier, which adds bulk to the product and helps it all mix together.

A mild powdered seasoning made from sweet red peppers, most paprika comes from Hungary, although some comes from Spain. It helps give the meat a nice mahogany color during the cooking process. If you look for paprika at a grocery store, the bottle will usually simply say "paprika." If you order your spices online or from a specialty store, you'll have more choices: sweet, half-sharp, or hot Hungarian paprika or hot Spanish paprika. The "hot" paprika isn't really hot at all, but it's darker in color and that means your meat will be slightly darker in color. My advice is to use the sweet version, although it probably won't make a noticeable difference.

SALT You'll need to decide if you want your dry rub to be on the sweet side or more on the salty side. I don't like my rub to be too salty, so I start with about a half-cup of salt. If you want to use kosher salt or sea salt, that's fine. Just be sure you give it a whirl in a spice grinder so the flakes won't be too large.

Some books will tell you to use flavor-enhanced salts like garlic salt or onion salt. I like to add those flavors with spices, not by using flavor-enhanced salts. But that's just my own personal preference. What you don't want to do is use charcoal, hickory, or any kind of salt with an artificial smoky flavoring. Any smoke flavor should be honest and come from the cooking process. In other words, smoke flavor should come from the wood, not from some flavoring in the rub.

SUGAR Next I add about a cup of sugar. You can use a mixture of different types if you want. Turbinado or raw sugar has a delicious cane flavor, but the granules are large, so you'll need to run it through the spice mill. Plain old granulated sugar will work, too. You might want to add some dehydrated honey or brown sugar to the mix, but be careful when you're using brown sugar. The flavor's great, but it's often moist; make sure it mixes in well. You might want to spread it on a baking sheet and dry it in the oven before you add it to your rub.

CHILI POWDER AND PEPPER Add 1 or 2 tablespoons each of chili powder and pepper to give a little kick to your recipe.

HERBS AND SPICES Here's where you put your own stamp on the recipe. Pull out all of your dried herbs and spices—well, not all of them; see "Mike's Spice Dos and Don'ts" on the opposite page—and start experimenting with your favorite flavors. You'll want to add a teaspoon or less of each herb or spice you choose.

Not all spices go well together. An excellent resource for learning about spices and what they complement is *Culinary Artistry* by Andrew Dornenburg and Karen Page.

Mike's Spice Dos and Don'ts

DO USE

Barbecue spice	Horseradish powder
Basil	Jalapeño powder
Cayenne	Mustard powder
Celery seed (bruise with a rolling pin)	Nutmeg
	Onion (granulated works best)
Cilantro	Oregano
Cinnamon (the ground stuff)	Parsley
Cumin (adds a chili flavor)	Red pepper flakes
Curry powder	Sage
Fennel seed (ground)	Tarragon
Garlic (granulated works best)	Thyme
Ginger (dried and powdered)	White pepper (adds a hotter taste)

DON'T USE

Allspice (I wouldn't)	Dill (use for seafood, not barbecue)
Anise seed	Lemon pepper or lemon zest (Some people like it. Personally, I use it only in rubs for fish and vegetables.)
Bay leaf	
Caraway seeds	
Coriander (will kill a maggot, but some people do use it)	Mace
	Marjoram
Chervil	Mint
Chives	Orange zest
Citric acid	Rosemary (only for poultry and seafood)
Cloves (will gag a maggot, but some people do use it)	Savory
	Turmeric

If you look at the labels of various dry rubs, you'll notice that some contain MSG, which is an excellent flavor enhancer. I don't use MSG in my recipes because it affects so many people in a negative way.

Another similarity among most dry rubs is that all of the ingredients are finely ground. If you have larger pieces of certain spices, the rub won't spread evenly and you'll get a distinct taste when you bite into certain sections of meat. The goal here is to have even flavor. One should not dominate another. That's why, for example, you don't want to use coarsely ground pepper or large flakes of sea salt in the rub you're making at home.

Your Basic Dry Rub

Here's an all-purpose dry rub that you can use as the basis for experimentation. To start experimenting, choose from the "Do Use" list of ingredients on page 65. Start by adding just ¼ teaspoon of a particular ingredient. Taste, decide if you'd like to have more of that flavor, and adjust the amount as necessary. You'll notice that this particular recipe has no sugar, but you can add some if you like.

3 tablespoons paprika

1 tablespoon ground black pepper

2 teaspoons chili powder

½ teaspoon salt

¼ teaspoon celery seed, bruised

½ teaspoon cayenne

½ teaspoon granulated garlic

¼ teaspoon mustard powder

Mix all ingredients and store in a tightly covered container.

MAKES ABOUT ⅓ CUP

Sprinkle on a Little Magic

Dry rubs can also be used for foods other than barbecue. I substitute Magic Dust anywhere I might sprinkle paprika, as you may have seen in the recipe for My Sister Jeanette's Deviled Eggs (see page 9). Use your favorite dry rub when you're smoking or grilling vegetables. Sprinkle some on popcorn (see page 69), baked potatoes, corn on the cob, french fries, and baked or fried sweet potatoes. Use it on anything but ice cream, I like to say.

Magic Dust

There's a big shaker of Magic Dust right next to the salt and pepper in my own kitchen and at all my restaurants. I wish I could figure out a way to attach the bottle to the restaurant tables because, at my restaurants, it's the most frequently stolen item!

To make it a little more hot and spicy, increase the mustard powder and black pepper to ¼ cup each.

½ cup paprika

¼ cup kosher salt, finely ground

¼ cup sugar

2 tablespoons mustard powder

¼ cup chili powder

¼ cup ground cumin

2 tablespoons ground black pepper

¼ cup granulated garlic

2 tablespoons cayenne

Mix all ingredients and store in a tightly covered container. You'll want to keep some in a shaker next to the grill or stove. Keeps indefinitely but won't last long.

MAKES ABOUT 2½ CUPS

Holy Cow Dry Rub for Beef

This easy and distinctive rub is typical of what's used on beef in Texas. The idea is to enhance the flavor of the meat, not to taste the rub.

¾ cup paprika

½ cup kosher salt, finely ground

½ cup coarsely ground pepper

1 tablespoon cayenne

Pour all ingredients into a sifter and sift to combine. Store in an airtight container. Use on all kinds of beef prior to smoking.

MAKES 1¾ CUPS

Ruben's Spicy Rub

Bonnie and Ruben Gomez live near Albuquerque, New Mexico, and they're working hard to raise awareness of barbecue in that area of the country. They have a catering company, and they've started quite a successful cook-off. Ruben has lived three colorful lives—that I know of. But I can't tell you the best parts because they're top secret. Now he's working on his barbecue story.

"Down here in the Southwest, there are Mexican restaurants on every street corner," Ruben tells me. "Barbecue is something new and different, and people love it."

One thing that really impresses me about Ruben is his knowledge of spices and chiles. He generously shared some of his rub recipes with me. The chili powder you buy from a grocery store is usually made from a blend of various types of chiles. Ruben prefers to use dried red Anaheim chiles (sometimes referred to as New Mexico Hatch chiles after the town where they're grown), which can be found in most Latino or Spanish markets across the country.

SEASON SALT

- ½ cup sea salt, finely ground
- ¼ cup paprika
- 2 teaspoons mustard powder (preferably Colman's)
- 1 teaspoon granulated garlic
- 1 teaspoon curry powder
- 1 teaspoon granulated onion
- 1 teaspoon dried thyme
- ¼ teaspoon dried oregano

RUB

- ½ cup packed brown sugar
- ½ cup sugar
- ½ cup kosher salt, finely ground
- ½ cup Season Salt
- 2 tablespoons ground dried Anaheim chiles or New Mexico Hatch chiles
- 1 teaspoon mustard powder (preferably Colman's)
- 1 tablespoon ground black pepper
- 1 tablespoon ground cumin
- 1 tablespoon granulated onion
- 1 teaspoon granulated garlic
- 1 teaspoon dried thyme

Make the season salt: Combine salt ingredients and run them through a spice mill if necessary. Pour into a sifter and sift to combine. Store in an airtight container. Use on all kinds of poultry prior to smoking.

Make the rub: Pour all rub ingredients into a sifter and sift to combine. Store in an airtight container. Use on all kinds of pork or beef prior to smoking.

MAKES ABOUT 2 CUPS

Woody's Bar-B-Q Dip

Woody's wife, Cecelia Wood, came up with this recipe to use for sampling at a fancy food show. Gourmet shops all over the country ordered their dry rub after sampling this zippy dip. You'll read more about Woody Wood in Chapter 4.

1 container (8 ounces) sour cream

2 tablespoons Miracle Whip salad dressing

⅛ teaspoon cayenne (optional)

2 tablespoons your favorite dry rub recipe

Combine all the ingredients in a bowl and mix well. Refrigerate at least 4 hours. Best made a day in advance. Serve with chips or raw vegetables.

MAKES I CUP

17th Street Barbecue Popcorn

Savory and spicy flavors make this popcorn an extra-special movie treat.

4 cups popped corn (best popped with oil)

4 tablespoons (½ stick) unsalted butter, melted

¼ cup grated Parmesan cheese

Magic Dust (page 67), or use your favorite dry rub

Pour the popcorn into a large bowl and toss with the butter. Add the Parmesan cheese and Magic Dust to taste and toss again.

MAKES 4 CUPS

Chapter
Three

LIV
LEG

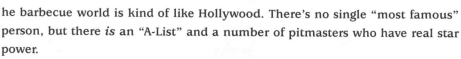

The barbecue world is kind of like Hollywood. There's no single "most famous" person, but there *is* an "A-List" and a number of pitmasters who have real star power.

I eat barbecue wherever I travel, and over the years I've met some of these folks by just stopping in for a meal and a visit. I've met still others while cooking at an event or competing on the circuit. We trade a lot of tall tales, drink like fish, and eat some of the best barbecue in the world when we're together.

Before we go any further, I have to insert a disclaimer. There are more barbecue legends in this country than I'm including in these pages. Some of them are friends I simply haven't met yet. If you feel I've left you out, give me a holler. A man can never have too many friends.

When I meet up with my barbecue buddies, the talk ranges from history to recipes we've "invented" to cooking disasters and how we miraculously saved the day. Mostly we try to get inside of each other's minds, to learn a little about each other's thought processes. The Bible says, "An honest answer is like a kiss on the lips" (Proverbs 24:26). I don't expect to get too many kisses from these people, but I do learn something new every time we have a conversation. We tend to get a little philosophical at times, talking about authenticity and pureness and what barbecue means to us. I don't know of anybody in this business who doesn't feel deeply grateful for the lifestyle and experiences barbecue has provided. It's hard work, that's for sure. But none of us know any other way we'd rather spend our days.

These pitmasters are scattered all over the country. Their operations range from small to large. But they all have a few things in common: a passion for the culture of barbecue, food steeped in tradition, and the respect and admiration of the food world. I feel fortunate to call them my friends.

Don McLemore and Chris Lilly

BIG BOB GIBSON BAR-B-Q

Decatur, Alabama

You will meet no finer people on this planet than the McLemore and Lilly families, who own Big Bob Gibson Bar-B-Q. Big Bob Gibson has been in operation, to much acclaim, since 1925.

Don McLemore is the grandson of Big Bob, founder of the original restaurant. Big Bob was a pretty colorful character. He had six children with his first wife and then three more wives after that. Don's lovely wife, Carolyn, and his son-in-law Chris Lilly work side by side with him, running his two restaurants and competing on the barbecue circuit. "This restaurant has always been in the family, and it will hopefully continue to be," Chris says. "We think that simplicity describes us. We serve barbecue staples: pork, chicken, ribs, beef. We recently added smoked turkey, and our side orders are potato salad, cole slaw, and baked beans. Barbecue-stuffed baked potatoes are new on the menu, also."

"Slaw and chips. Don's grandfather had only these two sides, and I still think that's as good with pork as anything," adds Carolyn.

While Big Bob Gibson's has been cleaning up on the barbecue circuit, in this neck of the woods they're known for their chicken with white sauce. Their chicken is some of the best I've ever put in my mouth.

"You see a lot of white sauce in Alabama," Carolyn tells me. "And it originated here. Don's grandfather invented it. We're real proud of it. Unfortunately, he gave out that recipe to anybody who'd ask. It's all over Alabama."

Don and I chat about some of the experiences we've shared, and Don says, "Think about the people you've met. Have you ever met such nice people? And some of the places we've gone? Who would've ever dreamed that we'd go to some of those places and cook? Little barbecue places from Decatur, Alabama, and Murphysboro, Illinois, cooking on the streets of New York City? And at the James Beard House? In 2003, I spent my 40th wedding anniversary cooking on the streets of New York City. I'll never forget that. And that was hard work. But did you ever have so much fun working so hard? There's such a sense of accomplishment after it's over with. We pulled it off, didn't we? We pulled it off."

I'm enjoying our unhurried meal and our time together. But I'm not used to this leisurely pace. I say to Don, "I'm about half-ass feeling guilty about being off work right now. I can't tell you the last day I was off. I go in seven days a week. I have to keep reminding myself that this here's a business trip."

"That's me!" Don agrees. "If I'm in town, I come in. Maybe not all day, but I'm here. I want to see that the customers are being taken care of. I want to see that the meat's being cooked right. And I've got good managers. But I still just want to see for myself.

"See that lady over there?" Don points to Mattie Johnston. "I don't tell that lady what to do. I don't have to, and really I just have so much respect for her that I don't try to. I was just a little kid when she first started working here."

Big Bob's barbecue is world-class; that's for sure. Their pies also have a sterling reputation. They serve lemon, coconut, and chocolate pies daily.

I'm thrilled to meet the pie ladies in person and pay them some compliments on those pies. Don tells me, "The pie ladies come in at four in the morning. I don't want 'em here alone, so the cleanup crew or some of the male cooks come in then, too. Times have changed, and you just have to be more careful today. They come in and have their coffee and do their thing."

We go back to shooting the breeze about the cook-off circuit for a bit. I retired from the circuit in 1994, and Don and Chris began competing in '96, so we never did compete together. I judge the contest every year, and that's how we first met.

"Really," Chris says, "we entered a contest as an afterthought, and we were fortunate enough to do well and we got hooked. We did not get hooked on competing; we did not get hooked on winning . . ."

Don and I look at each other. "Well," says Don, "it is awful nice to have your name called out."

"You bet it is," I say.

Chris agrees, but he continues. "Yeah, but what we really got hooked on was the camaraderie and the new friends we made out on the circuit. We're fortunate to do well, and we use that publicity to promote our restaurants and our sauces. But it all goes back to that camaraderie. That is barbecue and that is what defines Big Bob Gibson."

Reminiscent of Big Bob Gibson's Peanut Butter Pie

When Big Bob Gibson competes at Memphis in May, Carolyn very carefully packs up 16 pies, all flavors, to take on the trip, and friends flock to the tent on Friday night just to get a taste. The choice is so overwhelming; I've seen people stand there for 5 minutes trying to make up their minds. Smart people know to have a thin sliver of each kind. That's what I do.

The pie ladies don't make peanut butter pie every day; it's reserved for special occasions like competitions. I couldn't sweet-talk Carolyn into giving me the recipe, so I'll give you a favorite from the 17th Street kitchen.

This pie has a peanut butter crumb layer, which adds a different texture. Just like Big Bob Gibson's pies, it always receives rave reviews.

2 cups confectioners' sugar	5 egg yolks
1 cup creamy peanut butter	4 cups water
2 baked pie shells (9 inches)	1 tablespoon butter
1 cup powdered milk	2 teaspoons vanilla extract
1/3 cup granulated sugar	Whipped cream (optional)
1/2 cup cornstarch	

Preheat the oven to 350 degrees.

Mix the confectioners' sugar and peanut butter together in a bowl until it resembles crumbs. Spread all but 1/2 cup of the crumb mixture in the bottom of the baked pie shells.

Stir the powdered milk, granulated sugar, cornstarch, egg yolks, and water together in a large saucepan. Cook over medium heat, stirring constantly, until the mixture thickens. Remove from the heat and stir in the butter and vanilla.

Pour the hot filling into the shells over the crumb mixture. Bake for 15 minutes. After the pie cools, top with the remaining crumb mixture and whipped cream, if desired.

SERVES 6 TO 8 PER PIE

I agree with you there," I tell Chris.

"Can you believe," Don asks, "how many people go year after year after year and never get their name called out? They never get to go up on stage. That's dedication."

"That's kind of like going on a hunting trip and coming home empty-handed," I say.

"For us, we treat it as a family vacation, too," says Don. "Some folks go to Florida, which is fine. Our family goes to Memphis in May. All of our girls come and the grandkids. And we have a great time." Don then asks, "You ever cook in KCBS [Kansas City Barbecue Society] contests?"

The Lilly children and cousins love going to Memphis in May.

"Not really," I tell him. "Just Jack Daniel's. I like the comparison score. You've still got to win the blind judging to win, but I liked puttin' on a show and explaining our process to a judge. In KCBS, you just have that one turn-in box. They put so much emphasis on that box, it's unbelievable."

Chris had just returned from cooking at the Houston Livestock and Rodeo. "He won first place ribs!" Don brags.

"Now that was some contest," Chris says. "They only give you two slabs of ribs. And they're tagged. They come to your cooker and watch you put them on and then they come back and watch you take 'em off."

"Two slabs?" I'm surprised. "You better be careful and you better be good." At a typical cook-off, you might cook many more ribs, so you'll have a choice when it comes to putting your box together.

Chris cooks in the shoulder division in competitions, and I don't think I've ever tasted a better shoulder. I ask him to tell me some of his secrets.

"We inject the meat for competition. We do that so when a judge comes to our booth and he or she wants to taste the inside morsel right next to the bone, it's going to be as nice and flavorful a taste as you get closer to the outside of the shoulder. You can't get that flavor on that very inside piece of pork by doing a dry rub and putting it on the pit. But I guarantee our injection is a pure flavor and one that doesn't hinder the wonderful flavor of the meat. We don't inject in the restaurant, though. It's just too time-consuming."

Talking about injection leads to a discussion about purity and regional styles. Chris gives his opinion. "You have to define the word 'pure.' What it means to me will be different from what it means to others. When I think of keeping barbecue pure, I think of how well dry rubs complement the meat. I think of how well our vinegar sauce or red sauce complements meat. I look at the final product. I love vinegar-based Carolina style, I love red sauces, I love dry rubs. I like it all. I like it to complement the flavor of pork. If I ever do anything to mess that up, that's when my barbecue stops being pure.

"Barbecue is more than just cooking at a low temperature for a long period of time," continues Chris. "It's the time and environment that envelops the process and, more importantly, the memories that are obtained. It's the new friendships that are born and perpetuated through the bonds of the word. Just look at us. Would we have ever known one another had it not been for barbecue?

"When I go back home after cooking at an event or competing at Memphis in May, I'm not going to remember the long lines and the sore muscles. I'm going to remember the talks me and Ed Mitchell had about pits. I'm going to remember hanging out with Mike Mills until way late at night talking of barbecue and such. I'm going to remember the delectable taste of the wonderful barbecue I've eaten. These will be my memories. And this is barbecue. It is more than the final plate."

I just about have tears in my eyes.

Big Bob Gibson's Grand World Championship Pork Shoulder

Chris Lilly has mastered the art of injecting meat. The secret is to avoid leaving a whole syringe worth of fluid in any one spot in the shoulder. Start off slowly and release the fluid into the meat as you're drawing the needle out. This is trickier than it sounds and requires some practice.

1 pork shoulder (18 to 20 pounds)

DRY RUB

½ cup sugar

½ cup paprika

⅓ cup garlic salt

⅓ cup kosher salt, finely ground

¼ cup packed brown sugar

1 tablespoon chili powder

1 teaspoon cayenne

1 teaspoon ground black pepper

1 teaspoon dried oregano

1 teaspoon ground cumin

INJECTION BASTE

¾ cup apple juice

½ cup water

½ cup sugar

¼ cup kosher salt, finely ground

2 tablespoons Worcestershire sauce

Make the dry rub: Combine all the ingredients in a small bowl. Transfer to a shaker. Store leftover rub in an airtight container.

Make the baste: Whisk together the apple juice, water, sugar, salt, and Worcestershire sauce in a bowl. Fill a basting syringe and begin injecting the meat. You'll want to use about ½ ounce (1 tablespoon) per pound of shoulder. Coat the shoulder well with the dry rub and refrigerate overnight.

Cook on a pit or smoker for about 1 hour per pound or to an internal temperature of 195 degrees. Pull or chop the meat. Pile the meat onto buns for sandwiches or use for some of the other recipes in the book that call for leftover barbecue. Leftovers can be frozen for up to 1 month.

MAKES ENOUGH FOR ABOUT 30 GENEROUS SANDWICHES

Carolyn McLemore's Cornbread Salad

The flavors in this layered salad complement barbecue perfectly.

CORNBREAD

- 1 tablespoon vegetable oil
- 2 large eggs
- 3 cups buttermilk
- 2 cups yellow cornmeal
- 1 teaspoon baking soda
- 1 teaspoon baking powder
- 1 teaspoon kosher salt, finely ground
- 1 can (4 ounces) chopped jalapeño peppers

SALAD

- 1 package (1 ounce) ranch-style salad dressing mix
- 1 container (8 ounces) sour cream
- 1 cup mayonnaise
- 3 large tomatoes, chopped
- ½ cup chopped green bell pepper
- ½ cup chopped scallions
- 2 cans (16 ounces each) pinto beans, drained and rinsed
- 3 cups shredded cheddar cheese
- 1 can (15 ounces) corn, drained
- 1 pound bacon, cooked until crisp and crumbled

Make the cornbread: Preheat the oven to 450 degrees. Coat the bottom and sides of a 10-inch cast-iron skillet with the vegetable oil and place the skillet in the oven to heat.

Whisk the eggs and buttermilk together in a large bowl. Add the cornmeal, baking soda, baking powder, salt, and jalapeños while stirring briskly. Pour the batter into the hot skillet. Bake for 15 minutes or until lightly browned. Cool on a rack, then crumble into a bowl.

Make the salad: Combine the dressing mix, sour cream, and mayonnaise in a small bowl and set aside. Combine the tomatoes, bell pepper, and scallions in another bowl.

Place half of the crumbled cornbread in the bottom of a large serving bowl. Spoon on half of the pinto beans, then top with half of the tomato mixture, half of the cheese, half of the corn, and half of the bacon. Spread on half of the dressing. Repeat the layers, ending with the dressing. Cover with plastic wrap and chill for at least 2 hours before serving.

SERVES 6 TO 8

Desiree Robinson

COZY CORNER

Memphis, Tennessee

Desiree and Raymond Robinson got into the barbecue business when they were first married. They were living temporarily in Denver, and they simply couldn't find any barbecue fit to eat. So they experimented and came up with some barbecue that they liked. "We knew we had it when our friends were amazed by just how good it was," Desiree tells me. "We had other jobs, too. Barbecue was just something we did by the way. To make some extra money.

"When we moved from Denver back to Memphis, Ray barbecued in the backyard. One day I came home and he had nine shoulders on the pit, fixin' to cater for a fraternity party. I told him, 'You got to get that out of here! The neighbors are goin' to put us out with that smell!' So he looked around for a place to open as a restaurant."

Ray passed in 2000, and Desiree came out of retirement to work the business with her son, Ray Jr., and her daughter, Val. "They're running it," she says. "I'm just here to lend my support."

"You mean they're doing it and you're keeping your eye on them?" I ask.

"Exactly!" she says.

On this particular day, I tried to show up before the lunch crowd really got going. At 11:40 a.m., I was fifth in line. I placed my order at 11:50, and they were already out of sliced shoulder sandwiches. And strawberry soda.

"May is a busy month," Desiree tells me when I ask her about running out of pork shoulder. "And August, Elvis's death month, is real busy, too."

"I liked your beans, by the way. Tasted to me like you had pickle relish in there," I say.

"Yeah," she replies nonchalantly.

"I like it," I probe some more. "I thought, 'I believe that's what that is, a little pickle relish.'"

"Yeah," she says again, laughing.

"Tastes to me like it's the same pickle relish that's in that cole slaw," I try a third time. More laughter. She is good; she isn't going to give it up.

"I have a rule," Desiree explains. "And that rule is that whatever you say is in it, I say, 'yeah.'"

I finish off my meal with a slice of delicious sweet potato pie, the only dessert offered.

"My uncle makes that sweet potato pie," she tells me.

"You keep it in the family," I remark.

"Well, I like to keep it in the family because we got a lot of good cooks in our family," she explains. "I know he can make a pie. He learned from my great-grandmother."

The pie has excellent flavor, and it's a brighter orange than most. "I think I taste some condensed milk in here . . . and maybe rum extract instead of vanilla?" I ask casually.

"Yeah," she says. "I'm thinking about making pecan tarts in the future."

I jump on that. "Now that might be a good recipe to include in this book."

She gets a real sly look on her face. "I'll just make up some shells and put in a filling that I purchase in a can and put some pecans on top of that."

"Purchase in a can?"

"Yeah."

Here I am in front of Cozy Corner with Desiree Robinson and her daughter, Val Bryant.

Sweet Potato Pie à la Cozy Corner

You'll be proud to serve this quintessentially Southern dessert anywhere. The sweet potato flavor is not overpowering.

CRUST

- 5 tablespoons ice water
- 1 tablespoon apple cider vinegar
- 1 large egg
- 2 cups all-purpose flour
- ½ teaspoon baking powder
- ½ teaspoon kosher salt, finely ground
- 1 cup solid vegetable shortening, well chilled

FILLING

- 2 cups cooked and mashed sweet potatoes (about 3 large)
- 3 large egg yolks
- 1 cup sweetened condensed milk
- ½ cup sugar
- 2 tablespoons butter, melted
- 1 teaspoon ground cinnamon
- ¼ teaspoon ground nutmeg
- ½ teaspoon rum extract
- ⅛ teaspoon kosher salt, finely ground

Make the crust: Whisk the ice water, vinegar, and egg together in a small bowl. Set aside. Combine the flour, baking powder, and salt in a medium bowl. Mix well. Use a pastry blender or two knives to cut in the shortening until the mixture resembles coarse meal. Sprinkle the flour mixture with the liquid mixture, 1 tablespoon at a time. Toss with a fork after each addition of liquid until the flour is all moistened and the dough cleans the side of the bowl. Shape the dough into a ball. Divide the dough in half and shape each portion into a flat disk; wrap in plastic wrap. You'll be using only one crust for this pie, so put one away in the freezer for up to 1 month. Refrigerate the other for at least 1 hour.

Preheat the oven to 325 degrees.

Make the filling: Beat the sweet potatoes and egg yolks together in a medium bowl. Add the milk, sugar, butter, cinnamon, nutmeg, rum extract, and salt. Mix well until smooth.

Roll the pie crust out on a floured surface to about ¼ inch thick and line a 9-inch pie plate. Pour in the sweet potato mixture. Bake for 45 minutes or until the crust is well browned and a knife inserted into the center comes out clean.

SERVES 6 TO 8

Billy Bones Wall

Midland, Michigan

Billy Bones tests his sauce.

Billy Bones Wall is larger than life. "Constant dieting keeps me at 365 pounds."

"I know about that," I laugh, as I pat my own belly. "This here's a hazard of the job. Years of restaurant research."

Billy can spin some stories, and we started off talking about lies.

"You only lie to the ones you love," he says. "Think about it. Only your friends will lie to you. People who don't know you will tell you the truth. After all, what do you say when a woman asks, 'Does this make me look fat?'"

He's got a point.

Billy is what's known as a "ribber," a person who competes in rib burn-offs and rib sells, which are not sanctioned competition events. They're selling events purely for fun and profit.

"I have a golf cart called the 'Bonesmobile.' I used to team up with Smokin' Sam Ingros from Freedom, Pennsylvania. We'd open a bottle of Jack and mix it with healthy things like Gatorade. We'd tour around and cruise down the row of vendors. We'd stop and ask, 'Would you mind sharing a bite of your rib with us? We just want to see what we're up against.'

"We'd take a bite and then look real crestfallen. We'd tell 'em, 'This is the best thing we've ever had in our mouths. Boy, are we sorry we asked you about your ribs.' We'd really get 'em going. Then we'd drive away and laugh and laugh to ourselves and say, 'Ha ha! There's another sucker we're going to beat; there's another guy who doesn't stand a rat's-ass chance.

"Sometimes we'd just ask what they were cooking for turn-in. 'Barbecued shrimp on spaghetti? Mmm, what a wonderful idea. I'm sure you'll do real well with this idea.' Ugh! That was the sickest idea I ever heard in my life!"

Billy's favorite rib show is in Reno every Labor Day weekend. "There are 2,002 miles of bad road from Michigan to Reno, but I do it gladly. For me, it's the most fabulous selling show in the country," he tells me.

Billy tells me a funny story about our mutual friend Joey Sutphen, from Amarillo, Texas.

"Joey always accepts his trophy wearing Tenny Lamas—cowboy boot tops with tennis shoes for the foot part. And Mickey Mouse shorts. He's only 5'6" tall because he's weighted down with so much gold—like Mr. T.

"They always have a salute to the previous year's winner. They run videos; it's on national television. This one year he came in for his salute in a Texas duster coat, a big cowboy hat, white frilly shirt, boots, and Levi's. He said, 'I won last year, so I wanted to look special for this party.'

"Well, when they announced him, he went up on stage and took off his coat and he was packing a real .45 revolver. In a casino. In Reno. You should've seen 'em scramble! Steve Ascuaga, the organizer, handled it so cool. He said, 'Joey has always been a man of impeccable attire, but Joey, you've gone over the top tonight!'"

"Yep, that sounds just like Joey," I laugh. "He is one colorful character. He's lucky he didn't go to jail for that one!"

"Luckily they have a sense of humor out there," says Billy.

Now, I'm always interested in hearing about a person's younger years; how he became the person he is today. Billy shared some of his story.

"I'm a 'school of hard knocks' guy. I grew up in a family of butchers, and I've been cooking in one form or another all my life. Professionally, I started out as a men's sportswear buyer for Federated Department Stores of Cincinnati. I played golf at the country club. A lah-de-dah life. This life's a lot more fun.

"My first show on the road was in Cleveland back in '83. I was in food service management at the time. Vending machines, fancy catering, cafeteria lines. I did real well in that business. All the vegetables were gray until I came to town.

Homemade Sausage
with Michigan Cherries

Billy reminds me that Michigan is the number-one producer of tart cherries and the number-two producer of sweet red cherries in the country. He likes to add a little cherry burst to his sausage for a unique flavor.

10 pounds boneless pork butt

1 cup pitted fresh cherries (sweet or tart)

¾ cup kosher or sea salt, finely ground

½ cup coarsely ground black pepper

¼ cup rubbed sage

2 tablespoons cayenne

2 tablespoons red pepper flakes

¼ to ⅓ cup sugar

2 cups ice water

20 feet of hog casing, cleaned

Coarsely grind the pork butt using about a ⅜-inch plate. Grind the cherries and add them to the meat. Add the salt, pepper, sage, cayenne, pepper flakes, and sugar and work them into the meat with your hands. To help make this work in, add a little ice water, up to 2 cups, as necessary. The water will cook out.

For best results, let the mixture sit in the refrigerator for 6 to 8 hours. This lets the spices mellow out through the meat. Regrind the meat using a ³⁄₁₆-inch plate to make it more finely ground. Use a sausage stuffer to fill cleaned hog casings and tie off to whatever lengths seem right to you. You can also make sausage patties.

Hang on a sausage rod if possible and cook over apple or cherry wood at 225 to 250 degrees to an internal temperature of 160 degrees. This will take 2 to 2½ hours if the sausage is hanging and about 45 minutes if it's flat on the rack.

The sausages can be frozen, cooked or uncooked, for up to 1 month.

MAKES ABOUT 40 (¼-POUND) LINKS

"I was a fancy caterer at first. I didn't start doing barbecue until I moved to Midland. I ran into some cowboys from Texas, and I decided I really wanted to learn how to cook brisket. Some Texas moms sent me recipes, and I finally figured it out—but it took me awhile. The first time I ever did beef brisket for a catering job, I served 500 people. The next job was for 2,000 rib dinners. I'm semiretired, but I love catering; it's my passion."

"I know you've heard some stories in your time, Billy. What's the most outrageous lie you've ever heard?" I ask him.

"Well, there's a guy today claiming to be the winner of 500 world titles. Now think about that. If you settled the world championship once a year, this guy has to be 525 years old. Just think about that. He would've had to have won a contest every other weekend for 20 years."

I know exactly who he's talking about. We have a good laugh over that one.

Michigan does not have a barbecue culture, so to speak, so Billy got to choose his own. These days, he's concentrating on selling his sauce. "People want my sauce," he says. "It took me 16 years before I ever put it in a jar to sell. I had no former acquaintance with sauce," Billy admits. "I grew up only with ketchup and mustard and Heinz chili sauce."

I ask Billy if he has any favorite places.

"Texas is the epicenter of barbecue for me. My favorite place is North Main Bar BQ in Euless. It's a classic Texas scene. Hubert sits at the end of the counter with a fistful of cash. There's a sign right next to him that says, 'Hubert Green, Proprietor.'

"Hubert ran a sand and gravel business, and to entice his guys to work on Saturday, he'd cook up some beef brisket in the afternoon if they'd work in the morning. Eventually, people started asking, 'Can I bring my wife? Can I bring some home?' and it got so expensive he had to start charging. People started ordering incredible amounts of brisket. This was all happening outside in the parking lot.

"Well, there was a building next door where a religious group used to meet and they fell behind on their rent, so they left. It's not a lavish building; it's just a room filled with old chrome dinette sets so the religious people could sit around and stuff envelopes.

"It got awful hot outside in the summer, so they ended up in the building, where it was cooler. They finally realized they had a restaurant without a sign. They'd invite people in until the seats were filled, and they'd have two seatings on Saturday. Then they added Friday night. They're still only open two days."

"I've competed with Hubert," I nod. "He is a good cooker. His team is the Sweet Meat Cooking Team. I love that pit he has that looks like an armadillo."

"Hubert is wonderful," Billy agrees. "One time we were at a show and Hubert said to me, 'I know we ain't gonna make no money at this event, but this is the best excuse I could figure out to get close to you for a few days.'

"Now we all need to admit we do this because we enjoy drinking Jack Daniel's with our friends. Barbecue is really an excuse."

Billy's beloved wife, Sharon Wall, died in 2002, and her death has left a big hole in Billy's heart. She was as much a fixture at the rib burn-offs as Billy.

"She was everybody's mom," Billy told me. "She thought a lot of these men were little lost boys who didn't have an opportunity to have a real life. There are a lot of solitary men in this barbecue business. Every one of them had a place at her breakfast table.

"She really took care of Joey Sutphen, from Amarillo, in particular. Joey doesn't really have to work; his mom and dad made the money. He and his brother, Scotty, would do these shows, and they'd do just enough to make an appearance. They didn't work up a sweat. We were down in St. Petersburg, Florida, one night, and they started pouring cocktails at six o'clock in the evening. They just closed down when the lines got too deep. Sharon looked over and saw them and said, 'Look! They're getting out the lounge chairs! Their mother's going to run out of money some day!'

"She was so concerned that they were wasting their mom's money that she pulled ribs out of my smokehouse and gave them to Joey to sell. She stoked up their fire and made 'em get back to work. At about 11 o'clock that night, Scotty Sutphen came over and said, 'Jesus, Billy, I never worked that hard in my life! It nearly killed me working with her. And I never made so much money at a rib burn-off neither!'

I ask, "What do you think it is about barbecue that makes all of us so crazy about it?"

"I just love the diversity in this world of barbecue," he tells me. "I'm a big German guy from the Midwest. I'm most bored with my own kind.

"When I was a boy, I could go fishing if I could dig enough worms. When I got older, I could buy the worms, but there were times when I couldn't afford enough worms to go fishing for a whole day. I always thought if I could afford to buy enough worms and a bologna sandwich, I'd be a rich man. Now I can buy the worms for two days of fishing and have a beer, too. God has been good to me.

"You can grow up one way and you get satisfied and you have a life that's predictable. I like the color in my life. I've always wanted to walk into a Pentecostal church. I've stood outside on a summer night and listened to those folks sing and praise God. I want to be in there among 'em, but I'm not brave enough to walk in and I don't sing well."

Amen, Billy Bones.

Rick Schmidt

KREUZ MARKET

Lockhart, Texas

Many central Texas barbecue places started out as meat markets or grocery stores. Kreuz Market is one such place, and it's been an icon of Texas barbecue since 1900.

You have to remember that there wasn't much in the way of refrigeration back in 1900, so it was common for meat markets to smoke the meats that didn't sell. Lockhart, Taylor, Gonzales, and Luling were in the cotton belt, and literally thousands of cotton pickers would land in the area for the six to eight weeks of cotton season. Being black, Hispanic, and poor whites, they were not allowed to eat in restaurants, and they got their daily food from the meat markets. The meat markets served up the barbecue on sheets of butcher paper, and the workers would buy other items in the store to eat with it: cheese, saltine crackers, white bread, jalapeños, and pickles. There were no utensils; these were finger foods. There was no sauce, as that would've been too messy to eat with your fingers. Kreuz did have some community knives, chained to the walls, that could be used as necessary. Probably not too sanitary, but people weren't worrying so much about germs back then.

I had the pleasure of cooking with Rick Schmidt of Kreuz (pronounced "krites") at the first Big Apple Barbecue Block Party in New York City. I had heard about the fight he'd had with his sister, that she'd thrown him out of his own joint, and I asked him about it.

"That so-called feud? It wasn't a feud. It was just 'get out,' and I got out! After 99 years at the same location. I'm not proud of it, but family deals happen. When my dad died, he left the business to me and the building to my sister, so she wound up being my landlady. She decided she wanted to be in the barbecue business, and I couldn't get along with her and negotiate the lease. And I couldn't buy the property.

"She thought I would just go away, and I might have, except I have two sons in their 30s and they've committed to me that they wanted to continue the tradition. So I just

Rick Schmidt poses with some of his famous brisket.

moved up the road four-tenths of a mile, and I built me a little barbecue stand. It's a little over 23,000 square feet, and it's working."

Rick's sister, Nina Sells, installed her son, James Fullilove, as the pitmaster and renamed her business "Smitty's" after her dad, Smitty Schmidt.

Robb Walsh, who's a journalist in Houston and a noted authority on Texas barbecue, told me a funny story: When Rick was building his massive structure, people would come into Smitty's and ask, "What denomination is that church they're building up the street?" To which the staff at Smitty's would reply, "Why, that's the Church of Kreuz!"

The pits at the new Kreuz location are exact replicas of the old ones. One tradition at Kreuz's is that fires never go out. So when it was time to fire up the pits, Rick and long-time employee Roy Perez staged a ceremonial carting of the coals up the street to fire up the new pits with authentic Kreuz coals. Barbecue is serious business in Lockhart, and that story was covered in local and national news.

"When you're in a small place, you can get by with a real limited menu because you have limited space," Rick tells me. "When you're in a place like we have now, with 600 seats, you get a lot of new customers, and they expect more. Up until recently, we didn't have any beans or potatoes of any kind. If people wanted potato salad, I told 'em it was in the Lay's potato chip bag. Now we have three sides: beans, German potato salad, and sauerkraut. We're counter service, and you get your meat on butcher paper with a choice of crackers or bread. You go to another counter and buy you some pickles and onions or tomatoes or rat cheese. These are all an evolution out of our meat market and grocery store.

"We're kind of barbecue purists, and when you ask what kind of barbecue we do, we're real basic. We're concerned with the quality of meat we start with. Everything I cook is graded choice, with the exception of the brisket. We use post oak; we like the flavor it gives. Most barbecue places where we are use mesquite, and I'm glad they do; they can leave post oak alone."

I noticed Rick's woodpile when I drove up. It's hard to miss it; it covers about an acre, and it's divided into three sections—fresh cut, two years old, and three years old. They only burn the three-year-old wood.

"What're you using for seasoning?" I ask. "Do you use a dry rub?"

"Our seasoning is simple. Salt and pepper. A good, strong black pepper. That and the right smoke is what we put our emphasis on. We don't use barbecue sauce; we serve our barbecue naked. There's nothing to hide or change. Not that people who do that are wrong. I think everybody oughta be proud of what they serve."

I ask Rick, "Don't you think a lot of people can cook, but not everybody can run a place? If you had time and money, would you do anything differently?"

"No, I wouldn't. I'm different from a lot of people. I cook fast. I take a 15-pound shoulder clod and cook it in 3½ or 4 hours. It takes attention. You can't just put it on and go have a cup of coffee for 2 hours. You've got to check it every 15 to 20 minutes, maybe turn it. We start it fast and bring it on slowly at the end. That's the way we do things. We place importance on the quality of meat and seasoning and wood.

"I wouldn't change anything. If I had all the time in the world, I'd still do it the same way. That's the way the Kreuzes have been doin' it for over 100 years, and I'm gonna dance with the one what brung me."

The town of Lockhart has a population of 11,000 and four outstanding barbecue joints: Kreuz, Smitty's, Black's, and Chisholm Trail. Combined, they serve over 250,000 people a year.

PEACE, LOVE, AND BARBECUE

Kreuz Market Shoulder Clod

Shoulder clod is simple to prep; the secret is a quality piece of meat and careful cooking. This is a big piece of meat, so make sure you have a large enough cooking area on your pit. Invite some friends for supper because you're going to have plenty to share.

Rick cooks his shoulder clod hot and fast. You'll notice this recipe calls for a higher temperature and shorter cooking time than I normally advise.

1 beef shoulder clod, preferably USDA choice (15 pounds)

½ cup kosher salt, finely ground

¼ cup cracked black pepper

1 to 2 teaspoons cayenne

Bring the meat to room temperature. Combine the salt, pepper, and cayenne in a small bowl. Season the meat liberally and allow it to stand for 30 minutes. Smoke with post oak at 400 degrees for about 4 hours or to an internal temperature of 160 to 170 degrees for slicing. Allow the clod to rest for 30 minutes before slicing.

Serve with jalapeños and crackers. Leftovers can be used in other recipes in the book that call for barbecue or frozen for about 1 month.

SERVES 20 TO 25

Vencil Mares
THE TAYLOR CAFÉ
Taylor, Texas

Vencil Mares is widely regarded as the dean of the Central Texas pit bosses. When I first meet Vencil, I tell him that I'm a friend of Kenny Callaghan's from Blue Smoke. "You taught him how to do brisket, huh?" I ask.

"Yeah, I taught him. And if he just does what I told him, it'll be good."

I assure Vencil that Kenny has taken his lessons to heart and his brisket is indeed good.

While Vencil is getting my food, one of his regulars brags on him a little bit. "Did you read about Vencil in *USA Today*?" he asked. "His brisket was named in the top 10 in the country."

Vencil brings me a sampler plate right off the pit. Smoky, succulent sliced brisket so tender it melts in my mouth. There's no doubt in my mind that it's among the top 10; in fact, it's probably among the top 5.

There are two other well-regarded barbecue restaurants in Taylor—Louis Mueller's and Rudy Mikeska's—but to me, Vencil's is the real deal. This is truly a joint. A little dark, a little dingy. The screen door slams every time someone enters. The walls are covered with mounted game, handwritten signs, and framed articles and other memorabilia. No two bar stools are alike—there are various colors of old, ripped vinyl alternating with old tractor seats. A holdover from the days of segregation, the U-shaped bar divides the room into two sides—the black side and the white/Hispanic side. I notice that everybody still sits on his particular side. And nobody seems too bothered about it. There are even two jukeboxes, each stocked with music that might appeal to each racial group. The Amtrak train roars past hourly.

"They call me up from the train when they're about 30 minutes out, and I fix up their orders and somebody runs 'em down to the station," Vencil tells me.

"Pitmaster Vencil Mares, who was featured in Texas Taste on July 17, 2002, has become quite the rage among New York foodies."
—AUSTIN CHRONICLE

Vencil Mares shows off a plate of barbecue.

Vencil takes me back to his office. These are some tight quarters; the two of us can barely fit in there. It is also very eclectic, just like the restaurant. Mounted game on the walls, photos from the war. High up on one shelf is a collection of old cigar boxes, each one marked with a year.

"You've got some old cigar boxes, don't you?" I ask.

"Yep. Notice the dates? I keep real good records. Everything I've done for every year is in each box. If the IRS or anybody wants to come and ask a question, I just get down the box. If I did it, it's in there. If it's not in there, I didn't do it."

I ask Vencil if that's his secret to success.

"No, my secret's that you get that pit heated up and you put your briskets on there fat side up and you never turn 'em. That fat melts and your seasoning cooks down in there. If you turn 'em, the seasoning gets burned off. Also," he cautions, "don't poke your meat. The juice comes out, and it'll get dry. And if it don't turn out right and I wouldn't have it myself, I just throw it away."

"How much do you throw away?" I ask.

"Not much," he answers.

Vencil seasons his brisket overnight with a little salt, black pepper, chili pepper, and garlic.

"After I take it off the pit, I wrap it in butcher paper to keep it juicy, and I put it in an Igloo cooler. It'll stay hot for about six hours in a cooler. That steams it and makes it good and tender."

"Do you have children who'll take over your business?" I wonder.

"No. I got me a son, but if he worked here, he'd be divorced in 30 days. You never know when you're gonna be home. I have to be here all the time. If I'm not here, people think I don't need no business."

Vencil and I talk about sausage and chili and side dishes. He's particularly proud of his chili.

"Let me give you my chili recipe. It just has four ingredients. One hundred pounds of ground meat, 25 pounds of onions, 25 pounds of Mexene chili powder, and 25 pounds of tomatoes. I gave this recipe to Kenny to use at Blue Smoke. It's real good; people really like this chili."

I explain that I'm looking for a recipe that just feeds a family, not 200 people. So he gives me this one for traditional Texas pit beans.

Texas Pit Beans

Real Texas-style pit beans aren't at all sweet like traditional Southern baked beans. Vencil's secret to good pit beans is starting with dried beans. "Beans out of a can just don't taste the same," Vencil tells me. These are best served with sliced smoked sausage on top.

1 pound dried pinto beans	¼ cup chili powder
2 cups minced yellow onions	1 tablespoon kosher salt, finely ground
1 cup chopped bacon	

Wash the beans and sort through them to remove any foreign particles and broken beans.

Put the beans in a large bowl or saucepan and cover with cool water by at least 3 inches. Soak the beans overnight.

Drain and rinse the beans and put them in a large saucepan. Add the onions, bacon, chili powder, and salt and cover with cool water by 3 inches. Bring the beans to a boil, then lower the heat and simmer, stirring occasionally, for 2 hours, until the beans are very tender.

You can also cook the beans in a slow cooker or Crockpot. Prepare as above, but add 6 cups water. Cook on medium for 6 to 8 hours, adding water if necessary to keep the beans covered.

SERVES 6 TO 8

Paul Kirk
THE BARON OF BARBECUE
Kansas City, Kansas

Paul Kirk, otherwise known as the Kansas City Baron of Barbecue, is probably the most confident pitmaster I know.

"Those people who are always bragging about their world championships, what are they? Anyone who knows me knows I don't brag. I'll talk about it one-on-one, but I'm just not like that. Actually, I'm a recluse at a barbecue contest. I keep to myself. I'm there to cook, not there to party. I'm a hermit; I hide. I get a lot of publicity, and I can perform well at it. But I don't toot my own horn.

"Have you read Doug Worgul's book about Kansas City Barbecue? I'm so embarrassed. He equates my contribution to barbecue with Vince Lombardi's to football and Jack Nicklaus's to golf. Combined. It's very flattering.

"I have a knack that I can look at a recipe and convert it to barbecue on paper. I can write one up and not even test it, and I know it'll be good. I win recipe contests all the time. There are a few of 'em who won't let me enter anymore because I always win."

Paul's first contest was the American Royal back in 1981. He was a chef at a roadhouse restaurant where he cooked barbecue, fried chicken steaks, the whole nine yards. "My employers said, 'Paul, you're pretty good at barbecue. Why don't you get into that American Royal and we'll reimburse you.'"

He thinks for a minute. "In fact, when the mail gets here Monday, I'll see if that reimbursement check has finally arrived."

Paul borrowed two grills, a Hasty-Bake and a Weber Kettle, and headed to Kansas City in a pickup truck. "I stopped for a cocktail and came out at midnight to a flat tire with no spare. I had to get a ride home and borrow a van for the next day.

"The next morning at 7 a.m., I realized I forgot the charcoal. I went over to a store across the highway, came back out, and the van wouldn't start. I called my sous chef, and he arrived at 8:30. I was in a panic by then. I finally got the grill started and got to cooking. I ended up getting the ribs done several hours ahead of time. I just took an apple and sliced it real thin, laid it over the ribs, and wrapped them in plastic. They'll stay moist that way, in a cooler. I also did marinated Hawaiian-style chicken. I took first in chicken and second in ribs. It's been downhill ever since.

"I still compete; three contests a year is the least I've ever done. I've cooked in every Kansas State championship and in all American Royals except the first one."

The talk turns to Kansas City barbecue restaurants. I'm curious as to which ones he thinks are the best.

"I think the best barbecue place in Kansas City is Oklahoma Joe's. I'd have to pick Arthur Bryant's for my last supper, though."

That surprises me. While Arthur Bryant's is considered a barbecue mecca, it's not quite the same as it was in the old days. Paul agrees with me, but it's his benchmark, and his memory of Arthur Bryant's will always be warm and fuzzy.

"It's an iconic Kansas City place. I knew Arthur personally; he was a very gentle man. You either love it or you hate it. I've never found anyplace close to it. I get a Bryant's attack about every month, and I go down and have a sandwich."

Barbecue legends at the Jack:
Front row: Paul Kirk, Jim Tabb, Pat Burke, and me
Middle: Myron Mixon, Garry Rourk, and Roger Wagner
Back: Don McLemore and Chris Lilly

Strawberry Margarita Barbecue Sauce

Fruit-based sauces are very popular and are best paired with pork and poultry. Paul uses his knowledge of spices and ingredients to make all kinds of rubs and sauces that aren't exactly authentic barbecue, but they are just plain good.

- 2 cups strawberry jelly
- 1 quart fresh strawberries, sliced
- 2 cups sugar
- 1 quart ketchup
- 1 cup light corn syrup (like Karo)
- 1 cup raspberry balsamic vinegar
- ½ cup frozen limeade concentrate
- 1 can (6 ounces) tomato paste
- 1 tablespoon peeled, grated fresh ginger
- 2 tablespoons tequila
- 2 tablespoons triple sec
- 1 to 2 tablespoons sea salt, finely ground
- 1 tablespoon chipotle powder
- 1 teaspoon finely ground black pepper

Combine all the ingredients in a large saucepan over medium heat. Bring to a simmer, reduce the heat, and simmer for 30 minutes. Puree in batches in a blender until smooth.

MAKES ABOUT 3 QUARTS

Secrets and Lies

Creating recipes is Paul's passion. "I'm going to give you a real recipe; I always give away the real thing. I want people to be able to make good food, good quality food. I'm not going to mess that up by giving someone a partial recipe. It's not gonna be the same thing. You're ahead already because of your ability. I would never give away a bad recipe or sabotage any food. That's my name. Every time I put a dish together, it's my reputation. I'm not gonna lie just to stroke my ego. I want people to have good food and to enjoy it."

These days, Paul makes his living by consulting with barbecue restaurants, writing books, catering, and teaching cooking classes across the country.

"My classes are intense. Twelve full hours. I'm not doing it for the money; I want to pass on my knowledge. I want to make the sport of barbecue better. I teach authentic, old-style barbecue. I do not allow use of the Oklahoma or Texas crutch: wrapping barbecue in foil. That's barbecue as pot roast."

"I agree with you there," I tell him. "That's just plain wrong. The only thing that's worse is parboiling your meat first."

"We have a lot of fun in my classes. If I don't have a bunch of ladies present, I tell 'em it's okay to feel your meat and find out where the fat is."

"What's really funny," Paul says, "is I get asked to critique a lot of barbecue. But if you don't want my opinion, don't ask me. I try not to be brutal, but if it's bad, it's bad. Some people use lighter fluid. I have a very good palate, and I can pick it up. It's really hard to get rid of that flavor. You can do it, but not too many people know how. I'll say, 'That's not too bad except for the lighter fluid.' And they'll say, 'I didn't use lighter fluid!' and I'll say, 'Yes, you did.' And then they'll admit it.

"And another thing that a lot of people do is use Adolph's meat tenderizer. There's nothing illegal about it, but you'll never find anybody that admits they use it."

Paul's been around a long time, so I know he's heard it all. "What's the biggest lie you've ever heard?" I ask him.

He laughs. "That you're a good barbecuer."

Ollie Gates

GATES AND SONS BAR-B-Q

Kansas City, Missouri

I'm more than a little in awe of Ollie Gates.

Kansas City's reigning living legend presides over six Kansas City–area Gates and Sons Bar-B-Q restaurants. Ollie's mother and father got into the barbecue business in 1946, and 2004 marked 58 years in business.

"So how does it feel to be Kansas City's living barbecue legend?" I ask him.

"I guess I'm probably one of the oldest guys still in the business," Ollie answers humbly, "but I don't know if that makes me a legend. I don't even know that I am successful. It just depends on who you compare me with. We've been lucky."

"Luck is huge," I agree. "People don't always understand how much of success is being in the right place at the right time and being really lucky. I always say the barbecue gods have smiled on me."

"There you go," he laughs. "The barbecue gods. I like that."

I ask Ollie if he eats other barbecue. He certainly has his pick of 90 some-odd places.

"What I do is taste," he tells me. "I have tasted some of the competitors from time to time. Those I have respect for."

"I make it a point to never to pass up a sign that says 'BBQ' if I can help it," I say. "Therefore I always have a hard time getting out of Kansas City and Memphis on schedule. I do like to eat barbecue."

Ollie knows what I mean. "It's all good, as long as it's done with some feeling," he says. "Barbecue allows people to express themselves. Every barbecue has a different personality. I like 'em all. I'm sure I'd like yours. I just prefer mine. That's the taste that I like."

I like Ollie's barbecue, too. And I especially like his sauce. He graciously shares the recipe on page 60.

I'm certain Ollie has heard some good stories over the years and I wonder how many he's told himself.

"Oh," Ollie nods knowingly. "You're lookin' for fish tales."

"Yes, sir, I am," I laugh. "You got any?"

"I know a few tales, but I don't tell any lies," he says with a straight face. "Maybe a white lie or two, but not any whoppers."

"Me, either," I assure him.

"Probably the biggest lie I ever told was when I left Kansas City in 1949 and headed off to Durham, North Carolina, on a football scholarship," Ollie tells me. "I said that I was going to be something else; I was not going to be in the barbecue business. I wanted to be a builder more than anything else.

"In those days there was not too much potential for black kids in Kansas City because the professions were doctors, lawyers, teachers, and preachers. The barbecue restaurant or speakeasy restaurant kind of thing was not looked upon with admiration or considered a good professional business by the select few society folk."

I can tell by the way Ollie carries himself that he is a man filled with pride. His dress and speech are impeccable. His staff and customers treat him with reverence. And he, in turn, treats them with great respect. In fact, the word "respect" is frequently spoken by Ollie Gates.

"I like to think that I made the business respectable," he says. " Barbecue was pretty primitive when I left town in 1949. Now we have systems and a clean environment. We operate as a business. We have tried to move the standard from the lower end of the totem pole in the restaurant business. We wanted to become more than just a shack by the track.

"And we wanted to make the hometown folk proud of what we tried to do," he concludes.

"I know for a fact that your hometown folk are proud," I assure him. "I hear you talked about with great admiration all of the time."

"Is that right?" he asks. "Well, at least the atmosphere is better. I got air conditioning now. And exhaust fans. So smoke isn't getting in my eyes as much as it used to."

Looking around, I can see that Ollie has a lot to be proud of. "If you have to choose one thing," I question. "What would you say is your main point of pride?"

"My kids," Ollie answers, without skipping a beat. "Four of my five kids work with me. The barbecue business, as you know it, is not a business. It's kind of a way of life and you don't want to get into that unless you take your whole family into that way of life. I have to have my family here to be around them. You don't bring your wife in, then you'll be separated, like I have been since the 1970s."

"I can relate to that," I tell him.

"You can't have everything," Ollie shrugs. "But I have peace."

"Well, if you have peace, then you're doing okay," I say, as we exchange a knowing smile.

Maurice Bessinger

MAURICE'S BBQ/PIGGIE PARK

West Columbia, South Carolina

The original Maurice's BBQ restaurant certainly makes a statement. Actually, it makes itself known way before you arrive in town. I counted no fewer than 18 billboards, all with Maurice's larger-than-life image, leading the way to Piggie Park. The original restaurant occupies a good part of a peninsula-type piece of property, and his operation is actually more of a compound. There's the restaurant, which also has drive-through service, an old-fashioned drive-in area, and a park with picnic tables. Another building houses his corporate offices and a church. One whole area is filled with logs. He has his own log-splitting machinery. A fleet of trucks, decorated with giant bottles of Maurice's Gold sauce, is parked by a warehouse. Maurice even had his own hog farm at one point, but that just got to be too much work.

Maurice has been stirring up a storm with his politics for years. On July 1, 2000, when the Confederate flag was lowered forever at the State Capitol Building, Maurice raised a giant Confederate flag at each of his locations. And smaller versions, alternating with the American flag, march along the roofline of the buildings. All those flags make some people a little uneasy, and others find them downright offensive. Much has been written about this controversy; Maurice even wrote a whole book about it himself. But that's not what I want to talk to him about. No matter what you think about his politics, the fact remains that the man can smoke a pig. Maurice is definitely a legend in the barbecue world.

The last time I caught up with Maurice, he was on his way to a Civil War reenactment. Luckily, he had a little time to talk.

"Sherman came through here—guess you've heard of Sherman?" he asks me.

"Yes," I assure him. "I've heard of Sherman."

"I'm suing all of these chain stores," he launches right in.

As much as that's part of Maurice's story, I try to veer away from all that Confederate flag and lawsuit business. "Tell me about your sauce," I ask.

"It's a different sauce, mustard based. But it doesn't taste too much like mustard," Maurice tells me.

I stare at him in disbelief: His sauce is called "Maurice's Gold," and it's just about the color of a dark yellow crayon because of all the mustard in it. It's sweet and tart and tastes heavily of mustard—in a very good way.

"Mustard is the great earth, and the Bible speaks a lot about the mustard seed. As a matter of fact, most of my recipe comes from the Bible," says Maurice. "My daddy come up with it, that's the story.

"My father was a farmer, and I was born in the beginning of the Depression. I thank God for that. I think that taught me a lot, going through those real hard times."

I laugh. "You know, everybody has their own version of hard times. I grew up in the early '40s, and until the '70s I thought we were still in the Depression! I thought it ended in the '70s!"

During a stint in the Army, Maurice tells me, he made $33 a month. "I kept $5 or $10 to live on and sent the rest back home to the bank. Those other boys, they spent it all right away, and then they wanted to borrow from me. I'd gone through the Depression; I valued money. I had $8,000 cash when I was discharged. I came home and bought a new car and still had $7,000 left. I used that money to start my business."

Maurice Bessinger

I tell him, "My brother did that, too; he was a loan shark. He loaned those other boys money, but they had to pay interest. He came home with money, too."

"Charging interest didn't occur to me," says Maurice thoughtfully. "That sounds like a lot of bookkeeping."

We talk a little bit about his troubles and lawsuits, then I bring him back around to the subject at hand. "Maurice, what do you think is so great about barbecue?"

"Well, it's probably one of the real American dishes. The original American dish, certainly in the South."

Maurice continues, "The hog has done more for this country than it's been given credit for, I tell you. It's sent many a boy to college, by raising pigs. Somebody give me a pig when I was about 10 years old, and I raised that pig and he won first prize at the county fair. I fed him garbage from daddy's restaurant. Raising hogs, I wish that's all I had to do. I love pigs. There's just something special about pigs."

He's absolutely right.

Similar to Maurice's Carolina Mustard Barbecue Sauce

I didn't even bother to ask Maurice for a sauce recipe because I knew what the answer was gonna be. If you're craving an authentic South Carolina–style mustard sauce, you'll find this sauce tastes just as good as Maurice's. In fact, if Maurice had this recipe, I believe he'd change his.

1 ½ cups prepared yellow mustard (you should use French's)

7 tablespoons brown sugar

8 tablespoons tomato paste

5 tablespoons apple cider vinegar

1 tablespoon Worcestershire sauce

½ teaspoon cayenne

½ teaspoon ground black pepper

½ teaspoon granulated garlic

Whisk all the ingredients together in a saucepan over medium heat. Simmer until the sugar is dissolved. Don't overcook. Remove from the heat and let cool. Pour into a sterilized glass jar. Refrigerate between uses.

MAKES ABOUT 2 CUPS

The drive-up menu at Piggie Park

Like many people in barbecue, Maurice's family is heavily involved in the business, and they've worked long and hard for many years—2004 marked 51 years in that location. Now that's some longevity.

"My children have worked with me since an early age. Just like I worked with my dad, they stuck by me. Two sons and a daughter, 100 percent in the business, and I hope they'll carry it on. Some grandchildren are coming into it, too. How 'bout you? I see your daughter works with you. How 'bout your son?"

"He became a vegetarian," I tell him.

"Huh." Maurice chews on that one for a minute. He can't quite come up with a response.

Having your entire extended family dependent on you can weigh a man down. I ask Maurice if it makes him nervous sometimes.

"Well, sometimes it's a negative thing," he says. "You can't fire your family."

I laugh. "But you can threaten!"

"It's a commitment, and there's not a whole lot of home life. Your home life becomes here, and your friends are your customers. When you try to make plans or have an outside interest, it's interrupted so much and it frustrates you so much to change your plans so you just quit making those plans.

Maurice takes over my interview: "What is the single thing that caused me to be successful—why don't you ask me that?"

"Okay. What is the secret to your success?" I ask.

"I think the biggest secret to my success is that I love people. I didn't start in this business thinking I was going to get rich—I started out to have a lot of happy, satisfied customers. I wanted to have the best barbecue there was. I wanted to have the best food you could have and to satisfy my customers. That's the ingredient to being successful in the restaurant business and probably in every business. It's not about making 20 percent profit. If you start with that line of thinking, you're gonna go broke. Too much emphasis on making money. We didn't try to watch the food and labor cost too much; we just ran the business the best we could. The best product we could possibly produce ended up on the table. And the customers keep coming back.

"Now the other thing is that most people, when they start making money, start spending too much. I put all that money back in the business, 90 percent of the profits go right back in. We live very frugally. My wife still criticizes me today for that."

"We got a lot in common there," I tell him. "But you've still got a wife and I don't."

"Just barely," says Maurice.

Wayne Monk

LEXINGTON BARBECUE

Lexington, North Carolina

The last time I made my way through North Carolina, I called ahead to coordinate my schedule with Wayne Monk, who's widely regarded as having some of the best of Western North Carolina–style barbecue.

"He's semiretired now," the young fella who answered the phone tells me.

That was a new one on me, so I ask Wayne about his semiretirement when I see him.

Wayne just shakes his head. "Who'd you talk to? I work seven days a week, even though I'm only open six. I used to work 75- and 80-hour weeks; I'm working 35 to 40 now. Part-time. Half-days."

He continues, "Some people come in and say, 'I haven't seen you in here in two years,' and somebody else'll say, 'Don't you ever go home? You're here every time I come in!' It's what I do. I have a couple of buddies who come in for coffee in the mornings. We solve a few problems. Pigs in the city or war in Iraq. We're open. We have opinions on everything."

Lexington Barbecue is a family affair. Wayne has three children and nine grandchildren, and most of them work at the restaurant. "Now I've got 15 of my family working here," Wayne says. "I obligate each one and delegate a little authority to each one. So now I don't have to close every night. Here's who I got on the payroll: my son, son-in-law, brother, six grandchildren, wife, two daughters, four or five first cousins on my wife's side, and a couple first cousins once removed on my wife's side. My brother had a restaurant for 17 years, and he sold it to my daughter and son-in-law. They stayed there for a few years, and then they came back here. Like a mother hen, I take 'em all in.

"The grandchildren, they want cars, so they work. I don't overwork anybody, though. We switch out. School kids can make their ball games. My son and son-in-law work a 40-hour week."

Puffs of smoke billow overhead as Wayne Monk poses in front of his woodpile.

I nod. "You worked harder so they can work that schedule."

"Yeah," he says. "They don't know that, but that's what I do.

"You have to have an anchor. Just like at a grocery story or service station. Somebody has to be there to anchor things. That's what I do. And it works for us.

"I enjoy what I do," Wayne tells me. "This is my life now. This is all I've done for the last 50 years and I enjoy it. Guess I've just been in it so long I don't know any better!"

"Yep," I agree. "I've used that expression before."

"I got into it by accident, anyway. I was about 15 and I was in a car with two other guys. And the owner of a business came out and tried to hire the driver and then the other guy, and they turned him down. I was the third choice. That's how I got my first job. The driver works here right now; he works for me."

"So he made the wrong decision?" I laugh.

"Yeah. I got in and tried to get out for 10 years. I worked two and three jobs. And I was in the Air Force. But I ended up back here, and even when I was home on leave, I worked in the restaurant. I needed the money. After about 10, 11 years, I came out here, and somebody unloaded the place on me really."

Chopped barbecue is the most popular menu item at Lexington. Wayne cooks nothing but shoulders, smoked over hot coals. They burn their own oak and hickory wood. Wayne told me the shoulders take about 10 hours to cook.

"I don't do ribs," he says. "I keep it simple. I've had to back off of some items. We had some beef on the menu for a time, and we sold the heck out of it. But everybody who wanted it ordered differently. We worked our butts off."

Wayne has had to keep Lexington's homemade cobblers on the menu, even though they are both a blessing and a curse. People linger too long over dessert, so they can't move the tables fast enough. People have to stand and wait a bit. The wait's worth it, though, especially for that cobbler.

"My wife and I worked on the recipe, and my daughter makes it every day. We have cherry, berry-berry, and peach, and we sell the heck out of it."

Lexington Barbecue Red Slaw

According to Wayne Monk, their unusual red slaw is the most popular side dish. In the 1920s, a lady named Miss Dale came up with the slaw recipe. Cabbage was cheap and plentiful year 'round, and the dressing uses some of the same ingredients as the sauce. "Everything we do here is all tied together like a can of worms," says Wayne.

Just like with his kitchen dip, Wayne told me the ingredients in the slaw, just not the proportions. I think you'll find this an acceptable rendition.

½ cup apple cider vinegar

¼ cup sugar

½ cup ketchup

½ teaspoon kosher salt, finely ground

5 to 6 cups finely chopped cabbage

1 teaspoon ground black pepper

1 tablespoon hot sauce (like Texas Pete or Frank's Red Hot), optional

Whisk the vinegar, sugar, ketchup, and salt together in a small bowl until the sugar dissolves. Combine the cabbage and the dressing in a large bowl. Add the pepper and hot sauce, if desired, and taste for spiciness. Add more pepper or hot sauce if you want a little more heat.

SERVES 8

Wayne has noticed that his clientele has aged right along with him. "I'm not complaining; it's just the way it is," he explains. "I'm serving the third generation of some of my original customers. We don't do the rush-rush-rush that we used to do, because our prices have increased. We're not an economy restaurant anymore. But we still cook every bit of our food the hard way. Lots of labor."

"You have any tall tales or lies to tell me?" I ask.

"Oh . . . that'll take a little time." Wayne thinks for a minute. "I'll tell you the most recent one. Somebody came in and told me the bus driver wanted to see me outside. I just knew he wanted a discount, those bus drivers and tour directors are always wantin' to eat for free. I went out prepared to tell him 'no!' and there stood Kenny Rogers. That's why they called me out there. And then I didn't know what to say!"

"Isn't it amazing the people that barbecue attracts?" I ask.

"I've had some interesting people come through. Johnny Unitas, Andre the Giant, Dexter Manley, lots of state governors. Robert Duvall, he went back to see the pits and stayed and talked for an hour. There was a rumor that Tom Cruise was coming in, too, and all of the teeny boppers sat for a few days, waiting on Tom Cruise. But he didn't show.

"I met Ronald Reagan when I went to Williamsburg, Virginia, to cook at an economic summit meeting. Margaret Thatcher and Pierre Trudeau and François Mitterand were there, too. They wanted to feed 'em some authentic American food. That was quite an honor. We don't have nothing about it on the walls, but we'll talk about it."

Wherever I go, I eat barbecue, and I'm surprised to find out that some of my colleagues don't like to do that so much. Wayne explains his reasoning. "If I'm a few hundred miles away, I do," he says. "But if it's around here, they'll recognize me and I'll be treated differently. I don't want 'em to know who I am. Frankly, on my time off, I don't want to eat barbecue. I drive 30 miles to eat Chinese food 'bout once a week. I've been invited to go and judge lots of cook-offs, too, but I don't do that either. On my time off, I don't want to be around barbecue.

"This place has been good to me. I've traveled, I've met a lot of big wheels, and I've been able to be my own person, and that's what I want to be. I enjoy it. I'm doin' what I want to do."

Wilber Shirley

WILBER'S
Goldsboro, North Carolina

When you hear about North Carolina barbecue, Wilber Shirley's name is consistently mentioned near the top of the heap. Where Wayne Monk rules in the western part of the state, Wilber is king of Eastern North Carolina barbecue.

Rocky Mount, North Carolina, is considered the dividing line between Eastern and Western North Carolina-style barbecue. In the eastern part of the state, the whole hog reigns. The meat is chopped and mixed up, so you get bites of all parts of the pig in a sandwich. Both regions use a peppery vinegar-based sauce.

My daughter, my good buddy Jim Tabb, and I drove halfway across the state, mostly through a pelting rainstorm, to visit with Wilber one Sunday afternoon. The parking lot was packed full, in spite of the weather.

The plain, no-nonsense building seats 325 people, and Wilber usually has a full house. Wilber's uniform from his service in North Korea is framed and hangs on the wall. "I had to put a little spotlight on it so you can see what it is."

I explain to Wilber that I'm collecting stories, tall tales, and lies for this book. He gives me that look of his. "When you've been around it as long as I have, most of it stopped being funny a long time ago."

"Now, if you really want to hear some lies," Wilber says, "there's a table over there in the corner, that's where all the lies are told. I don't sit back there. Mornings about 7:30 or 8 o'clock, the lyin' loafers come in, and they solve all the problems in the world from then 'til about 10 o'clock. They talk about politics; they have resolved the tobacco problem down here. The only problem they ain't got solved is the Iraq war. They don't know quite what to do with this war in Iraq. They're hung up on that one.

"I told 'em the other day that if the president called me and asked me what to do about Iraq, I'd tell him to throw tomatoes. They can pretty well solve any problem. Then about 10 or 10:30, they'll leave, and then the lunch crowd comes in. And that's a continuous turnover."

"I think most restaurants have one of those special tables. We've got one of those, too," I tell him.

"There's a fellow sits there all the time; he's retired now, he used to work with heavy equipment in the military, and that fellow, undoubtedly, no matter what story you're tellin', he knows somebody or he's done something far greater than what you're tellin'. You know the type. He's been there, done that, or done something greater.

"Well, a few years ago, you may remember this, there was a sailor that got swept off a ship right off the coast here in North Carolina. And they finally found him and rescued him, which I thought was amazing. He treaded water out there for hours. We were talking about that one day.

"So this guy says, 'That ain't nothing. We were down here off the coast one day and it was so rough they told us, 'Don't nobody go on deck or you'll get washed off.' And a fella didn't pay no attention and the waves washed him off into the ocean. And there was another ship about 500 yards behind him and that wave brought him up and he landed on the deck of that other ship!'"

"I told him, 'Well, Gerald, that takes the cake. But that story I was talking about, that *actually* happened.'

"We're good around here when it comes to coming up with those lies."

There's a story about Wilber on the Goldsboro city Web site. It says there that his mama used to tie a rib bone around his neck just to get his dog to play with him. "Is that true?" I ask. "That's what I told 'em," he grins.

Half-hogs are transferred from the refrigerator room to the smokehouse.

You'll realize by now that I'm always curious to hear how people end up in the barbecue business, so I ask Wilber. "What made you get into barbecuing?"

"Lack of sense," he tells me.

Now there's an honest answer.

"I was driving a linen truck, and I had the hatefulest boss you'd ever want to see. It was either I was gonna have to quit or I was gonna have to kill 'im, so I decided to quit. And so I went down to the unemployment office and they had two jobs. One was at a barbecue place called Griffin's. So I went over and started there. That was back in 1949.

"I worked at Griffin's for 13 years. Then I got so deep in it that I couldn't get out of it. Got the barbecue fever. Me and another fellow bought this place. The night we bought it, he said, 'Wilber, you must've lost your mind!'"

When I ask Wilber what his most popular menu item is, he laughs. "Besides me? Most people come to see me!

"Most people come for my wit and wisdom, but I tell everybody barbecue is a big seller. And the chicken is good, too. Believe it or not, our recipes are so simple, I'm about ashamed of 'em. We have a daily special and our chicken and barbecue plates are real popular. Particularly in the summer. We're on the highway, on the way to Morehead City. The perfect stopping-off point when people are leaving the beach. People can get on the road and drive awhile before they eat. It's worked out over the years."

Wilber has had lots of offers to be involved in barbecue cook-offs, but he hasn't had the time to take anyone up on those invites.

"They talked me into being a judge down at the Hog Happenin' in Kinston a few years ago, and I did that. Man, that was hard. It must've been a year later there come a fellow in here and he said, 'I want to ask you something! What was wrong with my pig down at the Hog Happenin'?' I said, 'Man, I have no idea what pig you're talking about; I ate so many pigs.' Now that's some serious business."

We switch gears and trade opinions about the gas-versus-wood debate.

"I went to this Taste of North Carolina Barbecue thang up there in Raleigh awhile back. Some barbecue boy stood beside my pit the whole time. He kept saying, 'I really wish I could go back to wood.' He even stopped here and bought my barbecue to carry back home.

Wilber's Hush Puppies

"Most popular side dish? Slaw is our big thang. You gotta have cole slaw. I won't even sell somebody a barbecue unless they get cole slaw. If they want a barbecue and they don't want cole slaw, there's something wrong with that person. It all goes together. You've got to have cole slaw and hush puppies with barbecue." Wilber uses a commercial mix from Lakeside Mills for his hush puppies. "The secret is in the mix," Wilber tells me. Lakeside Mills will sell you some mix, but it's only available in 25-pound bags. If you want to make these at home, you can use their retail brand, Yelton's Best. If it's not available in your area, they'll ship you some.

1 cup Yelton's Best Self-Rising Corn Meal	1 large egg, beaten
½ cup Yelton's Best Self-Rising Flour	¾ cup buttermilk
2 tablespoons vegetable oil	1 teaspoon Magic Dust (see page 67)
1 small chopped onion	Peanut oil for deep frying

Mix the cornmeal, flour, vegetable oil, onion, egg, buttermilk, and Magic Dust together to make a thick batter.

Heat at least 3 inches of oil to 360 degrees in a large saucepan. Drop the batter into the hot oil by tablespoons. Fry to a golden brown, about 3 to 4 minutes. Drain on paper towels.

MAKES ABOUT 15 MEDIUM HUSH PUPPIES

"If I had to change, I'd go to electricity instead of gas. You're gonna get an odor with gas. Why do they make you vent your house when you've got gas heat? It's the same thing when you're cooking a pig. That smell has to go somewhere.

"When I worked at Griffin's, he cooked with gas, and I got accustomed to that smell. One night we gave out a little early, and I called over there and asked him for some help. I sent someone over to fetch some barbecue. I was sitting on that stool over there when they brought it in, and as soon as they dumped it in the serving pan, I smelled that gas. I had got away from it, but I could smell it."

Wilber and I talk a lot about rules and regulations and how new people can't really cook the old way. Luckily Wilber's grandfathered in.

"Nobody's said anything to me about it in recent years. Now several years ago in Greensboro, they claimed they stopped 'em from using wood at all. I don't know if that's a fact. They said it was a local county ordinance they've passed."

I'm always in awe of these men who have devoted more than 40 years of their life to the barbecue business and who have done it right. This, to me, is like having an audience with the Pope. I ask Wilber, "What do you think your major contribution has been to the barbecue world?"

Jim Tabb, me, and Wilber Shirley pose in his smokehouse.

"My major contribution? Well, I hope that I have kept the tradition of what I think is the original barbecue, the way I feel that it's supposed to be when it's barbecue. During my lifetime I hope that I have in some way contributed to keeping that tradition alive through the years and generations. Because, as we've discussed, there's all kind of methods to cooking. So when you come back to the basic thang of cooking it, I believe in doin' it the traditional way.

"I don't know who cooked the first pig, but I know it goes back to the very basic thing of what I remember. Dig a hole and put wire over it and burn the wood. Shovel the coals and put 'em in there and cook the pig.

"I'd like to pass the torch on to the next people and hope that it'll be continued. Because the way the trend is going, there's only six or seven of us in the state left who're still cooking with wood. So you see, we're becoming a dying breed. We're becoming extinct."

"Do you think your son-in-law'll still keep cooking with wood?"

"I would suspect so. Now, see he's come along, too, and that's all he knows. He's like I was when I got started. It's all I knew at the time. Electric cookers and gas and all of that, that was new to me. And I reckon I was too skeptical to try it. I've always lived on the theory that if you've got something and it ain't broke, don't fix it.

"One day there come a guy with one of those electric cookers on a trailer, and I said, 'Pull that thing around the back! I'm afraid if somebody comes along and sees it, they'll think I bought it. Drive around the back and park. Don't leave that thang sitting out there in the front!'"

Ed Mitchell
MITCHELL'S RIBS, CHICKEN & BBQ
Wilson, North Carolina

"Good times," pronounces Ed Mitchell, "are always associated with barbecue.

"Doesn't make any difference who you are, where you are, or what you're doing. It's the only product I know that gives you that feeling. Takes you into a natural high. When something great happens, somebody'll say, 'Let's barbecue.' Because it brings happiness."

"Joy and happiness," I nod my head in agreement. "You are absolutely right." Ed Mitchell is a man after my own heart.

Of all the pitmasters I know, Ed Mitchell wins the prize for looking the part. Black, smooth skin, and gray hair. Trademark overalls. He's so photogenic he could be a supermodel.

Yep, he's got that good-ole-boy look down pat. When he opens his mouth, however, you learn just what a smart individual you're dealing with. The man has been doing some thinking. Ed came to barbecue later in life, just like I did. He's quickly made up for lost time.

Ed tells it this way: "Having been growing up in the South in the '40s and '50s, we didn't go out to eat barbecue, so I didn't really get the chance to eat a lot of barbecue until later on in my years. So those times when we cooked barbecue, that to me was just the best times of my life.

"I'm the oldest of four sons. I had the responsibility to make sure the younger ones were fed at a certain time when Mom and Dad were off to work. At 7 o'clock, get up and heat this pan of grits up and put in these biscuits. And then it got to where I'd be able to make the biscuits. The same thing with lunch. Make sure they're fed by 11 or 12 o'clock. So I became very accustomed to working in a kitchen, and I hated it. God knows I hated it. But that was part of life. So lo and behold, in my mind, when I was a senior, I says,

'Whenever I graduate, I'm going away from here.' I went to Fayetteville State and played football, and I graduated with a degree in administrative services with the intention of teaching and working in some company.

"Ford Motor Company was coming around, and they were looking for junior officers, minority officers, to get into their accelerated management program; to allow them an opportunity to get into the mainstream. I got into their program, and they stationed me in Waltham, Massachusetts. I stayed there for 12 or 14 years. The job was super. They treated me real nice. I accelerated real high and I was very comfortable.

"I was working in corporate America and doing administrative work. Didn't have no cooking on my mind anymore. But the time turned and my father became ill, and my mama called me and said, 'I want you to come home.' I took a leave of absence, came back to North Carolina, and spent some time with her while Daddy had an operation. My parents had a small grocery store at that time, and I came home and helped her run the store.

"Mama said, 'Why don't you go into business here?' And I sent my resignation back to Boston and went into the real estate business. Because, quite frankly, it's too cold up there! Can you imagine a poor black boy coming from the South going up in all that snow? Oh, my. It didn't take a lot of persuasion to come back home.

Ed Mitchell

"My father became ill again, and finally he passed in 1990. I was working for the government labor department by then, up in Raleigh. One day, I stopped by the store to check on Mom, and she was sitting there in a daze. She told me, 'I just don't know what I want to eat. I think I want some barbecue.' That meant we needed to cook it with the wood, like we do on special occasions.

"So I went to the local supermarket and got a 34-pound pig and came back and pulled out a little cooker. I went down and got five dollars' worth of oak wood and put the pig on. Maybe about 4 o'clock it finished cooking and I brought it inside, and Mom took it back and chopped it up and seasoned it. I fixed me up a plate of barbecue, butter beans, and collard greens and mustard greens. I'll never forget, I was sitting there just putting it away.

"Someone came in to buy hot dogs and saw that barbecue sitting back there, and that guy said, 'You got barbecue, too?' And Mom looked back at me and said, 'Well . . . ?' My jaws were full, but I was bobbing my head up and down. Uh huh! Sell 'em some, Mom! There's more than enough for you and me. I was just trying to generate some cash for her. And make her happy.

"Every few days I went back to the butcher and I bought a bigger pig each time. Got to where I was driving home from Raleigh like a wild man, pulling my tie off as I was driving down the highway. Had to get home to put the pig on."

"I'm not at all sure that Mr. Mitchell doesn't use some of that moonshine on his hogs, because their flavor will definitely take you to a higher place."
—CHRIS LILLY, BIG BOB GIBSON BAR-B-Q

When Ed finally saw that this could turn into a lucrative business, he quit his job, called in two of his brothers, Aubrey and Stevie, and began to set down a plan.

Ed points to a man named James Kirby as his barbecue mentor, the one who taught him the fine points of the trade. Ed's only hesitation about getting into the barbecue business was that he didn't want to stay up all night.

"Then I found out that you don't have to stay up all night, that was just a way to get out of the house and take a shot of some moonshine. When I was little, I'd ask for a drink of water out of those jugs, and my daddy would frown and say, 'No, that's real bad water.' I later discovered it was moonshine. Cooking good barbecue and moonshine was just a traditional thing.

"So James Kirby, he started teaching me. The first night I went home and got coffee and got ready to stay up all night. James got a kick out of that. He came in, got the fire started, put

James Kirby, Ed Mitchell's friend and mentor

on the pig, and then he put on his coat and hat and walked toward the door. I said, 'Where you going?' and he said, 'I'm going home.' He taught me about a process called 'banking.'"

"Banking is not easy," I say.

"No," Ed agrees. "It's not easy to keep temperature all night long. When you had the old coal and wood stoves, those people needed to keep warm all night. Those people knew how to bank a fire. My daddy did it. I did it so many times I could do it in my sleep because it was my responsibility. I was 10, 11, 12 years old and I was the lead person in the family. I had to get up and make the fire in the stove. I learned very quickly how to bank the fire when my daddy showed me.

"The long process of cooking with the charcoal and wood takes time—an 8-, 10-, 12-hour process. We'll put the pigs on about 7:30 at night and bank 'em and come back in about four in the morning and flip 'em over and start putting the joy juice to 'em to season 'em."

I notice a photo of Ed sitting with a guy I recognize from television. "This guy visit you?" I ask. "What'd he think?"

"Yeah, that's Anthony Bourdain; he came here and filmed a show." Ed laughs. "We roughed him up pretty good. I'm just glad he likes exotic kind of foods. We had chitlins and cracklins and pickled pig feet."

I'm surprised by how many people turn up their nose at those things. They've just never heard of 'em or never tasted 'em, or the sound of 'em doesn't sound good. Some people just don't know what's good. Ed agrees with me.

"Yeah, Anthony, he's a hot shot. I didn't know anything about him or I wouldn't have agreed for him to come. He could say something that could destroy you. But I always go out every day and try to do the best I can. So I wasn't fearful of it. But I learned about him after he was gone, and if I'da thought more about it, I would've realized it didn't make good business sense. It all turned out okay, though."

121

LIVING LEGENDS

"You know, Ed," I tell him, "there's more business out there than any one of us could ever handle. I do my thing, you do your thing. If you're doing better than I am, then that means I'm not doing my job. I've slacked off."

Ed agrees with me. "That's exactly right. And what keeps me separate is that most people don't want to deal with the whole hog, and that's my specialty.

"Here, the same guy that's cooking at the pits in the back is the same guy who's running it up front. That's Ed Mitchell and so that business is going to be consistent all the way through."

"At some point in time, you've got to bring somebody on. You've got to train somebody, and you can't get removed from the heart of it. But you've got to back off a little, too, and train somebody in case something happens to you," I point out.

Ed nods. "That's why I got my son Ryan and my two brothers. I've told Ryan, 'You are the future,' and he banks and he cooks and I teach him the same way. What I'm doing now is I'm going to back all the way off. That's the only way his idea is going to work. I'm going to run my catering operation and I'm going to go around the circuit, and he's going to take the weight like I did. Because if he doesn't, he won't learn. I'm not going to live forever. He has to learn it."

Ed has transformed this building into the Taj Mahal of barbecue. There are classrooms on the second floor with windows looking down into the kitchen. "That's where I'll hold classes for people who want to open franchises. That's my son's future plan. They'll have to come to school here to learn every aspect of the business."

The private party room has two main features. The pig bar is Ed's pride and joy. It's set up for a pig pickin', so you can get the bits you like, instead of eating the meat chopped in a sandwich. "You can set up here with a whole hog sprawled out," says Ed. "We can pick it for you, or your guests can walk around and pick it themselves."

"Once you got the reputation that you were a good barbecue cooker man, you were, as the saying goes, in high cotton."
—ED MITCHELL

Ed Mitchell's Butter Beans and Black-Eyed Peas

Ed knows that people like to eat simple, fresh vegetables and side dishes, and he makes his from scratch daily. His butter beans and black-eyed peas are fresh and fragrant with just a hint of ham flavoring. Just like my mama used to make.

If you can find butter beans or black-eyed peas in the pod, you can shell them for this recipe; you'll need about 4 pounds of beans in the pods. But frozen is so much easier.

- 6 cups water
- 1 ham steak (14 to 16 ounces), cut into 1-inch pieces
- 2 bags (16 ounces each) frozen black-eyed peas or butter beans
- 1/2 cup chopped onion
- 1 1/2 teaspoons kosher salt, finely ground
- 1 teaspoon coarsely ground black pepper
- 1 small chile (jalapeño or habanero), seeded and finely chopped, or 1/2 teaspoon red pepper flakes (optional)
- 2 teaspoons all-purpose flour stirred into 1/2 cup cold water to make a slurry

Put the water, ham, and beans into a large saucepan and bring to a boil. Reduce the heat to medium and simmer until the beans are tender, about 2 hours. Add the onion, salt, pepper, and chile or pepper flakes, if desired, and bring back to a simmer.

Pour in the flour-water slurry, stirring constantly, and bring back to a simmer. Cook for another 30 minutes.

SERVES 12 TO 15

TIP: You can use dried butter beans or black-eyed peas in this recipe; you'll need two 1-pound bags. Cover the beans with cold water by at least 3 inches and soak overnight. The next day, drain and rinse the beans and proceed with the recipe.

The focal point of the room is a mural that depicts the North Carolina barbecue heritage, from planting the fields to the barbecue that celebrates the harvest. "Lotta people don't know about our heritage. That's why I have that mural on the wall. Lotta people don't know. I don't know what my son will do with it, but as long as I'm here, it's gonna stay on the wall. Because it tells the story. It tells you how to do it and why to do it. It's who we are.

"It's an awesome story," I say. "That mural belongs here."

My barbecue buddy, Jim Tabb, tagged along on my visit to Mitchell's and he was just as impressed with Ed's operation as I was. After our tour, we settled around the pig bar for some more conversation.

"I hosted the Niman Ranch people here just a few weeks ago," Ed tells us. "They were having a meetin', talking about that Ossabaw pig they brought over from Spain. They've just about got him back to what they think they cooked some 30 years ago."

Jim Tabb perks up. "Ooh, I went to see that pig! I went on the field trip to the farm where they're raising them. It's a real unusual looking pig. Has a long nose and hair is growing straight up out of the middle of its back. The fat content is what's supposed to make it taste absolutely wonderful. They sent one to some chef in New York City to cook, and they said it's 'orgasmic.' A fantastic-tasting pig."

"Now why would they send that pig to somebody in New York City?" I wonder. "How would he know how to cook that pig? I can tell you right now, he put that dude in the oven."

"Yeah," says Ed, shaking his head. "You know he did."

"A nice gas oven," adds Jim. "They gassed him up."

We just shake our heads. What a shame. And what a waste of a perfectly good pig.

I'm interested in hearing what Ed thinks is the secret to his success. So I ask him.

"Consistency. Determination. I don't do it to please anyone else. I just do it to please me. And I think most of the original guys that really do this thing, they get an enjoyment out of it. What'd they say about that pig? Orgasmic? It does that to me to do it right. I feel good about what I've done.

"And then again, you've probably noticed, I like to do the research. There was a reason why they did what they did and the way they did it way back when. So far, the old-timers

"People like to eat real food."
—ED MITCHELL

weren't wrong. All in all, if you omit any of the steps, then you're not keeping the originality of what they intended it to be. Case in point: Barbecue was not intended to be cooked with gas, even though you can do a fairly decent job. They started cooking it from the heat that was generated from the wood cinders."

"That's right," says Jim. "Gas is not mentioned in the government definition of barbecue."

"But again," continues Ed, "because of all the rules and regulations and things we have to deal with now, you do have to compromise to get inside the guidelines, to keep these people who are creating all of these rigid restraints happy. To satisfy them."

"You have really thought your pits through," I tell Ed. "Those are impressive."

When I researched pits, I decided to go the Ole Hickory route. There is a misconception that all commercial pits mean you're cooking with gas, but that's not true. I burn charcoal and wood. The only thing the gas lets you do is go to sleep at night, if necessary. It eliminates the need for the third shift.

"Now there might be some people who are just taking the lazy way out during the day. I hear rumors about them all the time. But most people I know, the ones who have pride and the ones whose barbecue tastes right, are still cooking with wood and charcoal. Actually, it's pretty tricky to work with a commercial pit and achieve good flavor. You've still got to know what you're doing," I tell Ed.

"I agree with that," says Ed. "And you got the gift. I tasted those ribs."

"Well, thank you," I say. "That means a lot, coming from you." A compliment from one of my colleagues always causes me to just puff up with pride.

The three of us are having a real good time, sitting at the pig bar, having a beer. Ed is enjoying showing off his place and his creations, and Jim and I are happy with the VIP treatment. We thank Ed for his time.

Ed pays us the ultimate compliment. "When you find someone who really searches out the true art of the trade, that's special. This is like an elite group here. A very special group."

We all nod in agreement. And we're all thankful to be part of such a group.

Chapter Four

SHRINES, JOINTS, Right Restaurants

SHACKS,

and

Respectable

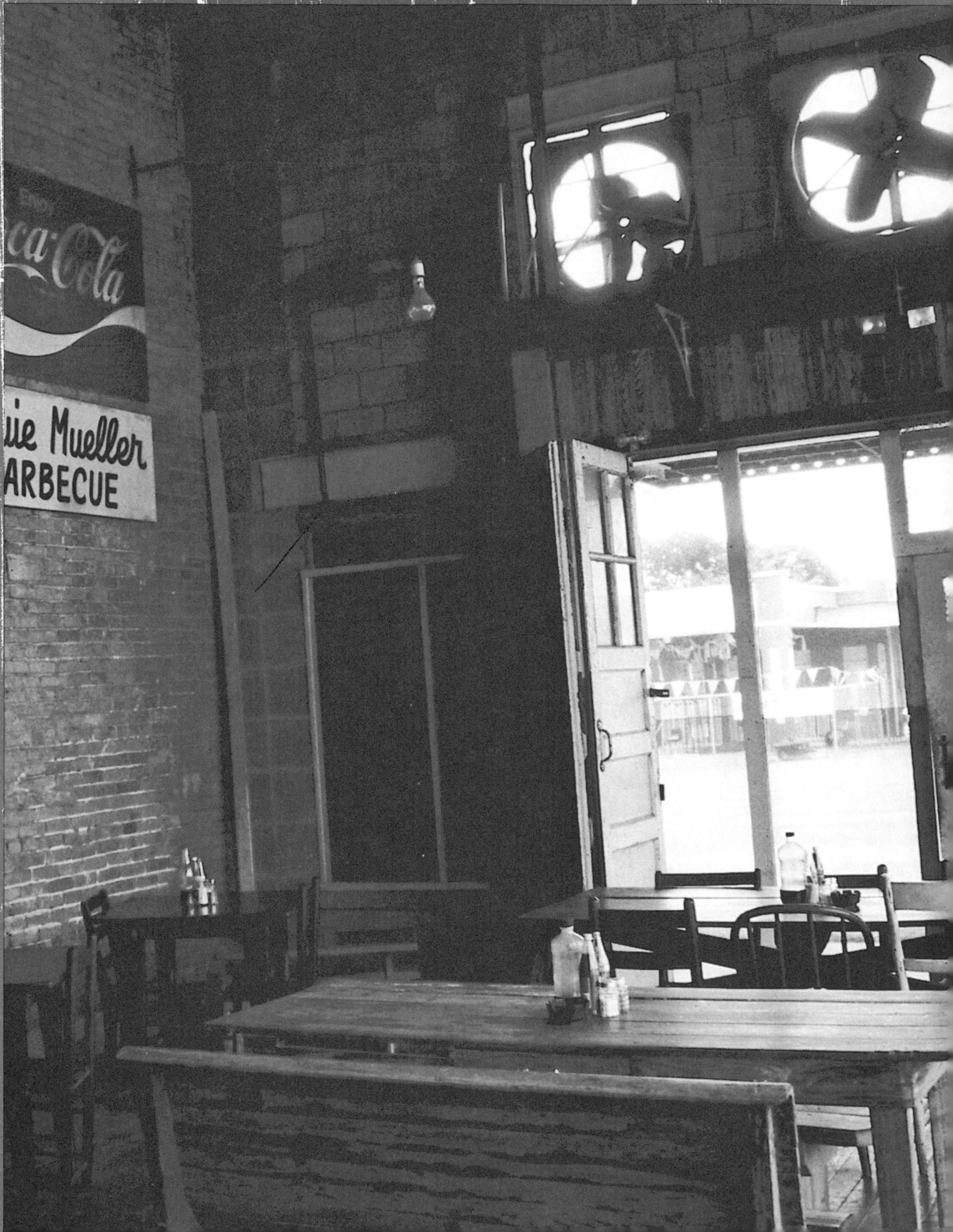

Coca-Cola
ie Mueller
ARBECUE

Barbecue is the world's great equalizer. It's America's most democratic food, and it crosses all racial, social, and economic lines. Any good barbecue restaurant will have a parking lot filled with all kinds of cars, from Mercedes to hunks of junk. The customers will be wearing everything from cutaways to cutoffs. You hang your title at the door when you walk into a barbecue joint, and you get down to the business of getting real and relaxed and personal. This isn't just my opinion; anyone in the barbecue business will agree with me here.

My buddy Wiley McCrary, of the Q Company in Atlanta, says that if he ever opens up another barbecue joint, he's going to call it "Memories." I know just what he's talking about. There are two types of people in the world: those who grew up eating barbecue, and those poor souls who were deprived. Without fail, people will always be partial to the memory of the first barbecue they ever ate, the barbecue they ate as a child. After all, we never forget our first love, do we? So when a guest in one of my restaurants starts telling me about the best barbecue or side dish he's ever eaten, I don't even try to compete. I just say, "I hope this will be the second or third best you've ever tasted." Trying to convince the person otherwise will just be useless. And really, if you can come in second to someone's treasured memory, then you're doing okay.

Often another pitmaster or competitor will ask for my advice or opinion on his food. If he wants to know a technique or how to do something, I'll give all the advice or suggestions I can come up with. But if that person just needs some reassurance or is fishing for a compliment, I know the person isn't really likely to change things. So then I just say, "I wouldn't change a thing." There's an unwritten gentlemen's code among pitmasters. Ask any of them about food eaten in another restaurant and they'll say, "It was good."

When I'm trying new barbecue, I always try to find that good thing to say. But sometimes, the best I can do is say, "Well, they got good rolls" or "They got good ice tea." Anyone in the know will understand what that means. But listen, just because I don't like it doesn't mean it isn't good. Every joint, from the best to the worst, seems to have people who think the food served there is the very best. Even bad barbecue is somebody's favorite.

Some say the measure of a good barbecue restaurant is how far you'll drive to get there. I've crisscrossed the country and eaten at literally every barbecue joint in my path and way off the beaten path. If I see a sign or billboard that says "barbecue," I pull over. I've rarely regretted it. You'll do well to go miles out of your way to eat at any of the places listed in this chapter. I may not have made my way to your personal favorite. You can call or write to me; I'm always looking for my next good meal.

SHRINES, SHACKS, JOINTS, AND RIGHT RESPECTABLE RESTAURANTS

The Shrines

During my travels over the years, there have been certain barbecue joints I've heard of again and again. At some point in my life, I've personally visited each one of the restaurants on this list. These are the "big boys"—the "shrines"—and it has taken them many years to develop and earn their reputations. Each has a unique story and its own unique food. You read about some of the living legends who run a few of these places in Chapter 3.

Once again, I must insert a disclaimer. As you're reading this list, you may feel I've left off a legendary place in your neck of the woods. Be sure to let me know and I'll add the name to my list for future barbecue road trips.

Being considered a barbecue "shrine" is a mixed blessing. These people have worked for years or even generations to achieve a level of success and visibility. But everyone's a food critic, and as we all know, people fall off pedestals all the time. When you combine high expectations with hundreds of subtly different barbecue variations, there's no doubt that you're going to disappoint some people. And they're going to talk about it. How often have you heard someone rave about a place, only to find it mediocre or not to your taste when you ate there? The more raves you hear, the higher your expectations. The fact is, everybody has a different palate. What tastes good to me may not taste as good to you. That's happened to me a number of times. Is the restaurant just having a bad day? Has something changed? Did the pitmaster go to the big pig pickin' in the sky? Maintaining a level of quality and consistency over a long period of time is very difficult.

That said, if you're in the vicinity, you ought to visit some of these places. Just so you can say you've been there.

I had to think about whether or not I could, in all good conscience, list 17th Street Bar & Grill in the "shrine" category. I'm of two minds about this. Barbecue has been served on and off in this location, under various owners, for almost a hundred years, starting back in 1915 when it was known as Ellis' Barbecue. My own family's barbecue heritage would support the claim. And over the past 15 years, I've certainly won enough awards and accolades to swell my head.

Then I went on the Texas Hill Country Food & Wine Festival's Big Bad Barbecue & Beer bus tour in the spring of 2004. Houston journalist Robb Walsh was leading the tour and answering questions. Someone pointed out the window to a barbecue joint in the town of Luling, a place that wasn't on our list of scheduled stops. "What about that place over there?" the guy asked. "That any good?"

Robb looked out the window and shrugged his shoulders. "I don't know, that place has only been there for 20 years," he told the guy. "When it's been there another 10, we'll stop by and see how it is."

So there's my answer. Have I continuously been in the barbecue business for 30, 40, or 50-plus years? No. But I have every intention of being listed with those big boys some day.

BARBECUE SHRINES

KANSAS CITY
Arthur Bryant's, Gates*

NORTH CAROLINA
Wilber's*, King's,
Lexington Barbecue*,
Stamey's, Alston Bridges,
Allen & Son

SOUTH CAROLINA
Sweatman's,
Maurice's BBQ/Piggie Park*

MEMPHIS
Cozy Corner*, Rendezvous,
Corky's (the original on Poplar),
Neely's Interstate Bar-B-Que

ALABAMA
Big Bob Gibson Bar-B-Q*,
Dreamland

TEXAS
Sonny Bryan's, Angelos Bar-B-Q,
Kreuz Market*, Smitty's Market,
Black's, Taylor Café*, Louis Mueller's,
Cooper's, the Salt Lick

KENTUCKY
Moonlite Bar-B-Q

ARKANSAS
McClard's Bar.B.Q.

*profiled in Chapter 3. See Resources on
page 313 for a complete list of addresses.

B·B·Q

Pepsi-Cola

DREAMLAND *Drive*

Pepsi
DREAMLAND

Smitty's

Cold Sausage (under 25)	1.30 ea.
Cold Sausage (over 25)	1.20 ea.
Box of Cold Sausage (25)	30.00 no tax
Hot Sausage	1.50 ea. +tax
Box of Hot Sausage (25)	37.50 +tax
Lean Beef (Shoulder)	7.90/lb. +tax
Fat Beef (Brisket)	7.90/lb. +tax
Pork Chops	7.90/lb. +tax
Prime Rib (Boneless)	12.90/lb. +tax
Pork Ribs (Sat. & Sun. ONLY)	7.90/lb. +tax

McCLARD'S
BAR·B·Q
FINE FOODS

Evelyn Harvel and Dorothy Hames show off a case of their homemade pies at Big Bob Gibson Bar-B-Q.

Shacks, Joints, and Plain Good Eating

Just like Moses and his people wandered the desert, I've been traveling the back roads of this country on my own journey to the Barbecue Promised Land. I'd have taken better notes had I known I'd be writing a book.

I've met the most interesting people and heard the most unusual barbecue success stories over the years. One of the most fascinating aspects I've noticed is the new breed of people from all walks of life who are getting into the barbecue business. Some are older and they've left the corporate world to start a restaurant. A surprising number are young, culinary-trained chefs who are opening barbecue joints instead of aspiring to fine dining. You'll read about several of these individuals in this chapter.

The stories that follow are about some of my favorite people and some of my favorite places. But in my life I've loved a few good women and a lot of good barbecue. I simply couldn't write about everywhere I've eaten or everyone I know. Starting on page 316, you'll find a list of additional places where I've enjoyed fine food and friendly folks during my travels.

Pork, Beef or
Chicken   -Jumbo   6.25

SANDWICH PLATTERS
➤ Includes: Baked Beans & Fries
Pork, Beef or
Chicken   Reg.   5.45
                           -Jumbo   6.25

NOTICE!!
SLAW SERVED ON ALL SANDWICHES
UNLESS TOLD OTHERWISE

B·B·Q & RIBS CO.

WHOLE HOG CAFÉ
WORLD CHAMPION BBQ

DEMO'S
BARBEQUE
& SMOKEHOUSE

Demo's Barbeque & Smokehouse
JONESBORO, ARKANSAS

I met Demo Gambill at a National Barbecue Convention, and when I heard him give some opinions during a seminar, I knew I had to get to know him a little better. We were talking about trends in food, and he said he sells a lot of Baked Lay's.

"All these women kept asking for Baked Lay's, and I thought, 'What the hell are you doin' in a barbecue joint if you're wantin' Baked Lay's?' But I had the guy bring 'em to me. I'll take their money."

Demo is a classic overnight barbecue success story that took 12 years to achieve. "I *evolved* into all this," he tells me.

Demo was in the convenience store business in 1991 and things weren't going so well. On his one-year anniversary, his banker called him up and congratulated him for being in business for a year. But, he told him, "you're $800 overdrawn and I can't carry you any longer."

"That's a tough conversation to have," I remark. "What did you tell him?"

"I told him, 'If you'll have faith in me, everything'll work out,'" Demo says. "He questioned me some more and he kept asking what I was gonna do, and I said, 'You don't need to worry about what I'm gonna do. What you need to worry about is that you done loaned me too much money. But I'll promise you that if you just hang with me for 30 days, I'm gonna turn this business around. I'm already in so deep with you now you can't hardly refuse.'

"I'd always had the idea of learning to cook barbecue when I started that convenience store. Now going broke and having no customers and no money, I had plenty of time and plenty of motivation to teach myself how to barbecue."

Demo borrowed a grill from his uncle and got to learning. "My first product wasn't the best, but it was good enough to sell, and my customers kept coming back for it. Two months later, I was in the black financially.

Demo and me, May 2004

"When people complain about my prices, I tell 'em, good food ain't cheap and cheap food ain't good. You want cheap food, you go on down the street to McDonald's."

—DEMO GAMBILL

"Those first months I kept looking at the stock on the store shelves. Each day I'd sell $200 to $300 worth of barbecue, and those cans of chicken noodle soup just sat there. I said to myself, 'Hell, this don't take no rocket science. I got to get in the barbecue business!'"

Before long, people started asking for side dishes to go with the barbecue, so Demo asked his grandma to make him some slaw and baked beans. He worked with her recipes until he had something he thought tasted real good. He started cooking baby back ribs and chicken on Saturdays, but customers wanted them every day.

Demo alternated between two borrowed grills for over a year. At one point, he had them both going at the same time, and he thought he was really in the big time then. He finally decided to take the plunge and buy his own smoker. He continued to barbecue at the convenience store until 1997, when he found the perfect location for a restaurant. Over the years, his banker had changed his tune, and he'd gotten real happy with Demo. So when Demo came across the building he wanted to buy, he called his banker.

A giant grin comes over Demo's face when he tells me this part of the story. "I went from broke and two borrowed grills to borrowing $250,000 over the phone."

What fascinates me most about Demo is the way he thinks things through. He always tells me he's not real smart, but I think he sells himself short. I remark on the state highway sign that advertises the restaurants at his exit. He's listed on there along with all the usual chains, and the sign simply says "BBQ."

"I did that on purpose," he tells me. "People don't know what 'Demo's' is, but they know 'BBQ,' and I got that in real big letters!"

The 40 × 40-foot building only seats 42 people, and I've been there at noontime when the line is out the door and down the steps. Demo works the cash register himself, and you can see the efficient line of workers preparing the orders.

A woman walks back up to the counter with her sandwich. "There's slaw on this sandwich," she starts to say.

Demo points at a large sign behind him: SLAW SERVED ON ALL SANDWICHES UNLESS TOLD OTHERWISE. "Ma'am, do you see that sign?" he asks. He gives her another sandwich and rolls his eyes. "You can tell. She ain't from around here."

The woman in front of me says, "Don't give me so many of those peppers; I only want one."

Special orders interfere with the flow on the line. "You don't want 'em, just throw 'em away," he says, handing her a plate with a handful of peppers. Everyone in line grins.

Another sign warns about cell phone use. "You'd better put the phone away," I hear someone say to his friend behind me. "If you're talking when you get to the counter, that guy'll make you step out of line."

Nobody seems to mind Demo's eccentricities, though, because they're there for the food, and he has quite a following.

"I'm just an average kind of guy, and lots of good things have happened for me. People think everything I touch turns to gold. They think, 'That guy makes things happen.' They don't have a clue what I've sacrificed," Demo says. Then he smiles. "And they don't have a clue what a good life this really is."

Demo's Hand-Squeezed Tart and Sweet Lemonade

Getting a recipe out of Demo for this book isn't easy. "The reason it's a secret is because I keep it a secret," he tells me. "I'll give you my lemonade recipe."

"Lemonade?" I question. "That's all you can come up with? Lemonade?"

"My lemonade's real good," he says. "Everybody brags on it."

Demo's lemonade is indeed tart, refreshing, and good. You also get free refills. His secret is using simple syrup so there aren't any granules of sugar at the bottom of the jug.

To avoid diluting the lemonade with ice, make an extra batch of lemonade and freeze it in ice cube trays. Add the lemonade cubes to your glass or pitcher.

1 cup water	Juice of 6 lemons, unstrained, but remove the seeds
1 cup sugar	4 cups cold water

Start by making the simple syrup: Combine 1 cup water and the sugar in a small saucepan and bring to a boil. Stir until the sugar dissolves completely. Let cool and refrigerate.

Mix the simple syrup with the lemon juice in a large pitcher. Stir well. Add the 4 cups cold water and stir again. Refrigerate until well chilled. Serve ice cold.

SERVES 6

Woody's Barbecue
WALDENBURG, ARKANSAS

Woody Wood is a former crop duster who started barbecuing in the late '80s to make a little extra fishin' money. He doesn't have time to do much fishin' anymore. He and his wife, Cecelia, run a most unusual barbecue business. They started off selling barbecue on the opening day of duck, deer, and pheasant hunting seasons. It got to be a tradition. Now on Wednesdays, Thursdays, and Fridays, you can find them at a four-way stop on U.S. Highway 49 in Waldenburg, Arkansas, population 80. They drive their motor home onto an acre parking lot with nothing on it except for electricity, water, and phone hookup. Oh, and a few picnic tables.

Woody smokes his barbecue on a pit that he pulls right alongside the motor home. You might wonder how much business they can do in such a small town, but appearances can be deceiving. Ten thousand people a day travel that highway, and truckers, especially, come from all over the United States to eat at Woody's. In 2003, he cooked over 30,000 pounds of barbecue. Now that's a lot of meat for only selling three days a week.

"We have a humongous truck business," Woody tells me. "That's why we've got an acre parking lot."

Their original RV was over 10 years old but only had 27,000 miles on it. They just plumb wore out the inside. They found an exact replica on eBay for $7,500, and they drove to Montana to pick it up. Not only is Woody Waldenburg's star entrepreneur, he's also been the mayor for the past 10 years. "There ain't nobody else who'll do it," he tells me. "And if we don't have a mayor, the town loses its charter and its state services. So I'll be the mayor as long as I have to. It don't take up too much time, really."

Cecelia shows me around the RV. It is small and efficient, with barely enough room for the two to work side by side.

Woody and Cecelia Wood outside their RV

"This is close quarters," I remark as I look around. "You must get along real well."

"We've worked together since we said, 'I do,'" she tells me. "I was a secretary in the crop dusting company.

"Some days we don't talk much," she admits. "And sometimes when we get home, we don't talk at all."

Woody's has real good ribs, but their most popular item is their barbecue sandwich. "We only sell one size," Woody explains. "We use a standard 4-inch restaurant bun, and we pile it high with meat. For years we had no name and no logo; we'd just set up for business. Finally I decided we had to get professional, and I had somebody draw me up a logo of a whole hog squished between a bun."

On the days Woody isn't selling barbecue, he's down the road working his sauce and dry rub business. This operation is impressive. Inside a plain brick warehouse is a laboratory-like setup for mixing, cooking, and bottling barbecue sauce and rub. Not only does he bottle and sell his own sauce, but he bottles sauce and rub for other people, too. Or he'll rent you the facility, and you can come in and do it yourself.

"What's different about me is that I'll use your exact ingredients," he tells me.

That's real smart. I know from experience that the bigger companies won't do that. For example, I use Hunt's ketchup in my sauce. My bottler uses what he *thinks* is the recipe to make Hunt's ketchup. Coming up with my exact taste took that company months. I wish I'd known about Woody Wood at that time, 'cause I would have asked him to be my bottler.

Woody uses old equipment from a pharmaceutical company in his plant. "I have a friend at this company, and his boss says to him periodically, 'Call your barbecue friend and see if he wants any of this equipment before we throw it away.' I just go down there with a truck and load it up."

He shows me two large stainless steel pots; one holds 40 gallons, the other 60. "I got these for a real good trade," he tells me. "This old man came by and asked me if I had any use for these pots. I traded him some bones for his dogs and cabbage leaves for his chickens. Another friend stopped by one time and asked me for some bones and I said, 'Whatcha got to trade?' He said, 'Oh. I forgot you use bones like currency around here!'"

Cecelia looks at me and laughs. "Poor folks do poor things," she says.

I look at all of the equipment around the plant and shake my head. "Looks like I need to make myself some new friends," I say. "Particularly ones who work for pharmaceutical companies."

"We put that safe in here and built that spot especially, not for money but for recipes. People come in here and first thing we do is sign a nondisclosure. If that recipe gets out of this building, we're responsible. People don't like for recipes to be laying around on a desk or in the plant or somewhere where somebody could see it."

—WOODY WOOD

Whole Hog Café

LITTLE ROCK, ARKANSAS

What's the biggest lie you ever told?" I ask Sarge Davis.

"Biggest lie I ever told?" he replies. "I've told so many I can't remember!"

"Most people, when I ask 'em this question, they say, 'I don't tell lies!'"

"Well, that'd be a big one right there," he laughs. Then he looks over my shoulder and calls out to a group of women hovering in the doorway of his restaurant, Whole Hog Café. "Come on in, girls, don't be bashful. I need the money!"

Sarge and I traveled the circuit together, and he provided some fierce competition for me. I'm not surprised that the food at Whole Hog Café is competition quality. He's relatively new to the restaurant business, but he's a retired military man and he's taken those lessons he learned in the Army and successfully applied them to this new venture.

"My biggest secret to success is my Army training. That can-do Army attitude. The Army teaches you not to be a failure. They give you a mission, and your job is to figure out how to accomplish the mission. Don't come dragging back home a quitter or a failure.

"I've been retired from the Army for 10 years, and I gave up everything I was doing, which was fishing, to start these restaurants," he tells me.

I laugh. "You gave up your whole life, didn't you? But did you ever have so much fun?"

"Nope," Sarge answers. "Something about this just gets in your blood. I got to liking this more than I liked my wife, and it ended up costin' me $300,000 to find that out."

Unfortunately, I know exactly what he means. "Yeah, buddy," I nod knowingly. "I've been there, done that, and gave back the T-shirt."

"Not a day goes by that somebody doesn't tell me, 'This is the greatest barbecue I've ever had!'" he continues. "99.9 percent of the people have something positive to say."

"That does it for me, too," I agree. "That's better than being handed a five-dollar bill."

Sarge Davis
and me at Whole
Hog Café

Sarge is an excellent cook, and during our competition days he routinely turned out some of the best barbecue I've ever eaten. He's quick to tell me he's self-taught.

"I had on-the-job food training, mostly just watching Texans burn stuff up. Every year for 20 years in the Army, we'd have an organizational picnic, and they'd want to grill something. And everywhere in the Army, I don't care where you're at, you've got a Texan there. And every Texan thinks he knows more about everything than anyone else does. And all they are is just a bag full of wind. They'll burn up more dadgum chicken and pork and stuff. Or else you cut a quarter of an inch in and you're eating something that's all raw and bloody. Every dadgum time. I've watched 'em for 20 years screw something up.

"So I watched and I took notes. I figured out that after we drank a quarter-keg of beer, them coals are just about right to cook on. And don't use lighter fuel. I can't tell you how many dadgum hamburgers and steaks we ate that was cooked over lighter fuel instead of charcoal.

"And then after I retired, I found out there are actual barbecue contests where you can find out just who really cooks the best. So that was just right down my alley. Get out here and drink some cold beer and have some fun. Talk a little trash and stuff. It's a whole new way of life."

We sample a little of everything on the menu, and I have nothing but the highest praise for Sarge's food. He mentions something about "double cooking" his brisket, and after tasting it, I want to know more about that. "This brisket is outstanding," I say. "Tell me more about this 'double cook.' You've got me curious."

Sarge tells me. "We were cooking beef brisket, and somehow we ended up with too much. I put it on and let it cook for about five hours and then pulled it out. Put a little extra seasoning on it and wrapped it up and chilled it down.

"To bring it back around, I left it in the plastic film and put it back in and cooked it for another four or five hours or whatever it took to get it back up to temperature, to 170. That chilling it and putting extra spices on it, the moisture pulled all those spices back down inside the brisket. Then when you cook it, it releases it again and it seems like it pulls out three times as much moisture, so you've got ready-made au jus down in the plastic. So if you've wrapped it tight enough where it won't leak, you just put it in a pan and slice the film open. Trim the excess fat and slice it up." Sounds like a tip to me, for someone ready to make use of it.

Sarge's Smoked Portobello Mushrooms

When vegetarians eat at barbecue joints, they usually have to fill up on side dishes. This substantial and well-seasoned portobello mushroom gives those folks a chance to eat something smoked and will please anyone who wants to take a break from meat.

- 3 tablespoons olive oil
- 2 tablespoons Worcestershire sauce
- 2 tablespoons butter
- ½ teaspoon ground black pepper

- ½ teaspoon Greek seasoning (Sarge uses Cavender's brand)
- ¼ teaspoon granulated garlic
- 2 portobello mushrooms, sliced

Mix the olive oil, Worcestershire sauce, butter, pepper, Greek seasoning, and garlic together in a small saucepan. Heat over medium heat for about 5 minutes. Set aside and cool this marinade down.

Place the sliced mushrooms in the bottom of a shallow pan and pour the cooled marinade over them. Marinate at room temperature for 10 to 20 minutes.

Smoke at 210 degrees for 20 minutes or until tender.

SERVES 1 OR 2

Dinosaur Bar-B-Que
SYRACUSE, NEW YORK

I knew John Stage has been in the barbecue business for over 20 years. So when I first met him, I was surprised to see that he was just in his early 40s. That surprise turned to admiration when I learned where he came from and just what all he's accomplished.

John grew up in New York state. By the time he was in his early 20s, he was living a hard and fast life on the road with his biker buddies.

"We'd go to all these biker rallies and tattoo shows, and the food was terrible," he tells me. "One night after a lot of drinkin', we came up with this idea to get in the business of selling food at the events. When we sobered up the next day, I said, 'Hey, remember what we talked about last night? Even sober, it's still a good idea.' I had done some cooking as a job once, and I liked seeing people enjoy my food.

"We didn't have any money, so we made a pit out of an old 55-gallon barrel, and we started cooking at these events and we were doing okay. Actually, we were charbroiling, but I didn't know that at the time. I was down in Baltimore and this old guy comes over and says, 'What's this you're calling barbecue? This is good, but it ain't barbecue.'

"That comment kind of set me off; I had no idea what the hell he was talking about. I got on my motorcycle and traveled the South and tried to find out what barbecue was all about. Back then, there were no cookbooks out. When I first tasted real barbecue, I was like, 'Whoa.' It was an epiphany. And then I started getting it. And then it became a work in progress."

"I'm still progressing," I tell him. "It's never-ending."

"We did pretty well, but it was hit-or-miss for a long while. We slept under our trailer for a long time. When we could afford a hotel room, we knew we'd hit the big time."

"Yeah, I know about that," I nod. "And the other end of the success is when you get to where you can afford the hotel, but you can't leave the pit. Somebody's gotta be there at night."

"Exactly!" John agrees.

If you're the least bit of a nervous type, you might feel uncomfortable walking up to Dinosaur Bar-B-Que. There are dozens of bikes lining the street, and the crowd is a bit different looking than you might see at your typical barbecue joint. Lots of piercing, lots of tattoos. If you look closely, though, you'll see lots of friendly smiles and some families and young children mixed in the crowd. The walls are covered with framed memorabilia and graffiti. The bathrooms are famous for wisdom on the walls. Every now and then, they whitewash the place and start over.

I asked John how he came up with the name of his joint.

"We are the original dinosaurs," he explains. "We drove old bikes, listened to old music. We were prehistoric. One partner was a 350-pound guy named Dino. The word 'dinosaur' just seemed to fit."

I invite John to visit us in Murphysboro sometime.

"Where is that?" he asks. "That near Marion?"

"Yes, just about 20 miles away," I explain. "I have a restaurant there, too."

"I went up through there one time," he says.

"You weren't in the pen, were you?" I joke.

"No, I went to visit a friend who was. I kept going south and there were all these casinos. South of Marion. All these riverboats? That ended up being a very weird week," John laughs. "It's just very strange down there. I picked up some very weird vibes. I ended up in some place called 'Skinheads' in Paducah, Kentucky. You ever heard of that place?"

"No," I shake my head. "Can't say that I have. There are a lot of rednecks in that area."

"Yeah, I got that," he grins and shakes his head. "That much I got."

Talk turns to the Dinosaur Bar-B-Que outpost in Harlem, and the overwhelming positive reaction to barbecue in New York City.

"When I first met Kenny Callaghan [the Blue Smoke pitmaster], he told me that someone said to him, 'Dinosaur Bar-B-Que is coming to New York! What's that going to do to your business?'" John says. "Kenny laughed and told the guy, 'Buddy, there are 3,000 restaurants in New York and only five of them serve barbecue. I think there's more than enough business to go around.'"

I laugh. "And actually, it's raising the awareness of and demand for barbecue. And competition is a good thing; it makes everyone work a little harder. Each time one opens, it just raises the bar. The good ones will continually improve."

It's about four o'clock on a Sunday afternoon, and this place is hopping. This young man went from a pretty tough life on the road to owning three busy restaurants, writing a book, and developing and bottling a line of sauces and rubs. Yet he's as humble and down-to-earth and hardworking as they come. I recognize the drive and hunger of a self-made man.

John tells me, "My secret to success is cooking the real deal and working my ass off. There's no magic bullet."

I agree wholeheartedly. "And you have to be careful," I add. "You can't get too big for your britches, especially in a small town."

"No doubt," John nods. "You've gotta be very humble in barbecue. You can't drive around in a Hummer or a Jaguar. You've gotta watch that stuff."

I look around this lively, noisy, bustling joint.

"Did you ever think . . . ?" I ask him.

"Barbecue saved me," John says simply, throwing up his hands. "Barbecue saved me."

State Fair Sausage-and-Pepper Sandwiches

The Dinosaur guys sold these sausage sandwiches at fairs and festivals up and down the East Coast before they retired from the circuit and opened their first restaurant in 1988. After a 10-year hiatus from the festival circuit, they teamed up with Gianelli sausage company of Syracuse, and they sell thousands of these hearty sandwiches each year at the New York State Fair.

2 pounds Italian sausage links, hot or sweet

1½ large onions, sliced into thick rounds

1 large red bell pepper, seeded and sliced into thick strips

1 large green bell pepper, seeded and sliced into thick strips

¼ cup olive oil

Finely ground kosher salt and ground black pepper

6 crusty submarine rolls

Barbecue sauce or mustard (optional)

Using a mixture of hickory and apple woods, smoke the sausages at 250 degrees for about an hour or so.

Toss the onions and bell peppers together with the olive oil in a bowl. Season with salt and pepper to taste. Transfer to a 13 × 9-inch baking pan. Smoke the onions and peppers alongside the sausages for 30 to 40 minutes or until tender but not limp or overcooked.

Stuff each roll with a sausage and top with some onions and peppers. Add your favorite barbecue sauce or mustard, if desired.

SERVES 6

Jake's Boss Barbecue

JAMAICA PLAIN, MASSACHUSETTS

Jake Jacobs was born in Maryland and moved to Boston when he was 10 years old.

"All my life I wanted to be a cowboy," he tells me. "Imagine me, a black kid raised up in Boston, dreaming about being a cowboy. I always wore cowboy boots, and on Saturdays I'd shovel stalls at a stable in Franklin Park so they'd let me ride horses when I was finished.

"I grew up and moved to Houston, and I worked for Eastern Airlines. I didn't become a cowboy, but I did become fascinated by barbecue. I begged an old-timer, Pop Bossett, to teach me. He didn't have a restaurant; he was just a barbecue fanatic."

When Eastern Airlines closed out of Houston Intercontinental Airport, Jake transferred back to Boston. He brought his smoker with him and started barbecuing on weekends in a parking lot in Jamaica Plain. This was back in the mid 1980s. Someone told a food writer about him in 1987, and he got written up in the *Boston Globe*.

"All of a sudden, I had these long lines on the weekends. Now I have my own place. Really, it's a dream come true," he tells me.

I nod. I know all about those barbecue dreams.

Jake and I met when we cooked together at Sakonnet Vineyards' Summer and Smoke soiree in Little Compton, Rhode Island. He strolled over to introduce himself, kindly bringing me a plate of his specialties to sample.

The first thing he says is, "I met your grandson."

"Oh, yeah?" I reply. My grandson, Woody, was 12 at the time and is filled with personality. I was getting a kick out of watching him work the room. Woody went around to each chef and introduced himself, and then he'd come back to report to me who was who and what was going on.

"He asked me where my smoker was," Jake continues. "I explained that my restaurant isn't too far away, so I cooked my food there and then brought it here. Then he asked me if I had any trophies, like from cook-offs, and did I ever go to Memphis in May? I told him no, I don't go to that.

"Then he pointed down your way and he said, 'Well, see that big smoker down there? That's my grandfather, Mike Mills, and he's got *a lot* of trophies!' He was marking your territory and making sure I know just who's important around here!"

We share a laugh over that one.

Jake's is located in Jamaica Plain, just outside Boston. He's known for his brisket, but I have to say that his ribs and pulled pork are smoky and succulent as well.

Jake Jacobs and me at Sakonnet Vineyards in Little Compton, Rhode Island

Sweet Potato Salad

Jake served this colorful dish at Sakonnet Vineyards. The slightly sweet potatoes are toned down with crunchy bell pepper and apples and a vinegar-based dressing. This salad is a new and different twist on regular potato salad.

8 medium sweet potatoes (about 3½ pounds)

1 cup tarragon or white wine vinegar

½ cup vegetable oil

2 tablespoons honey

2 cloves garlic, minced

½ teaspoon kosher salt, finely ground

¼ teaspoon ground black pepper

½ teaspoon grated orange zest

¼ teaspoon dried thyme

1 medium onion, halved and thinly sliced

1 medium green bell pepper, seeded and cut into thin strips

2 medium firm red apples, cored and chopped

Cook the sweet potatoes in boiling salted water just until tender, about 20 minutes. Drain and cool completely.

While the sweet potatoes are cooking, combine the vinegar, oil, honey, garlic, salt, black pepper, orange zest, and thyme in a bowl. Whisk to make a dressing.

When the sweet potatoes are cooled, peel them and cut in half lengthwise and then into ¼-inch slices. Put the sweet potatoes in a large bowl with the onion, bell pepper, and apples.

Add the dressing and gently toss to coat. Cover and refrigerate for at least 3 hours.

SERVES 14 TO 16

Oklahoma Joe's
KANSAS CITY, KANSAS

We're a bunch of middle-aged, overeducated white kids running a barbecue place in arguably one of the top barbecue cities in America," Jeff Stehney tells me. "We should know better."

"We all should," I laugh.

Jeff got his start on the competition circuit. His team, Slaughterhouse Five, cooks primarily in Kansas City Barbecue Society contests. He still cooks in a few contests each year, but he's slowed down on the contests because his restaurant, Oklahoma Joe's, is taking most of his time.

"When I had a real job, I had plenty of free time and we did a ton of cook-offs. Between 1993 and 1996, we'd compete in 15 to 25 cook-offs each year. We were the 1993 KCBS team of the year—we won six or seven grand championships that year. We just had a ball," Jeff remembers. "That was the funniest time of my life, competing almost every weekend from April to October.

"My wife, Joy, is addicted to winning, and if we don't win, it's my fault. It's a little bit of a spoiled attitude. In 2004, we hadn't competed in a while, and it took a few cook-offs for us to get our feet under us again. One night, at a pretty important contest, I overindulged and blew it. She chastised me all the way home. She told me if this was the way I was going to compete then she wasn't going to be a part of it."

"I bet that motivates you," I comment.

"You know it," he nods.

Oklahoma Joe's, which Jeff and Joy opened in 1996, is widely considered a top contender in a city dominated by the legendary Arthur Bryant's and Gates restaurants—not to mention more than 90 other barbecue joints.

"What were you thinking?" I joke. "How did you get up the nerve to open in this marketplace?"

"Honestly, we didn't think about it," Jeff admits. "We live here, and we knew it was a good barbecue town. It's hard to answer this without sounding arrogant, but we knew we could cook fantastic barbecue."

"That's not arrogant if it's the truth," I tell him. "What do you think sets you apart?"

Jeff thinks for a minute. "There's an elite group in town that's hit on flavor profiles that the public likes, and our flavors just so happen to have struck a chord with the market. We have some sandwiches that set us apart, especially the Carolina pork sandwich with a vinegar sauce and vinegar slaw. Most people in Kansas City slice their pork for sandwiches, but ours is pulled."

The sandwich is excellent. Another one of my favorites is called the Z-Man sandwich. Smoked beef brisket, smoked provolone cheese, and thick onion rings topped with barbecue sauce and served on a kaiser roll. I've never seen a sandwich like this on a barbecue menu, and Jeff tells me that it's one of his best sellers.

Jeff also uses different dry rubs on different types of meat. Most pitmasters use their signature dry rub on all types of meats, as do I. But I can see how he sets himself apart in this way.

"Let me ask you this: What is your barbecue dream?"

Jeff thinks for a minute. "I don't really have one."

"No dreams?" I question in surprise.

"No. I wish I could come up with something. I guess if I have an answer, it's that I'm living it."

Oklahoma Joe's Red Beans and Rice

The side dishes at Oklahoma Joe's are hearty and have a southern bent. This red-beans-and-rice dish goes perfectly with barbecue. This is served as a side dish, but you could make it an entrée by adding more andouille sausage to the top when serving.

½ teaspoon dried thyme

½ teaspoon chili powder

½ teaspoon coarsely ground black pepper

½ teaspoon ground white pepper

¼ teaspoon mustard powder

¼ teaspoon paprika

¼ teaspoon dried oregano

1 teaspoon kosher salt, finely ground

4 ounces andouille sausage, cut into ½-inch dice

1 cup diced onion

½ cup diced celery

½ cup diced green bell pepper

2 teaspoons minced garlic

2 bay leaves

2 cans (15 ounces each) red beans (not kidney beans), drained and rinsed

3 to 4 cups water (as needed)

1 tablespoon chicken base or 2 chicken bouillon cubes

1 tablespoon barbecue sauce (your choice)

1 teaspoon hot sauce (such as Tabasco)

2 cups cooked white rice

Combine the spices and seasonings, including the salt, and set aside.

Sauté the sausage in a large skillet over medium heat, with no oil, for 3 to 5 minutes. Add the onion, celery, bell pepper, garlic, and bay leaves and cook for another 5 to 10 minutes. Add the seasonings while cooking the vegetables and combine thoroughly. After the vegetables have cooked, add the red beans and just enough water to cover the beans.

Add the chicken base or bouillon cubes, barbecue sauce, and hot sauce. Stir to combine thoroughly, then raise the heat and bring the liquid to a boil. Turn the heat to low and simmer, uncovered, for 1½ to 2 hours. Stir every 20 to 30 minutes and add water if the beans get too thick.

The red beans are done when they have thickened slightly and made their own "gravy." Remove the bay leaves. Serve over the cooked rice.

SERVES 6

BBQ & Ribs Co.
GRAHAM, NORTH CAROLINA

Hilton Eades is a trained chef who's worked in restaurants all over the world. I met him at a barbecue convention, and when he gave me his card, I noticed that his title was "Director of Concept Development." I had never heard of such a thing in the barbecue world, and I asked Hilton to explain.

"I work for Boddie-Noell, the largest family-owned restaurant business in America. Some of the friendliest, finest folks I've ever come into contact with," he tells me. "They hired me to come up with a 'fast-casual' restaurant concept for them. I was off in a different direction with home-style comfort foods like roast beef and rotisserie chicken. We were getting ready to roll with that idea when one day Mayo Boddie walked into our concept development meeting and said, 'I want barbecue!'"

"I didn't know exactly what he meant. I said, 'Okay,' and I kept working. He said it again, 'No, I want barbecue!' and I said, 'You mean right now?' And he said, 'Yeah.' I asked, 'You mean you want for me to stop what I'm doing and start a barbecue concept?' And he said, 'Yeah, that's what I mean.' So I went back to the test kitchen and started over."

I visited Hilton at the BBQ & Ribs Co. in Graham, North Carolina, and I was duly impressed. The pulled pork was excellent. And the side dishes were really outstanding. There's nothing fast or casual about the way this food is cooked. I especially liked the name of their vinegar sauce. Pig Wyzz. Catchy name, don't you think?

"Baked beans are best sellers," Hilton tells me. "But I think the Brunswick stew is the best item on the menu. We make everything fresh daily. Red-skin potatoes. Cream-style corn. Green beans. We boil fatback for an hour and a half with salt, pepper, and butter before we put anything in it."

Now here's a man after my own heart. "You use a good fatback base and you're going to get some flavor." I nod approvingly.

GREAT VEGETABLES
COOKED FRESH
EVERY DAY

Hilton Eades and me in front of the BBQ & Ribs sign in Graham, North Carolina

Hilton agrees that the people in the barbecue world, both the restaurant people and the customers, are unlike any he's ever known.

"I worked in 15 different cities and countries, mostly in the Italian food sector," he tells me. "And those were nice people. But the people in this business are the friendliest, warmest people I've ever worked with or been around. They want to cook good food and they want to eat good food."

"We quickly developed some regulars here. There's one man who comes in every Monday, Wednesday, and Friday at exactly 3 o'clock, when he knows the pudding is coming out of the oven. He buys a quart, and he sits in the exact same booth and eats every bite. You just don't get customers like that in other types of restaurants," Hilton tells me.

"And don't you find," I ask, "that the customers treat a barbecue place like their own?"

"Exactly!" Hilton exclaims. "There's one lady who comes in every few days just to check the plants and see if they need watering. People are more careful and courteous even in helping keep the bathrooms clean. I've never seen anything like it."

Hilton's Collard Greens

Collard greens are one of the most popular side dishes at BBQ & Ribs Co., and Hilton cooks them in a slow, time-honored way.

- 4 quarts water
- 3 pounds salt pork or fatback—get some with streaks of meat in it
- 1 tablespoon kosher salt, finely ground
- 1 tablespoon coarsely ground black pepper

- 1 teaspoon red pepper flakes
- 2 cups sugar
- 4 to 6 bunches collards, chopped
- 2 tablespoons apple cider vinegar
- Pepper vinegar or vinegar-based barbecue sauce (optional)

Combine the water, salt pork or fatback, salt, pepper, pepper flakes, and sugar in a large stockpot. Bring to a gentle boil, then cover and simmer for 1 hour.

Wash your greens well. Fill a large dishpan or 5-gallon bucket with water and plunge the greens up and down, leaves first. Change the water often and do it again. And again, until well rinsed.

Split the leaves and remove the largest part of the stem to remove some of the bitterness. Then chop the collards however you like, preferably about the size of the nail on your pinkie. Add the collards to the pot. There will be way more collards than water, but don't worry; they'll cook down.

Return to a boil, then lower the heat and simmer the collards for several hours until they are done. Stir them every once in a while with a long-handled wooden spoon. You may need to add water from time to time, but not too much. After the collards start cooking down, you want them barely covered with water. When the collards are dark in color and pierce easily with a fork, add the cider vinegar, stir, cover, and remove from the heat.

After about 15 minutes, fish out the salt pork or fatback and drain the liquid from the greens. Transfer to a serving bowl or just eat them straight from the pot.

Hilton likes to serve collards with pepper vinegar or any good Eastern North Carolina vinegar-based barbecue sauce.

SERVES 8 TO 10

Eades Family Banana Pudding

Banana pudding is a traditional North Carolina barbecue dessert, and BBQ & Ribs Co. makes theirs fresh every day.

- 1 box (12 ounces) vanilla wafers
- 4 medium bananas
- 2 teaspoons vanilla extract
- ¼ teaspoon kosher salt, finely ground

CUSTARD

- 3 cups sugar
- ½ cup cornstarch
- 5 cups milk
- 8 egg yolks

MERINGUE

- 8 egg whites
- 1 cup sugar
- 1 teaspoon cream of tartar

Preheat the oven to 350 degrees. Fill a wide pot or the bottom of a double boiler with a couple inches of water and set it on the stove.

Line a 13 × 9-inch baking dish with a layer of vanilla wafers; you won't use the entire box. Top with the banana slices.

Make the custard: Combine the sugar, cornstarch, milk, and egg yolks in a large stainless steel bowl or the top of a double boiler. Whisk thoroughly to dissolve the sugar and cornstarch completely. Set the bowl onto the pot of water on the stove and check to make sure the water doesn't touch the bottom of the bowl. Turn on the heat. Don't boil the custard, but do bring the water in the lower pot to a slight perk. Cook the custard, stirring constantly, until it's just a little thicker than the consistency of French dressing. It should stick and cling to the whisk when it's done. Remove from the heat and add the vanilla and salt. Pour the custard over the bananas and cookies.

Make the meringue: Use a mixer to beat the egg whites in a cool, squeaky-clean metal or glass bowl on high speed until frothy. Gradually add the sugar and continue beating until combined. Add the cream of tartar and beat until the whites have tripled in volume and form stiff peaks. Using a rubber spatula, spread the meringue over the top of the pudding.

Bake for 10 to 15 minutes or until the meringue is lightly browned.

SERVES 10 TO 12

GONZALES
FOOD MKT.

HOT SAUSAGE
BAR-B-Q & BEER

BAR-E
BARBEQUE & SAUSAGE
CITY MARKET
LULING, TEXAS

**More Outposts along
the Barbecue Trail**

When you're on your own barbecue journey, try to stop
by and enjoy a meal at any of the worthy establishments
listed in Resources, starting on page 313. Be sure and tell
them Mike sent you.

OLE TIME BARBECUE

Jack McDavid of
Jack's Firehouse
in Philadelphia

Chapter Five

WHAT'S FRIENDLY COMPE AMONG

A LITTLE

TITION

FRIENDS?

Don Lefkowitz and Jim Tabb judging at the Jack

CHAMPIONSHIP JUDGING TIMES

SHOULDER	11:00 - 12:00
WHOLE HOG	12:00 - 1:00
PATIO PORKERS	12:30 - 1:30
RIBS	1:30 - 2:30
FINALS PATIO	3:30 - 4:30
CHAMPIONSHIP	2:00 - 5:30

n any given weekend, hundreds of enthusiastic barbecue teams are competing for prizes in cook-offs throughout the country. Until the late 1990s, most competitions were located primarily in the South and Midwest; but competition popularity has spread, and you can find a cook-off in just about every corner of the country. Teams, judges, and ambassadors travel for miles to participate in their favorite contests and join in the fun. The Grand Champion winners of sanctioned events are guaranteed an entry to cook in the best-of-the-best competitions: Memphis in May International Barbecue Cook-Off (MIM) and the American Royal in Kansas City—also known as the Super Bowl of Swine and the World Series of Barbecue, respectively. Winners of certain sanctioned events are entered into the lottery drawing for a coveted spot at the Jack Daniel's Invitational in Lynchburg, Tennessee, and at the Houston Livestock Show and Rodeo Bar-B-Que Contest. To give you an idea of the scope of these things, upward of 250 teams compete in Memphis and more than 450 compete in Kansas City, while the Jack is much smaller, with only about 60 teams competing each year. There are some other large regional events, but these four are the big ones.

The press likes to focus on the "yee-ha!" aspect of these weekends, the grown men wearing plastic pig snouts, the wild parties late into the night. I won't lie to you; some of that does go on. But that's only part of the picture. What really goes on behind the scenes is a lot of hard work. Perhaps that isn't quite as exciting or newsworthy.

Join the Club

The competition world is a club, and I may have been the first to compare it to country clubs and other expensive hobbies. But unlike other clubs or social outlets, everyone is welcome. In the world of barbecue, it doesn't matter much who you are, how much money you have, where you live, or what you do for a living. There's no set initiation fee, and you don't have to be sponsored. No one cares if you have a homemade barrel smoker or a $20,000 pit. All you need to belong is a passion for barbecue and the willingness to talk and share with other people. That's it. The circuit is really all about community, and every weekend is like a nice, slow-paced reunion. People take the time to talk and visit without the interruptions of television or other distractions. You never know who will be at any given cook-off. You'll meet up with old friends and make some new ones. In fact, when you show up at your first event, you'll make friends within about 30 minutes, unless there's something wrong with you. The people cooking, judging, and volunteering are from all walks of life. Politicians and businessmen, plumbers and firefighters, rich and poor, young and old cook, eat, and carry on, side by side.

It's all about the food. This group of people is united in one common cause, and that's the pursuit of the world's best barbecue.

How It Works

Figuring out this world can be a little confusing for the uninitiated. There are several different sanctioning organizations (see Resources on page 313), International Barbeque Cookers Association, Memphis in May, and Kansas City Barbeque Society being the largest. Each system has its own set of rules and regulations that competitors need to study carefully. If you have a question, even the smallest question, ask the organizers or the teams around you. Don't be embarrassed. Many a team has been disqualified for a minor infraction of the rules. Most infractions involve the "blind box" contents, and the infraction could be something as simple as using kale instead of lettuce for garnish. This is serious business.

> ## "You can put all of the sauce on it you want, but you still have to master the art of cooking barbecue."
> ## —MIKE MILLS

The main difference between the MIM and other sanctioned contests is the judging process. The MIM process is twofold. Teams submit meat for blind judging to one group of judges. The blind box must contain only meat, no garnish, though you can turn in a little container of sauce if you wish. Then a separate group of judges visits each booth. Each team gives a 15-minute demonstration to three different judges, one after the other. The two sets of scores are entered into a computer system for the final tally. The three teams with the highest scores in each category go through the whole process again for the finals judging. An MIM contest consists of three categories: shoulder, ribs, and whole hog. Teams can choose to compete in one, two, or all three of the categories. There is a winner in each category, and the team with the highest score of the three first-place winners is the grand champion overall. You could cook in only one category and still be the grand champion. Local contests may choose to have some other type of side contest, such as chicken, beef, or "anything but." Those scores don't count toward the championship.

At a KCBS-sanctioned event, only blind judging takes place, but there are many more categories in which to compete: ribs, shoulder, brisket, and chicken. The other barbecue sanctioning organizations have similar rules to KCBS. Individual contests may decide to add whole hog and dessert categories. The points are cumulative, so a team needs to compete in every category in order to be the grand champion. The blind boxes may be dressed up with lettuce, parsley, or cilantro—but not kale. Judges evaluate appearance, tenderness, and flavor. You must supply at least five portions of meat for judging, but if you're really considerate, you'll put in an extra serving for the table captain. IBCA contests are held mostly in Texas, and they have the distinction of triple blind judging. That means that not even the contest organizers know the names of the teams. The winners are called by number, not name.

One thing everyone agrees on in competition is that you have to barbecue the old way. You can't cook with any type of gas assistance or electricity. You use wood, charcoal, or both. You can use a propane torch to light the fire, though.

It's All About the Blind Box

All of the contests hinge on what's called the blind box. The blind box is a single-compartment hinged-lid Styrofoam container, the kind you might get when you take some food home from a restaurant. The boxes are supplied by the contest organizers, and they have a number on them, never a team's name. The judges refer to the boxes only by the numbers, so it's truly a fair and anonymous process. As an extra precaution, numbers are changed when the entry is turned in. If there are any markings or anything that looks suspicious, the box is literally dumped into another box, and that destroys the presentation. Teams may be disqualified for things like drawing a smiley face on the box or using a piece of fruit for garnish. There can't even be a piece of foil or anything that might be construed as a signal to the judges.

There are very specific rules about what goes into the box. In KCBS, the garnish is important. I've watched people spend 30 minutes or more pleating lettuce to decorate the edges. In MIM contests, garnish is strictly forbidden. Teams submit their meat already sauced in a KCBS contest, and sometimes I've seen 'em puddle the sauce; but that doesn't look good, so it won't help your score. MIM judges want the meat to stand alone on its own merits. They'll taste it plain, then they try a bite with the sauce to see how the sauce complements the meat.

Not Better, Just Different

There's a sense of rivalry between the MIM and KCBS crowds. The KCBS folks are covering more food categories, and they consider themselves "purists." The MIM crowd considers barbecue a pork product, and they think that the combination of two scores gives everyone a better chance. In MIM contests, you cook the whole product—a whole hog or a whole shoulder, for example. In KCBS, you can cook a butt instead of a shoulder.

I've cooked in both types of contests, and personally, I prefer the MIM system. I like interacting with the judges, putting on that dog-and-pony show. Answering their questions and undergoing their scrutiny keeps me on my toes. Some people worry about favoritism, but the bottom line in an MIM contest is that everybody could get high scores in the outside judging, but you've got to win the blind judging to win the contest. You simply can't talk your way to a trophy.

How to Play the Game

Two of the questions I'm most frequently asked are how to get started and how to win. Here's some of my best advice.

The number of people per team is up to you. I've seen winning teams of just one or two people and a charcoal grill, and I've seen teams with 30 people and big-time equipment who have a real good time but don't win many trophies. One thing's for sure: You're going to spend a lot of time together, so be sure to choose people you like. Then, you've got to have your Indians and you've got to have your chief. And it's real important for all of the Indians to know who the chief is.

In the days when Apple City Barbecue was competing, Pat Burke and I were the team captains, if you will. We had about 15 official team members, but only 6 or 8 would travel to each event, depending on who was available. We also had some honorary team members, people who wanted to come to see what all the fuss was about. Now, those people may not have gotten to contribute too many ideas, but they were welcome to be there.

Myron Mixon's world champion team, Jack's Old South, is a two-time Memphis in May Grand World Champion, and he's consistently near the top of virtually any contest he enters. Myron's secret is keeping his competition team lean. "You know how you decorate for your high school prom and there's 50 people who show up to help and only 5 do the actual work? Well, I only want those 5 on my team. The rest of those people will drink your booze and eat your food and just party. I'm only interested in the workers. You also got to have a good night man, someone who will follow your instructions exactly while you're getting some sleep."

Visit a few cook-offs and befriend some teams. Ask lots of questions. Most people will let you look at their equipment, their blind box, or anything else you're curious about. If you're well organized, you'll find that competing gets easier with practice. Allow yourself plenty of time to set up your area, to cook, to make extra trips to the store. Always cook extra meat so you'll have a choice when it comes to making up those blind boxes for the judges.

Cooking in a competition is nothing like cooking at home or cooking at a restaurant. You have the time to baby each piece of meat. You can inject, marinate, and use different spices and sauces. The judges are going to taste 10 to 20 different samples of meat. You want yours to stand out.

Teams can have a good time with clever names and booth themes. Some teams really go all out. One team of emergency care doctors and nurses was especially clever. Their booth and skit was like a MASH unit. They set up an old Army tent and arranged to fly their pig in by helicopter. They lowered it down on a stretcher and rushed in and performed an operation. The pig died, so they had to cook it.

They won the showmanship prize with that skit. They didn't win for the food, though. But it was cool.

Willingham's team members insert a hog spreader. The hog will hang in the W'ham Turbo Cooker.

Trophies lined up for the awards ceremony at the Murphysboro Barbecue Cook-Off

Smokers come in all shapes and sizes.

Elaborate booth at Memphis in May

If You Can't Stand the Heat . . .

Most barbecuers I know are typically not flashy people. Their cars aren't too fancy and neither are their clothes. Their one indulgence might be their smokers. Have you ever watched a group of men crowd around a new car? They usually have a can of beer in one hand. The owner throws open the hood, and everyone peers into the engine. The owner is real proud, as he points out the features. His friends pay compliments and ask questions. This allows the owner to brag a little and feel good about his purchase. You'll see a lot of this going on around smokers at a cook-off.

Once, down in Clarksdale, Mississippi, these guys were showing off their fancy new pit, one that had all kinds of controls. "This is so well insulated and holds the heat so well, we don't have to do hardly anything!" this guy told me.

Well, Pat Burke and I were sittin' there at about two o'clock in the morning, and we had a habit of watching smokestacks, seeing how smoke's drawing out of 'em. I said, "Pat, that one over there's drawing awful heavy."

We sat and watched it a little bit, and it kept getting stronger and stronger. I finally said, "There's something wrong with that pit, that damn thing's on fire!" It kept gettin' hotter and hotter, and it didn't shut down.

We walked over there and the team was partying pretty heavy. We walked around the corner and glanced over at the thermometer, and it was up to about 500 degrees. And we found the guy who'd showed the pit off to us earlier. I said, "Hey, buddy, you might want to check your pit. Looks to me like it's getting awful hot."

He staggered over there and saw that needle buried at over 500 degrees. He opened the lid and just about the second he did that, the fire caught some oxygen and it shot straight up in the air and across the metal bars holding up the tent. Well, that got everybody's attention right away. Three or four of us who were sober grabbed some fire extinguishers and threw open the lid to the firebox. We put that out first. Then we doused down the pit and the hog, which was just ruined.

Turning a Sow's Ear into a Silk Purse

John Willingham was using his W'ham cooker one time and the pig's ear got caught on the rotisserie. He almost burned that pig up. It ended up in three pieces, so they just sat it upright; stacked those three pieces on top of each other. They brought the judges over to look at the hog, and they never said a word about why it was positioned like that. They just acted like it was the most natural thing in the world. The meat tasted good. That hog won second place.

Funny thing though, it probably wasn't half an hour later those people were sobered up a bit and there they were, digging inside that hog to get the good meat out. All the chemicals and char were on the outside. By that point in time, it was well done. Letting it go to waste would've been a shame.

Getting by with a Little Help from Our Friends

While there is fierce competition, there's also a very unusual spirit of community. If something goes wrong, everyone will pitch in to help. Brand-new to this game? You will get all the help and coaching you need. Of course, you'll get 10 different opinions along the way. Burn up your meat? Three or four people around you will give you some of theirs. There has been more than one instance of someone placing in or winning a contest with "borrowed" meat. Lose your rig on the way to the contest? People will band together and help you build one out of concrete blocks.

One time down in Demopolis, Alabama, a team was traveling down the highway and the pit came unlatched. I think they might've had a little spirit in the cab of the truck, because no one noticed this occurrence. They pulled into the contest area and looked back and their pit wasn't there. They went searching for it and discovered it had rolled down a ditch and had plowed through a creek, then a fence, and then through a big billboard. They had to haul it out with a wrecker, and it was pretty damaged, to say the least. Another team had traveled with two pits, so they set up with a borrowed smoker. They found a lumberyard and bought some concrete blocks and a piece of plywood. Somebody else loaned a grate and a 55-gallon barrel that they rigged up to burn down their wood. The show did go on.

Stop by for Supper Friday Night

Most of the actual judging at a cook-off takes place on a Saturday, but teams start arriving a few days in advance. Most of these cook-offs have different activities going on so they can draw a crowd. At our cook-off in Murphysboro, for example, we have a fish fry on Thursday night and a barbecue buffet and street dance on Friday night.

Friday night is also the traditional visiting night for the teams. Once you get set up, it's time to walk around and see who's there. Cook some food and ice down some beer or mix up some beverages to share that evening.

We always enjoyed cooking something a little different for the Friday night party. Every now and then, we'd try something exotic like rabbit or pheasant. But mostly we had things like smoked prime rib, tenderloin, or chicken.

Cole slaw, baked beans, and potato salad were always on the Friday night menu in the Apple City tent. Various team members and friends would make their favorite foods, too. The main criteria for these dishes were: They had to be easy, hearty, able to cook or reheat on the pit, and they had to feed a crowd.

Smoked Canadian Loin Back Sausage

We probably had the most fun with Canadian loin back sausage, better known as bologna. Our friends would take a bite and get kind of a funny look on their faces. "Tastes just like bologna, doesn't it?" I'd ask. Then they'd get the joke. I've never met a piece of bologna whose taste can't be improved with a little smoke.

1 bologna bullet (10 to 12 pounds)	**FOR SERVING**
Magic Dust (see page 67) or your favorite dry rub	Soft white bread or hamburger buns
Apple City Barbecue Sauce (see page 54) or your favorite sauce	Cole slaw (optional)
	Sliced sweet onions and tomatoes (optional)

Remove the casing from the bologna and season with Magic Dust. Make long cuts, ½ inch deep, about every inch all around the bullet. As the bologna heats, these cuts will form little trenches and will catch the sauce as you baste it.

Maintain a pit temperature of 200 to 225 degrees. Smoke for 3 to 4 hours or to an internal temperature of 150 to 160 degrees. Bologna is already cooked; you're just adding smoke. Baste it with the sauce about every 10 minutes for the last 45 minutes of cooking. The outside should have a saucy flavor.

Slice into ½-inch-thick slices and make sandwiches with cheap white bread or buns. Top with cole slaw or sweet onion and tomato, if desired. Finish with barbecue sauce.

MAKES ENOUGH FOR 25 TO 30 SANDWICHES

Jean Tweedy's Hearty Broccoli, Rice, and Cheese Casserole

Spring and fall nights can get a little chilly, even when you're sitting by a fire. A serving of this cheesy casserole will warm you right up. And it does meet the Friday night criteria. Double or triple the recipe to serve a crowd.

½ cup chopped onion

8 tablespoons (1 stick) butter, melted

1 can (10½ ounces) condensed cream of mushroom soup

1 can (4 ounces) sliced mushrooms, drained

1 roll (6 ounces) garlic cheese, chopped

¼ cup slivered almonds

2 packages (10 ounces each, or about 3 cups total) frozen chopped broccoli

Finely ground kosher salt and ground black pepper

1 cup quick-cooking rice (like Minute rice)

2 cups herb-seasoned stuffing mix

Preheat the oven to 350 degrees. Butter a 2-quart casserole.

Cook the onion in 4 tablespoons butter in a heavy skillet over medium heat until the onion is tender. Transfer to a large bowl. Add the soup, mushrooms, cheese, almonds, and broccoli; season with salt and pepper to taste and mix well. Stir in the rice and transfer to the casserole.

Combine the stuffing mix and the remaining 4 tablespoons butter (you can use the same bowl) and spoon over the top. Bake for 30 minutes.

SERVES 6

Drinkin' and Smokin'

I would say that if you have a drinking problem, you should steer clear of cook-offs unless you have a whole lot of self-control. Personally, I never drank before a contest; I always waited until after all the judging was over and we'd collected our trophies. But I made sure everybody who visited, particularly people from other teams, had plenty to drink. There are a couple of unwritten rules about alcohol on the competition circuit, too. Drinking a beer each time you put a log on the fire is one of them. Another is, if you're cooking a whole hog, you need to finish off a fifth of whiskey per team member. The cook's got to be well basted, as my nephew, Chris Mills, is fond of saying.

Most people are perfectly satisfied with a big cooler of ice-cold beer. But a few teams go the extra mile and mix up some drinks and potions that pack a powerful punch.

You can imagine that lots of good stories follow all that drinking. Sometimes the night man drinks himself to sleep, or people are so busy partying that they don't pay attention to the pit and the meat burns up.

"There are a lot of subtle tricks to the trade. We make sure the smoke is the right color. And one guy rotates the beer in the cooler so at no time a guy gets a warm can of beer, because that could shut down the whole operation."

—BILLY BONES WALL

Strip and Go Naked Punch

There used to be a team from Murphysboro called "New Pigs on the Block." After partaking of a goodly amount of this punch, we'd be calling them "Nude Pigs" by about midnight.

I case beer (Bud Light is a barbecue favorite)

I bottle (I liter) vodka (the quality is up to you)

2 cans (8 ounces each) frozen lemonade concentrate, thawed

Mix all the ingredients together in a container. At a barbecue cook-off, you are most likely to see this served out of a clean new garbage can or a large stockpot.

SERVES A CROWD

Pink Pull Your Panties Down Punch

This fizzy punch is sometimes served in the judges' tent at Memphis in May. Don't let the girly name fool you. You'll be dancing in the streets after a few cups of this liquid refreshment.

I case beer (Bud Light is a barbecue favorite)

I bottle (I liter) rum (the quality is up to you)

2 cans (8 ounces each) frozen pink lemonade concentrate, thawed

½ cup lime juice

Mix all the ingredients together in a container. At a barbecue cook-off, you are most likely to see this served out of a clean new garbage can or a large stockpot.

SERVES A CROWD

Rebel Yell Jell-O Shots

The Swine and Dine team hails from Memphis, and they have 80 people on their team. This is one well-organized group, and they work for weeks to get ready for Memphis in May. One committee's job is to make up the Jell-O shooters the team consumes and shares during the festivities. That committee meeting is an all-nighter. More than one member has been reported lost along the way due to the need to taste-test throughout the night.

Swine and Dine reports making 2,004 shooters for the 2003 competition. If each shooter is 1 ounce, then that's about 7½ gallons each of Jell-O and alcohol cooked and cooled in multiple batches and then carefully poured into individual cups. Sounds like fun, doesn't it?

1 cup boiling water	1 cup whiskey (preferably Jack Daniel's) or bourbon
1 package (4-serving size) peach Jell-O	

Mix the boiling water and Jell-O. Stir in the bourbon. Pour into 1-ounce soufflé cups, shot glasses, or ice cube trays. Refrigerate for 2 hours or until the Jell-O has set.

MAKES 16 SHOTS

VARIATION: Other popular flavor/liquor combinations that complement barbecue are cherry Jell-O with cherry brandy, or lime Jell-O with ⅔ cup tequila and ⅓ cup Triple Sec.

"For every beer you drink,
throw on about six lumps of charcoal
or one small stick of wood."
—MIKE MILLS

Pork 4-Skins Grey Goose Vodka Martinis

The Pork 4-Skins from Steeleville, Illinois, are famous on the circuit for their hospitality. Not too many people turn down an invitation to visit their martini bar. Long toothpicks threaded with homemade pickles and olives provide a tasty garnish for the martinis. A couple of these will have you dancing on the table before the night is through.

2 ounces Grey Goose vodka

½ ounce dry vermouth

Shake the vodka and vermouth with ice in a cocktail shaker to chill. Strain into a cocktail glass. Garnish as desired.

SERVES 1

Cliff Knop shows off one of his famous Pork 4-Skins martinis.

Welcome to Our World

The barbecue competition circuit is filled with people who are fanatical about barbecue. Most of them are weekend warriors who are hell-bent on cooking and perfecting the ultimate barbecue, though there are a few who own their own restaurants, too. Over the years I have met hundreds of mighty fine barbecuers, many of whom have become trusted friends and respected colleagues. You'll meet some of the people I admire the most on the pages that follow. What's interesting is that each does things differently, yet each consistently takes home the top trophies.

Helping Roger Wagner position his hog on his pit

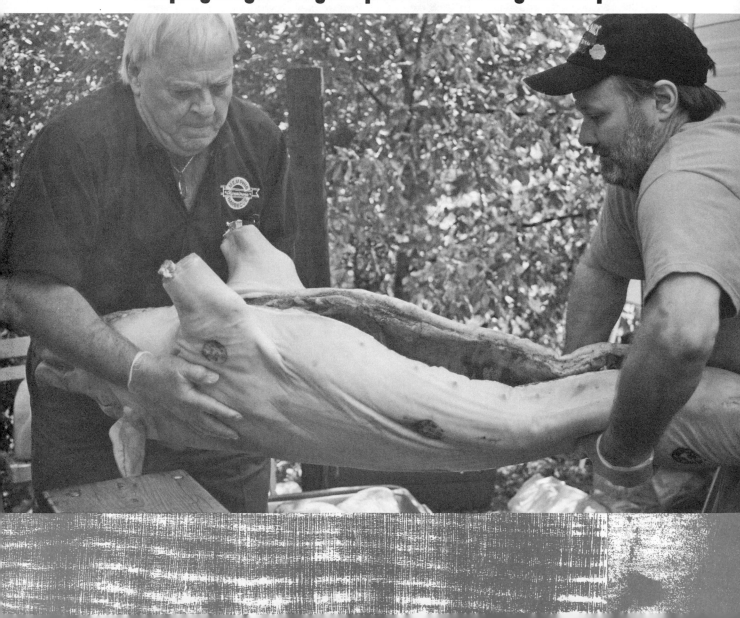

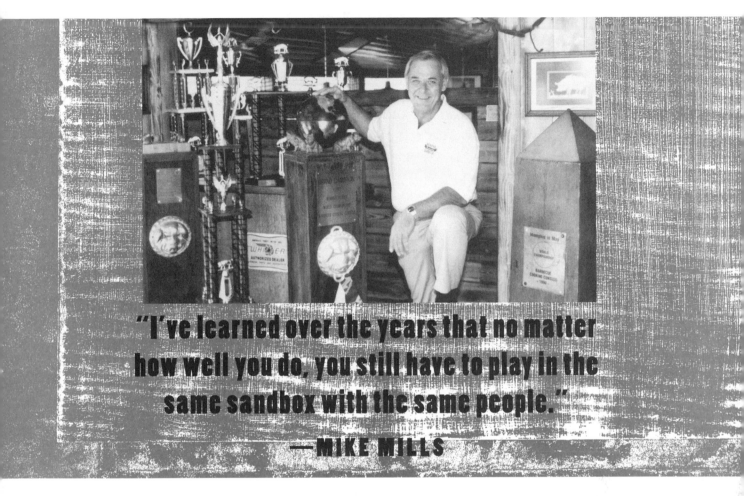

"I've learned over the years that no matter how well you do, you still have to play in the same sandbox with the same people."

—MIKE MILLS

Apple City Barbecue

From 1989 to 1994, the Apple City Barbecue team was the winningest team on the circuit. And boy, did we have a good time.

I can honestly say that I owe all I have today to my family and to competition. Obviously, my family is where I learned the secrets. But competition is where I sharpened the skill. Virtually everyone you meet at a competition is willing to talk to you all day long about barbecue. Most will tell you every secret they have. Of course, there might be some omissions or lies in there, too, so it's up to you to figure out what to believe. But the bottom line is that no two people will ever smoke exactly the same way. Variations in meat, spices, equipment, proportions, intelligence, sweat equity, and just plain common sense will always result in subtle differences in taste. The best advice I can give you is to try everything you hear. You'll soon figure out what works best for you.

Sometimes I learned from the most unlikely sources. There was one guy we called Snoop, because he'd nose around everybody's area and then go report back to his team.

He came around one day and we made small talk. We happened to be cooking in all three categories and he asked, "You got your hog on?"

"Yep," I told him.

"You got your shoulders on?" he asked.

"Nope, not yet," I answered.

"Oh," he said, nodding and looking real thoughtful. "You're cookin' them to take home?"

I straightened up a bit and thought, "You old cuss . . ." But you know what, he was right. The shoulders weren't done on time and we ended up takin' 'em home. Lesson learned.

We've had our share of cooking disasters. One night in Batesville, Arkansas, I had the late shift, and I closed my eyes for just one minute. When I opened them up, our whole hog was covered in flames. We were cooking it in a crouched position so it would look real pretty during judging. I threw the pit door open and the whole side of that hog's head was on fire. I threw some water on it and thought, "Man, what am I gonna do here?" I was not looking forward to Pat coming back, and I had about three hours to think about what he was going to say. I rounded up some shoulder skin and any piece of fat I could find from neighboring teams and I started grafting skin. We performed plastic surgery and reconstructed the whole side of that pig's face. We finished up by coloring the raw fat with some Magic Dust.

He was missing an eye and an ear, and we didn't even discuss the head when the judges came around. We won with that hog, too.

The next week, I got a summons in the mail for performing surgery without a medical license. Doc Stalker, a local heart surgeon and organizer of the Batesville contest, must've been the one who turned me in.

In 1992, we helped Doc Stalker and his committee in Batesville start a barbecue cook-off that's become a successful annual event. As a thank-you, the state of Arkansas honored the Apple City Barbecue Team with the Arkansas Traveler award, which "represents the friendliness and hospitality that Arkansas extends to out-of-state visitors who have contributed to the progress, enjoyment, or well-being of the State of Arkansas or its people." It was signed by Governor Bill Clinton on September 26, 1992. He signed it again when he visited 17th Street as president of the United States.

"We've been knowing Mike for a long time. If the truth were known, we taught Mike and Pat everything they know. They came to Caruthersville and taped everything we did, and they brought it back and reviewed it and they did everything we did. That weekend, four of us won whole hog, shoulders, ribs, and grand champion. With just four of us. But we've never won in Murphysboro."

—JAMES LANTRIP, SUPER SWINE SIZZLERS, SOUTHAVEN, MISSISSIPPI

We retired the Apple City Barbecue team in 1994, after we were fortunate enough to win our fourth World Champion and third Grand World Champion titles. We wanted to go out on top. And besides, we had to get back to work.

A few teams now have two Grand World Champion titles. If a team ties our record, I guess we'll have to go back and defend it. Actually, I'm surprised we've held on to the record this long.

Apple City Barbecue Team Record

DECEMBER 1989 TO MAY 1994
69 competitions
64 First Place awards
22 Second Place awards
9 Third Place awards
32 Grand Champion awards
1 Grand Sauce award at Jack Daniel's
2 First Place awards at Jack Daniel's
1 Grand Champion award at Jack Daniel's
2 Perfect Scores at Memphis in May (first time ever)
4 times World Champion at Memphis in May
3 times Grand World Champion at Memphis in May (only team ever)

Tower Rock Barbecue

Pat Burke, my Apple City teammate, continues to rack up the awards with his new team, Tower Rock Barbecue. After we retired Apple City, Pat took a year off.

"I thought I was done cooking," he says.

But Pat came back with a vengeance. The Tower Rock team is both revered and feared on the circuit. When other teams see Pat's trailer pull up, they know there will be some especially fierce competition that weekend.

Above: Pat Burke, Chuck Fager, Tom Welton, Merrill Fuller, and Patty Burke. Below: Patty garnishes a whole hog in preparation for on-site judging.

Classic Church Supper Seven-Layer Salad

You can always count on being well fed when you visit the Tower Rock booth. Pat's wife, Aliene, and his daughter, Patty, often bring this popular salad to serve alongside their award-winning barbecue. Double or triple this when you're serving a crowd.

1 head iceberg lettuce, torn into small pieces

1 cup diced celery

1 medium onion, diced

1 box (10 ounces) frozen peas, thawed

8 slices bacon, cooked until crisp and crumbled

2 cups mayonnaise

2 tablespoons sugar

½ cup shredded mild cheddar cheese

Take out a tall glass bowl and make even layers of the ingredients in this order: lettuce, celery, onion, peas, and bacon. Stir the mayonnaise and sugar together and spread over the top. Scatter the cheese over the mayo. Cover with plastic wrap and refrigerate for 4 hours or overnight.

SERVES 6

Pig Pickin' Cake

Various versions of this luscious cake have been floating around for years. The name alone makes it the perfect cake to finish a barbecue meal.

1 package (18.25 ounces) yellow cake mix

4 large eggs

¼ cup vegetable oil

1 cup chopped walnuts

1 can (11 ounces) mandarin oranges

1 tub (16 ounces) frozen whipped topping, thawed

1 can (15 ounces) crushed pineapple, drained

1 package (4-serving size) instant vanilla pudding mix

Preheat the oven to 350 degrees. Butter and flour two 8-inch round cake pans.

Mix together the cake mix, eggs, oil, walnuts, and the canned oranges with their juice. Divide the batter between the cake pans and bake for 25 to 30 minutes or until the cake tests done. Remove the cake layers from the pans and cool on wire racks.

Mix together the whipped topping, drained pineapple, and instant pudding mix. Fill and frost the cooled cake. Refrigerate until ready to eat.

SERVES 8

Jack's Old South

Myron Mixon is one serious competitor, at the top of his game, and he runs a tight ship with his cooking team, Jack's Old South. He's also had to learn to deal with the envy of others.

"People say, 'You win everything.' They think I've already gotten rich off of this deal. They don't realize that if you win gas money to get home, you're lucky!" Myron says. "You and I know we're not doing it for the money. This is our entertainment."

"That's right," I agree. "But unless a person has been on the stage and gotten a trophy, he'll never understand that. That trophy is the biggest deal in the world to someone who hasn't won one. Most people would rather have the trophy than the check. The first few times, anyway."

I ask Myron to tell me some of his secrets.

"There's no one magic secret," he says. "The top teams are doing basically the same things. The best teams find the shortcuts. They find a way to make a difference. I have a lot of teams ask me how to get started and what's the magic thing to making it better. There are a lot of little things that make a difference. You just have to learn. And if you don't learn, you don't win."

Myron uses a water pan in his smoker, and he maintains constant temperature in the pit as opposed to starting off high and then bringing the temperature down.

Myron believes in injecting his hogs. One of his secrets is an injection solution made with Georgia peach nectar and curing salts. Curing salts contain nitrate and/or nitrite, curing agents that are the old-time method of curing hams and bacon. Meat used to literally be soaked or injected with this cure. You can use a product like Morton Tender Quick right off the grocery store shelf. I like to use something called BHM-20 from Townsend Supply in Oxford, Arkansas. It has a little brown sugar in it, and that gives a good flavor.

Myron contemplates the contents of his pit.

Myron is the Johnny Cash of barbecue. He's got the look. He always wears a black shirt and black jeans, and he has thick, wavy, grayish hair. I usually wear brightly colored shirts, but I wore a black shirt one day, and Myron called me right out.

"You can't wear that," he says. "I've got that look trademarked!"

"I just wanted to see what it felt like to be you, Myron," I tell him. "I want to be just like you when I grow up.

Myron's Grand World Champion Peach Injection

If you want to add a little different flavor, you can substitute a different fruit nectar or juice (nectar will be a little more potent than juice). You can also add spices as long as they're fine enough to pass through the injection needle.

If your meat is low in fat content, you can also put a little oil in the brine to help add moisture.

You can't overinject. It'll cook out some during the cooking process.

½ cup Morton Tender Quick	1 quart peach nectar
3 quarts water	

Pour all ingredients into a large bucket and mix well to thoroughly combine. Fill the syringe unit with fluid and inject liberally, all over the piece of meat. Don't start pressing down the plunger until you're drawing the needle out of the meat. You don't want to inject "puddles" of fluid. It should be dispersed as evenly as possible throughout the meat. Let the piece of meat rest for 30 minutes or so to let the injection settle into the meat. Store leftover solution in the refrigerator for up to 2 weeks.

MAKES ENOUGH FOR AT LEAST 4 TO 6 SHOULDERS OR 1 WHOLE HOG

Myron injects shoulders with some of his magic potion.

The Rib Doctor

"I've been cooking since I was knee-high to a five-cent stamp," Hayward Harris tells me with a grin.

"But that's not your 'real' job, is it?" I ask. "I heard you were some sort of attorney or something like that."

"I will just say I'm a professional bureaucrat," he hedges.

My curiosity was piqued a few years ago at a National Barbecue Convention. Hayward dresses in overalls, and he's got the hayseed look down pat. But at dinner that evening, he appeared all decked out in a fine suit. When I remind him of that evening, he's surprised.

"You saw me dressed like that? I do my best to keep that away from people." He thinks for a minute. "But Eva feels I have to attire appropriately for dinner. That must be why I dressed up."

"I believe Joe Oaster [a barbecue caterer out of York, Pennsylvania] is the person who told me you're an attorney," I dig a little deeper.

"Joe Oaster's been trying to figure out what I do for 10 years! He has gotten right in my face and asked me. I keep telling him, 'Joe, I've known you for 10 years. My answer is not going to change. I barbecue.'

"What I do is so controversial, I just don't want to talk about it. It would take away from my relaxation at barbecue. When I barbecue, I like to unwind and just be myself," Hayward continues. "I'll tell you this much: I work in a building that has probably 7,500 to 10,000 people in it, and I do my level best to keep out of sight, because when people recognize me in the corporate world, they say, 'Can I have two minutes of your time?' and it winds up being two or three hours. I use only the private elevators and back stairs in that building just so I can avoid being seen."

"So that's your barbecue secret," I joke.

"That's one of 'em!"

Hayward is known as the Rib Doctor, and he and his wife, Eva, have a barbecue catering company in Riverside, California. They both have those warm, genuine smiles, and they just light up like they're so happy to see you. They're also champions on the competition circuit. Hayward comes from a long line of barbecuers. Even though he was raised in Compton, California, his bloodline is Southern. His father is from Florida and his mother from Mississippi. His family has always barbecued.

"My auntie is the matriarch of the barbecue family, though," Hayward tells me. "She was raised in Mobile, Alabama. She could take a washtub with some coal in it and use a rack from the oven and cook the best barbecue on the planet. In later years, she had a barbecue restaurant in San Diego. That's where I got the pride. Even my dad would tell you she was the better cook."

Hayward has been catering almost every weekend since 1989. His barbecue is a marriage of Florida and Mississippi styles. People in California love his Southern-style side dishes, too.

"What would you call Florida-style?" I ask.

"My sauce is real different," he explains. "It has a serious tang to it. A vinegar, lemony tang."

"You got lemon in your sauce?" I question.

"It does have a lemon tang to it," he says evasively.

"When I got started, my mom wouldn't give me the recipe for the barbecue sauce. She flat out said no. So I went to work on my own sauce, and believe it or not, the first time out of the box I came up with the sauce I still use today," he continues. "She has tasted the sauce and she subsequently offered to give me her recipe. But I told her I don't want it. I have my own sauce now. She likes my sauce so much, but I won't give her the sauce. She buys it from me."

"You sell your sauce to your own mother?" I question.

"Yes. And I give it to her as a gift three times a year—for Mother's Day, her birthday, and Christmas. Three bottles of sauce for each holiday."

Hayward and Eva have been judging and competing in cook-offs since the early 1990s, but they didn't even dream of competing in the American Royal until Paul Kirk goaded Hayward into it.

"One day I'm at the Royal just as a judge, and Paul says to me, 'Hayward, that yellow stripe don't look good on your big black body. You took my class twice and you won't cook here, you big chicken!' That's all it took. I competed the next year."

"Sometimes you just need a little push, don't you?" I say.

"In 2004 we had competed at the Royal for 10 years in a row, and we had never had our name called out. We were so busy that year that we decided we just weren't going to go, but at the last minute we changed our minds. We packed up right when it was over and headed out. We travel in an RV, and it's a long way back to California. We were five hours down the road and my brother-in-law called me on the cell phone. He was busting with excitement. 'You got seventh place chicken! I got your ribbon for you!'

"Wouldn't you know, the one year we pull out early and we got our name called out," Hayward shakes his head. "Then a friend called to tell me, too, and he said, 'You should've seen your brother-in-law going to pick up your ribbon. His feet never touched a step from the balcony all the way down!'"

The Flying Pigs

"You have pounds of barbecue knowledge, but you only give me a few ounces at a time!" accuses my great-nephew, Chris Mills.

"If I just told you everything, how would you ever learn?" I ask.

Chris was born and raised in Memphis, and we were never real close with his branch of the family. We reunited on the barbecue circuit, and one of my proudest moments was at Memphis in May in 1992 when Apple City was first in ribs and Flying Pigs was first in shoulders. We had a family affair up on that stage.

Chris is in the computer business, and instead of taking clients to lunch, he brings his best clients to Memphis in May each year. *Inc.* magazine even did an article about Chris and his unique method of business entertaining.

The Flying Pigs crew always figures out how to have a good time. One year for Memphis in May, they had some "Wild on Camera Crew" T-shirts made up. They stood outside their tents with video cameras and tried to get girls to perform for the camera.

"We got a couple of girls to lift up their shirts and do a little dance," he says. "But it didn't work out as well as we thought it would."

My nephew, Chris Mills, and me
at Memphis in May 2004

"You've been doing this for a long time," I say to Chris. "Do you still feel the pressure when you compete?"

"A little bit," he answers. "But a good kind of pressure. I know that I'm going to put out a good product, and on any given day, it's anybody's chance to win. I enjoy the competition and I enjoy knowing I can go up and compete with the best. We only cook in six contests a year; I'm hanging with these guys who compete consistently—or who barbecue for a living. Super Smokers cooks 6,000 slabs of ribs a month in his restaurant. If I can cook 60 slabs of ribs better than someone who can cook 6,000 a month, that makes me feel good."

"What's one of the biggest lies you've ever heard?" I ask Chris.

"Here's a good one," he tells me. "A couple of years ago at Memphis in May, this guy comes up and starts talking about his team and how well they do. I asked him, 'How'd you do last year?' and he said, 'We got real close; we were fourth in shoulder.'

"'Really?' I said. 'Then you must have a trophy just like that!' and I pointed at our fourth place trophy in shoulder from last year. He got real red in the face and got out of there pretty quickly."

"We have a new guy on our team and he's 76 years old. He got bit by the bug. We keep him around; tell him he's our chaperone. He wanted to take over and start cooking the ribs. He found this cooker on the Internet and paid several thousand dollars for it. Drove 700 miles to go pick it up. Had to tell his wife it wasn't his personally, that the team bought it. At 76 years old, he's still having to lie to his wife about barbecue."

—CHRIS MILLS

Colorful Pasta Primavera Salad

After you eat a lot of smoked meat, some vegetables and cold dishes are refreshing. Chris often serves this chilled salad, which is always a crowd pleaser.

1 package (16 ounces) pasta (choose your favorite shape)

2 cans (2 ounces each) sliced black olives

1 cup frozen petite peas, thawed

1 cup cubed Genoa salami

1 cup cherry tomatoes, halved

¾ cup chopped scallions

¾ cup chopped celery

½ cup chopped fresh parsley

1 package (0.7 ounce) Italian-style salad dressing mix

1 cup mayonnaise

1 cup sour cream

2 tablespoons milk

Cook the pasta until al dente, following the package directions. Rinse under cold water and drain. Transfer to a large bowl and stir in the olives, peas, salami, tomatoes, scallions, celery, and parsley.

Make a dressing by stirring the salad dressing mix, mayonnaise, sour cream, and milk together. Reserve ½ cup of the dressing and stir the rest into the salad.

Cover with plastic wrap and refrigerate overnight. Stir once more before serving and add reserved dressing if necessary.

SERVES 6

Porky's IV

Charlie Hagene is a fierce competitor and the brains behind the Porky's IV team, which hails from Pinckneyville, Illinois. Charlie's brain works in mysterious ways.

"How many eggs does an armadillo lay?" Charlie asks me as he hands me an armadillo egg to sample one Friday night.

"I have no idea," I tell him. "Maybe you oughta check the Internet."

These are so good, I hope those armadillos keep laying plenty of eggs.

Armadillo Eggs

These armadillo eggs are one of the best ideas I've seen recently. Spicy bratwurst sausage is molded around a jalapeño pepper stuffed with cream cheese to form an egg.

12 jalapeño peppers

1 package (8 ounces) cream cheese, softened

Wilton Golden Yellow paste food coloring (or yellow food coloring)

3 pounds spicy bratwurst sausage, casings removed

17th Street Special All-Purpose Dressing (see page 38), optional

Cut the stem ends off the jalapeños and use a small knife to cut the seeds out. Keep the peppers whole.

Put the cream cheese into a small bowl and use a toothpick to add a tiny bit of the paste food coloring (this paste is very concentrated, so a little goes a long way). Mix the coloring thoroughly into the cream cheese. Add more, if you need it, to achieve a bright golden color, like the yolk of an egg.

Transfer the cream cheese to a pastry bag fitted with a wide tip and pipe the cheese into the jalapeños. (You can make your own pastry bag by using a small zippered plastic bag and snipping off one corner.)

Divide the sausage into 12 pieces. Flatten each piece into a disk, place a filled jalapeño in the center, and wrap the sausage around it, pressing the edges to seal. Form the sausage into the shape of a large egg.

Smoke for 1½ hours at 250 degrees.

Slice to serve. The slices will resemble sliced hard-cooked eggs, with the colored cream cheese looking like the yolk. Serve with the dressing, if desired.

SERVES 12 TO 18

Ubon's

Garry Roark shows me a real nice picture of himself standing on his porch, surrounded by dozens of trophies.

"You know how to count those trophies?" I ask him. "One thousand, two thousand, three thousand . . ."

Garry gets a real sick look on his face. "I've never thought of it that way, but that's scary. That's really scary. Golly. I wisht you hadn't told me that. Because every time we cook, it's at least $1,000."

He keeps shaking his head. "That just makes me really sick to think about how much money we spent over the years doing this."

"I know," I tell him. "I've counted my trophies, too. And I don't know where I ever came up with that money, either. But you know, we would've spent it anyway, on golf or fishing or some kind of entertainment."

"That's true," he says, still shaking his head. "You just kinda ruined this picture for me, though. I'm never gonna look at it quite the same way."

"Sorry about that, buddy," I say.

The talk turns to keeping secrets. "Do your daughters know your recipes?" I ask.

"My son-in-laws, they know 'em," he tells me.

"You must really trust 'em," I say.

"I do trust 'em; they're good boys. I took 'em hunting a couple of years ago and I said, 'Guys, I want to tell you one thing. Daddy-in-laws don't normally tell son-in-laws this, but I want you to know I love ya. I appreciate ya'll taking care of my babies and loving my girls the way I want 'em loved and the way I love 'em. I want you to both know I love you. You are my friends first and my son-in-laws second.' And they both got quiet and they didn't say anything. But they know. I've been truly, truly blessed. My girls did good."

"What do you hope your legacy is?" I ask.

"Huh. I don't really know. I guess really that people will remember me as somebody who was a good guy all the time, never tried to beat anybody. I want to instill this in my girls so they'll pass it on to their kids. I want to be somebody people want to be around. Out on the circuit, if you want to sit down or you want something cold to drink, I want people to come to my place. This is an extension of my kitchen at home. I want people to think, 'Garry was a good guy.'"

I can assure Garry that his legacy is already firmly in place. Everybody I know thinks Garry Roark is one fine man.

Ubon's Smoked Prime Rib

Prime rib smoked on the pit is a real treat. Garry likes his prime rib a little more on the done side. "I don't want to cook a hundred-dollar piece of meat and eat it raw. Just because one person wants his raw don't mean I do."

If you're not using Magic Dust, use a rub that's fairly heavy in salt, garlic, and coarsely ground black pepper. And be careful not to use too much wood. You don't want it to have an overpowering smoke flavor. Smoke should be like an ingredient. Garry prefers apple or any fruit wood.

> 1 boneless rib eye roast (12 to 14 pounds)
> Magic Dust (see page 67) or the dry rub of your choice

Trim some of the excess fat and remove the thin membrane covering the top side of the rib eye. Season with a thick layer of Magic Dust.

Maintain a pit temperature between 200 and 225 degrees. Cook for about 4 hours or to an internal temperature of 135 degrees for rare, 140 for medium, or 145 for well done.

Remove from the pit and let the meat rest for about 15 minutes before carving.

SERVES 18 TO 20

The Perfect Sandwich

Ubon's team member Brian Campbell made up some prime rib sandwiches and passed 'em around one afternoon. One guy took a bite and said, "Now that's a perfect sandwich!" So it's been known as "The Perfect Sandwich" ever since.

"All of our friends stop by at some point on Saturday to have one," says Garry.

> Onion rolls
> Horseradish
> Mayonnaise
>
> Smoked prime rib, cooked medium-rare, sliced thin
> Sliced sweet onions (like Vidalias)

Spread the onion rolls with a thin layer of horseradish and mayonnaise. Layer slices of smoked prime rib and top with onion to taste.

The Arizona Kid

Roger Wagner is an outstanding barbecuer, and his restaurant, Thee Pitts Again, in Glendale, Arizona, is top-notch.

"I started competing in 1979," Roger reminds me. "I'm probably the oldest running barbecue team. Not the oldest individual, but the oldest team."

I'd say he's correct. Roger cooks in all types of sanctioned contests, and he wins consistently. What's unusual is that he's always been a one-man show and that he cooks all categories on one pit. Back in the late '80s, he'd have his small kids with him, and when I say small, I mean six and seven years old. They'd stay right with him and camp out in the cooking area.

Early on, people were surprised to always hear his name called out. He's not the kind of guy who's out partying or bragging. He's as friendly as can be, but very private and intense.

I was happy to run into him at the Jack when I was judging in 2003. His wife, Cheryl, was with him on that trip. I arrived at his booth just in time to help him turn his hog. He's added a small Backwoods Smoker to his collection, and he had five racks of ribs and some salmon smoking in there. Juggling all of these different categories by yourself is tricky.

"You have a very small window of perfection, don't you?" I comment. "You've got to have this timed perfectly."

Roger nods. "You get to the peak with the ribs and then it's downhill. Salmon only has about a 15-minute window where it's really good."

"This is one beautiful hog," I say as we lift and reposition. "I might be looking at the first-place hog here."

"Even though people have done a pig before, there are still things they don't know, things you don't want to tell 'em," Roger says as we lift and turn the hog.

"Like what?" I ask.

"I like to season it three to five hours ahead of time so the seasoning soaks into the meat. A lot of people don't do that because once you get that pig out and get ready to go, there's no place to keep it cold," he explains.

He didn't give me quite enough information to be fully helpful, so I have to ask how he keeps it cold.

"Ice bags. I put the pig on a table, season it, and pile bags of ice on top," he tells me.

That's obviously worked for Roger, because he has over 260 trophies to show for his efforts. Keep in mind that he only cooks in about six contests a year; the most he's ever competed in one year is 11. And by the way, that hog placed fifth in the 2003 Jack Daniel's.

I ask Roger if he has a recipe to share, maybe something he cooks for the Friday night parties?

"We don't socialize, remember?" he reminds me. "I'm here to compete."

He decides to part with the recipe for his chili, one of the most popular items at his restaurant.

Cheryl Wagner's Heart-Healthy Chili

This is probably the only recipe in this book that can be called heart-smart, because it uses lean ground turkey instead of ground beef. Even though the fat may be missing, the spices and seasoning give it great flavor. This chili is a perennial favorite at Roger's restaurant, Thee Pitts Again.

1 tablespoon olive oil

2 pounds ground turkey

1 small onion, diced

1 tablespoon minced garlic

2 tablespoons chili powder

1 tablespoon ground cumin

1 teaspoon kosher salt, finely ground

1 teaspoon ground black pepper

1 can (15 ounces) tomato sauce

2 cans (14 ounces each) diced tomatoes

1 can (14 ounces) stewed tomatoes

1 bottle (10 to 12 ounces) V-8 or tomato juice

2 tablespoons dill pickle juice

2 cans (15 ounces each) chili beans (such as Bush's)

Heat the olive oil in a large pot over medium heat and add the turkey, onion, garlic, chili powder, cumin, salt, and pepper. Cook until the meat loses its pink color, stirring often to break up the meat and combine the spices. Add the tomato sauce, diced tomatoes, stewed tomatoes, V-8 or tomato juice, and pickle juice and bring to a simmer. Adjust the heat to low and simmer for 1 hour, stirring occasionally. Add the chili beans and stir gently to combine. Simmer another 10 minutes or so, just to heat the beans through. Leftovers can be frozen for up to 1 month.

SERVES 10

Cheryl and Roger Wagner at Jack Daniel's in October 2003

Super Smokers BBQ

Terry Black and Skip Steele of Super Smokers BBQ are working their tails off with three St. Louis–area locations. They also have a concession at Busch Stadium during the St. Louis Rams and Cardinals games. And then, there's their competition schedule.

"I can't believe I get paid to barbecue," Terry tells me. "It's like guys who get paid to play baseball for a living. They're getting paid to play a boy's game. I'm getting paid to do somebody's hobby. This is a pretty nice country we live in, when you know you can live in the USA and get paid to barbecue every day. I don't think that's going on over in Kosovo."

"No," I tell him. "I assure you it's not."

"B.S.—that's one of the biggest aspects of the business. With that being the case, and I say this with a smirk on my face, this industry was tailor-made for me."
—TERRY BLACK

The Super Smokers crew, left to right: Kernis Louviere, Neil Parker, Terry Black, Craig Basler, Andrew Selkirk, and Skip Steele

Super Smokers
Sweet and Spicy Chicken Wings

These chicken wings are one of the most popular appetizers at Super Smokers BBQ. The sweetness comes from honey, and the kick comes from using the hottest, spiciest barbecue sauce your taste buds can take.

You'll need apple wood chips and a disposable foil pan.

2½ tablespoons ground black pepper	5 pounds chicken wings, rinsed and dried
1 tablespoon onion powder	1 cup honey
1 tablespoon chili powder	½ cup hot barbecue sauce (or more to taste; use your favorite, the hottest sauce you can stand)
1 tablespoon garlic powder	
1 tablespoon seasoned salt	3 tablespoons apple juice

Make a dry rub by sifting the pepper, onion powder, chili powder, garlic powder, and seasoned salt into a bowl to blend.

Place the chicken wings in a large zippered plastic bag. Pour in the dry rub and shake to coat the wings well. Marinate for at least 30 minutes (at room temperature) or as long as 24 hours (in the refrigerator).

Prepare coals using 3 pounds of charcoal. Make sure the coals are in a pile to one side of your grill or smoker. After the coals have turned white, place 2 cups of soaked and drained apple wood chips on the pile of coals. Set the wings on the grate so they will cook by indirect heat—in other words, not over the coals—and smoke for 25 minutes. Turn the wings and smoke for another 20 to 25 minutes.

Mix the honey, barbecue sauce, and apple juice together in a small saucepan. Cook over medium heat until warmed through.

Place the wings in a disposable foil pan and pour the warm sauce over the wings. Toss to coat evenly. Cover and smoke for another 20 to 30 minutes, stirring occasionally, until the glaze is finished the way you like it. If you're using a grill, you can move the aluminum pan directly over the coals while you're glazing the wings.

SERVES A CROWD

Tall Tales from the Judges' Tent

Judges hear some tall tales and lies, too.

"You hear any lies today?" I ask Fred Gould, a well-seasoned judge.

"Yeah, my first two teams lied to me," he tells me. "They told me they had the best product. Well, I guess it's best to them. I've heard a lot of truth, too."

"Like what?" I ask.

"One team did have a good shoulder; they told the truth," he says. "A team will tell me, 'I cooked this rib for eight hours at 240 degrees' and come to find out if they'd cooked it another eight hours it might've been a good rib."

He continues, "I've told you this story before. I was a finals judge in ribs here last year, and I think you serve a better rib at 17th Street than any I ate in finals that day. And that's the truth. I just like what you do with your ribs."

I must have a big smile on my face because Fred asks, "You get a kick out of hearing that, don't you?"

"You bet I do."

Fred's a good judge. After the contest, he goes back and visits with his teams.

"I like to give 'em some pointers. Some are young teams just starting out, and anything I can do to help them, I'll do," he tells me. "Hey, I don't plan on quitting this for a long time, so when the old teams get tired and quit cooking, I want to see these young teams up on top."

> **"One of our stories was how we chose the most tender portion of the pig. At our local pig farm, the pigs have to walk on a steep hill, and the pigs walk around that hill counterclockwise, in fenced-off lines. The paths are so narrow that they can't turn around. This causes the right leg to be the one that gets the heaviest workout, and that leg ends up a little bit longer. The most tender meat comes from the left side of those particular pigs. All of that meat's going to taste good when I'm finished with it. But for competition purposes, I always used the meat from the left side of the pig, because it's just a little bit more tender."**
>
> **—Dave Fombell, Great Boars of Fire, Anna, Illinois**

"I've been lied to by judges," Terry Black of Super Smokers tells me. "After the contest, the judges come back 'round and give you suggestions. Some will say, 'I gave you perfect scores all the way down! You did great!' And then I'll get my scorecard, and I can see exactly how each judge scored me. And there won't be one column with all 10s. So they either gave us the wrong scorecard, or they entered our scores wrong, or that judge lied to me!"

I nod knowingly. I've heard that line before, too. "You'd think they know we get to see those cards. Maybe they just wanted to make us feel good?"

"They don't have to make me feel good. I'd rather hear, 'I almost gave you straight 10s, but your flavor was a little off.' I have more respect for them when they're honest with me."

Expert barbecue judge Hap Zook samples another bite of a rib.

Come Visit Us in Murphysboro

I ain't got no dog in this hunt these days, but I still get a thrill out of going to a cook-off. Judging at Memphis in May and hosting the Murphysboro Barbecue Cook-Off are the highlights of my year. I like to see all the people; I've met and cooked with a lot of those teams out there. I like to welcome them to Murphysboro and show them some hospitality.

I know most of the judges personally. Some of them plan their vacations around our contest in Murphysboro, and they love to come to Southern Illinois. We have judges and competitors who travel from New York, Arizona, Arkansas, Indiana, Kentucky, Missouri, Tennessee, even California. We have judges who've been here every single year since 1986. They've been trained and certified. It's kind of like the Olympics—somebody judging ice-skating or diving—they know what to look for.

In Murphysboro, more than 100 people serve as judges and ambassadors every year. These folks aren't paid; they come on their own dime. They do it for the love of barbecue, for the camaraderie.

Barbecue brings a lot of people to Southern Illinois. I love when people discover just how special this area is, and my hope is that somebody will fall in love with Murphysboro and open or relocate a company here.

I just enjoy being around people, and I like to smell the smoke.

Scenes from the circuit

Chapter Six

BAR BE CUE

Goes Uptown and Upscale

arbecue's down-home reputation usually makes you think of beer-drinking bubbas, Wrangler jeans, and paper plates. However, a passion for barbecue is gaining ground among a crowd leaning more toward Pinot Noir, Prada, and porcelain plates.

My daughter wrote those first two sentences, and I had to ask her what Prada is. I usually shop at Sears, myself. I don't know too many people who drink Pinot Noir either, especially not with barbecue.

What I do know is that all over the country, some high-profile people are embracing barbecue. Those of us who've been in the barbecue business for a while are more than a little amused and somewhat fascinated by some of the upscale directions barbecue is taking. But no matter how you dress it up, some things remain the same. People from all over the country are committed to preserving the tradition, lifting up the culture of barbecue, and sharing its unique flavor and goodness with a whole new crowd.

The Broadway Connection

Pat Daily and Tom Viertel are a theater couple with a passion for barbecue. Tom is a producer of Broadway plays such as *The Producers, Hairspray,* and *Smokey Joe's Cafe,* among others. Pat's company, Showtix, sells theater tickets. I first met them in Lynchburg, Tennessee, when I was cooking in the Jack Daniel's Invitational.

"Tom has always loved barbecue," Pat says. "But honestly, until we got involved in judging, what we thought was barbecue was either Chinese barbecue or Tony Roma's."

"That's true," agrees Tom. "But after all, I grew up in Stamford, Connecticut. So how would I know?"

In 1991, Pat saw a small article in the *New York Times* food section saying that the Jack Daniel's Invitational barbecue contest was looking for judges. You had to submit an essay telling why you thought you'd be qualified to judge. Pat thought Tom would really enjoy the experience, so she decided to nominate him.

"I labored over that essay," says Pat. "I even went so far as to say that his mother put Tabasco sauce in his baby bottle and he came out loving barbecue."

She never heard back from the contest, so she tracked down the phone number and called them. She was told that they were actually looking for celebrity judges; they'd already filled the spots for "regular" judges. Pat quickly set them straight. "Tom *is* a celebrity! He produced *Driving Miss Daisy!*"

"*Driving Miss Daisy* was just out in the theaters. But of course I didn't clarify that he produced the off-Broadway production, not the movie. But he'd had a lot of good publicity, so I sent her a bunch of his press clips and he got chosen to judge. The other celebrity judges that year were Rex Reed, Liz Smith, and Elinor Donohue from *Father Knows Best*. And so that's how it began."

The following spring, Tom and Pat were invited to Memphis in May, and they, along with Tom's brother, Jack Viertel, who's also a Broadway producer and barbecue fanatic, went through the official judging certification class. They spent a lot of time with us in the Apple City Barbecue booth.

"You know how important those friends are at a cook-off. If you don't have any friends, you won't get any food," Tom says. "You were one of our first barbecue friends."

I'm always curious about what "outsiders" think about the barbecue culture. These events are not like a New York City cocktail party. The food is out of this world, but it's served on paper plates. The people are the best people you'd ever meet in your life. And again, they're unlike most people you'd interact with in the city. If you can't be real, you'll never make it with the barbecue crowd. And if you can't be real, you probably wouldn't be too interested in it anyway.

"The Jack Daniel's event changed our lives," says Pat. "That experience was a real eye-opener. The food, the culture, the people. The 'bubbas.' So different from Northeasterners. Very friendly and warm and generous."

"A few people knew we were involved in theater, but what was really intriguing to people was that we were from the North," adds Tom. "Very few people came down from the North at that time. It was just unheard of."

Educating yourself about barbecue takes time, travel, an appetite, and a sense of adventure. Pat and Tom embraced the challenge.

"When we first started going to Memphis, we explored heavily," Tom tells me. "We'd go to four or five restaurants a day to sort of get it all. I'm glad we did that, because several have gone out of business now or the pitmasters have died. Hawkins Grill, for example. Now that was a great experience. I'll never forget sitting at the bar, waiting for our sandwiches to arrive. Listening to the jukebox. What a great memory."

"Oh, yeah," I nod. "I loved that place."

In addition to judging at the major competitions, Pat and Tom have judged at quite a number of other contests. "We've judged at the Kansas City Royal, Fort Worth Stockyards, five or six smaller contests in the South. Several times at Jack Daniel's. At least 10 times at Memphis in May. And each of has judged finals; now that's the pinnacle of judging."

"And you've judged in Murphysboro," I remind him.

"We'd read about the phenomenon of small towns being 'Wal-Marted' to death, but we'd never really seen it until we came to Murphysboro," remarks Tom. "Actually, coming to a contest where *you* weren't cooking was strange."

"I can't very well cook in my own contest," I joke. "Besides, I had to give those other people a chance to win something."

Second to barbecue, Pat's passion is Dairy Queen ice cream. Pat was a military brat, and when her family was stationed at Virginia Beach, her first job as a teenager was working at a Dairy Queen. My nephew Gary Mills just happens to own a Dairy Queen in Murphysboro, and it's conveniently located right across the street from 17th Street.

"When we judge at contests, we eat so much meat all day that we don't need a meal in the evening. So we just go to the Dairy Queen for dinner," says Tom.

Pat has often told me that her dream is to own a Dairy Queen in Manhattan. "Well, I probably don't have time to actually run one," Pat says. "But I wrote Warren Buffett a letter asking him to consider opening one in Manhattan. His office wrote back and said it wasn't feasible, considering the price of real estate. They just don't understand. It could be huge."

I started sending barbecue to New York for various parties Pat and Tom were having. "The first one was to celebrate a play I produced, *Smokey Joe's Cafe.* Having your barbecue for our parties became a tradition. We invite all of our friends and colleagues."

"Everyone was amazed," says Tom. "Nobody had tasted anything like this food. The only people who weren't completely floored were the ones who were originally from the South or Midwest. The others didn't know this barbecue world existed. The food was very exotic and interesting to them. Everybody loved it."

Tom is the board chairman of the Eugene O'Neill Theater Center in Waterford, Connecticut. Playwrights from all over the world apply for its prestigious summer residence program. When it came time for the O'Neill's thirtieth anniversary, he and Pat decided to have barbecue instead of the more traditional New England clambake.

They asked if I'd consider coming out to cook the barbecue, and I immediately said yes. That trip is one of my favorite barbecue memories. Pat decided she'd try to find a smoker somewhere close by so I wouldn't have to drive my pit out there. This was back in 1994, and there didn't seem to be a smoker to be found on the New England seaboard. Pat called to say thanks anyway, but she couldn't locate a pit. Let's not be hasty, I told her. I had another idea.

Ole Hickory, the manufacturer of my favorite pits, just so happened to have a pit that needed to be delivered to Washington, D.C. So we decided that I'd drive the pit to Connecticut, use it for the party, then clean it up and drive it on to D.C.

"I'll never forget when you pulled up after driving 1,200 miles," Pat remembers. "You were only 20 minutes late, and when you got out of the van, Doritos bags and Snickers wrappers came tumbling out with you."

"Hey, now," I stop her. "Don't tell all my secrets!"

"I thought you'd want to go to your room and get cleaned up, but the first thing you said was, 'Show me the meat,'" says Pat. "We went right to the kitchen and you looked it over."

"And after you cooked up the first round, you didn't think it was quite up to par," remembers Tom. "So you cooked a whole other batch. Everyone loved the food. And everyone still remembers August Wilson standing there by the cooker with a boneyard at his feet."

"You were willing to go to the ends of the earth for your friends," states Tom.

"That's what friends are for!" I tell them.

"At the O'Neill Theater Center's first barbecue in 1994, August Wilson stood by the pit the entire time and Mike just kept handing him ribs," says Tom Viertel. "He never sat down. He never ate any of the side dishes. Now we have 17th Street barbecue every year. It's just expected."

The Blue Smoke Story

The development of Blue Smoke is a perfect example of how a good barbecue story evolves. There are some tall tales involved, and certainly some lies, and as with all good ideas, several people are laying claim to this one. Jeffrey Steingarten is quick to point out that he was the first person to write about me in the national press, therefore he's sure Danny Meyer learned about me through his writing. Tom Viertel maintains that he approached Danny Meyer with the idea to open a barbecue restaurant in New York City. He reminds me that he had me ship some ribs so he could have Danny over for a taste-test. And Danny's version is that he conceived Blue Smoke as his ode to his love for barbecue and his midwestern childhood.

All three of these men have some valid points. They can each believe what they want to believe: I'm just grateful for the opportunity to call each one of them a friend. What's especially funny to me is that I didn't know any of these claims until we were well into the process of planning the restaurant.

"Well, I'll set the story straight," says Tom. "Pat and I had to travel a long way to eat the food we love. We simply got tired of not having great barbecue in New York.

"We approached three different, highly respected restaurateurs with the idea of bringing your barbecue to the city. We didn't know any of these people; they were all friends of friends. One guy wasn't interested at all. One guy just couldn't get his head around the numbers. Danny Meyer was the one who was interested in it on the culinary level. Being from St. Louis, he had a real love of genuine barbecue; he knew what it was about. He was intrigued enough to come over and sample the barbecue.

"Danny stayed for hours. We talked and talked about what it was and how it was made. He loved what he tasted. But he was very busy with opening Tabla and Eleven Madison Park at that time, so he couldn't commit to the barbecue idea for a while. He was even courteous enough to say, 'I'll understand if you want to take this idea to someone else.'

"But after meeting him, we thought Danny was the right guy," says Tom. "Really, I don't know anyone else who could've done it so successfully on any level. And the bonus was that he had the perfect location, because his cousin James Polsky owned that club, Jazz Standard. The music part was going great, but the food wasn't, and James wanted Danny to help him with the food.

"Now being Danny Meyer, he had to prove to himself that this was the best barbecue he could find. So he staged a nationwide investigation just to make sure."

"That was important, too," I interject. "Because they found lots of ideas and regional tastes. I couldn't have provided all of those. That research constitutes a huge part of his success. And it adds to his barbecue credibility. He did the research. He's eaten more different kinds of barbecue than 80 percent of the people in this business. I guarantee it."

"I don't doubt that," concedes Tom. "Blue Smoke is a dream come true for us. Now we have our favorite barbecue right nearby. That's *our* story and we're sticking to it."

Restaurateur Danny Meyer is well known for his elegant restaurants in New York City: Eleven Madison Park, Gramercy Tavern, the Modern, Tabla, and Union Square Cafe. Then, in 2002 he opened Blue Smoke, a barbecue and jazz joint, right in the middle of Manhattan. I've had a number of once-in-a-lifetime experiences, I can tell you, and being involved in Blue Smoke is one of them.

The first time Danny Meyer and Richard Coraine, one of his partners, visited Murphysboro, they were undercover. Incognito, if you will. Tom Viertel had suggested they come and have a meal. I never even knew they visited until they called me a few months later.

When they introduced themselves, I have to admit, I didn't know exactly who they were. I hadn't been to New York City since the early 1970s. I do read restaurant publications, but most of the articles that capture my attention are about casual dining. I had no personal reference point, so their names and the names of their restaurants didn't mean that much to me. Tom told me these were some powerful people. It didn't take me long to figure out for myself that they're pretty hot stuff.

Now, a number of people have told me they want me to help them start a barbecue restaurant. Out in Las Vegas, I've had dozens of people, especially from other countries, say, "I'm going to fly you over and you must teach us everything. We'll pay you!"

I'd gotten myself into one of these situations before, and frankly, it wasn't a good experience. The fancy chefs I was trying to train were not good students. They didn't think they had much to learn. This group, however, was different right from the start.

Danny sent another contingent, Union Square Cafe chef/partner Michael Romano and his sous chef, Kenny Callaghan (who would be the Blue Smoke pitmaster), to the Murphysboro Barbecue Cook-Off a few months later. This trip was an eye-opening experience—for Michael, especially. He'd traveled all over the country and all over the world, but Murphysboro was something new.

"I was struck by the small-town feel and the closeness of the people," Michael remembers. "But at the same time, there was a touch of sadness because many of the downtown businesses were closed. But all of a sudden, the town just came alive during the cook-off, and that was amazing to see. I was raised in Manhattan; the closest thing I could relate this to was maybe a street fair, like the San Gennaro festival I knew as a kid. But that was a religious thing."

"Barbecue's a religion," I remind him.

"Well, yeah, but you know what I mean," he says.

Yes, I sure do.

"I've had some amazing culinary moments all over the world; in Europe, Asia, this country," Michael tells me. "And I had one of them right here during that trip—when you took me back to one of the smokers, pulled off a slab of ribs, brushed it with sauce, and tore one off for me to try. I bit into it and was filled with a sense of amazement. I immediately knew *this* is what ribs are supposed to taste like."

I can confidently say that there is not a barbecue restaurant—or any restaurant, for that matter—that's as well researched as Blue Smoke. Those men traveled 62,044 miles over the course of three years learning about every style of barbecue in the country.

Some of the best times we had, I think, were the weeks Kenny and Michael spent in Murphysboro, learning the secrets of smoke, so to speak.

This was the training and testing stage, and I don't know of any other pitmasters-in-

> "Mike taught me his mantra:
> low, slow, and steady. Women like that as well.
> Cook your barbecue like you'd handle a woman.
> Low, slow, and steady."
>
> —KENNY CALLAGHAN

training who had the resources and the imagination to approach learning to barbecue in quite this way. Kenny and Michael ordered a mountain of meat from New York's finest purveyors. They smoked over 900 pounds of meat during each test week. Lamb, duck, boar, veal, pheasant, rabbit, beef, and, naturally, every part of the pig imaginable—several styles of ribs, shoulders, butts, bacon, loins, chops, jowls, tongue, and even tails! And then there was the fish—bonito, salmon, bluefish, sea bass, shark, mackerel, and scallops.

The opportunity to experiment prior to opening was invaluable.

"That gave us such a tremendous foundation," Kenny says. "Just to be able to work the pits ourselves with no other pressures. We figured out what would and wouldn't work. And we played and experimented with foods other than traditional barbecue. That gave us a leg up when we opened."

Kenny Callaghan shows off a smoked shoulder during one of our training sessions in Murphysboro.

Myself, I've never had the opportunity or need to work with some of these types of meat. I was especially fascinated by watching them use conventional cooking methods combined with a shorter time on the pit to add just a hint of smoke. You wouldn't necessarily call this barbecue, but you would definitely call it good.

Veal shanks, for example, will probably never make the menu at 17th Street, but should the occasion arise, I'll do what Michael did one day: He took the shanks, seasoned them with salt and pepper, and put them in a pan with white wine, veal stock, thyme, bay leaf, parsley, sage, and garlic. Rather than brown them first, as you would normally do, he braised them for 3 to 3½ hours, covered, so as not to dry out the meat. Then he took them out of the liquid and put them on the pit for about 2 hours. While they were on the pit, he heated the braising liquid, reduced and strained it, and made a delicious sauce. When the veal shanks came off the pit, they were a little dry, but he put them in the liquid and warmed them through, and they moistened perfectly. This dish is worthy of the finest restaurant, but the six of us who were gathered in the kitchen that day ate it right out of the pan, diving right in with our forks.

The training weeks were serious business, but we had a lot of laughs, too. These city boys got a kick out of my operation. My kitchen is not quite as well equipped as theirs. Luckily they traveled with their own knives. That's a fancy chef thing, I've come to learn.

"By the way," Michael asks. "Did you ever invest in some decent knives?"

"Nope, not yet," I laugh. "Every now and then I go down to the supermarket when they have a $5.99 special. I can pick 'em up at Wal-Mart sometimes, too. I don't want to spoil the cooks. They're working just fine with what they have. These knives were good enough for my mama, and they're good enough for me!"

Michael shudders.

"What amazes me," Kenny says, "is that you have this little barbecue empire, but if something breaks down, you roll up your sleeves and fix it yourself. You don't call a repairman."

This must be a difference in generations or the difference between country boys and city boys. Or both.

"Why would I call someone when I know how to fix it?" I shake my head. "When I was growing up, you learned to fix things. There was no money to call a repairman; today I don't have time to wait for one. And if I don't know how to fix something, I just call my brother. He's older than I am, so he's had more experience!"

Shopping for supplies was another small-town adventure. I never have much trouble finding what I need, but their list was pretty extensive. Our local grocery store doesn't have much in the way of fresh herbs, but luckily my sister had a good supply in her garden, so we were able to cut what they needed. Then Michael needed juniper berries for a brine recipe. Those aren't available either, so we just substituted a healthy splash of gin.

I never went to culinary school, but I got a little glimpse of what it must be like as I watched these two. Michael is very methodical. He kept a logbook of every single step—the method, seasoning, temperature, smoking time, and end result.

Sampling ribs right off the pit. Kenny and Michael learn it's all about peace, love, and barbecue.

In my world, there are the flavors and spices I grew up with. I know how to use them in the foods I prepare, but I don't have that vast knowledge that comes from cooking school. These chefs know exactly how particular spices will add or detract from other flavors. They also use some herbs and spices I would never use in barbecue. For example, I wouldn't have thought to use rosemary because it's so pungent, but I saw that when they use the proper amount, it didn't overpower a dish.

From the beginning of Blue Smoke's conception, Danny Meyer was adamant that his grandmother's prized potato salad recipe be on the menu.

"She, like so many in her generation, used to pride herself on special house recipes, and the trick—just like you, Mike!—was to never reveal the recipes. When she died, the only thing I wanted was her recipe book, and I still have it. It's made up of lots of index cards with recipes and scribbled notes, more or less specific," Danny tells me.

"Well, Kenny and Michael made a batch of her potato salad, and it put a huge smile on my face. I was so happy, it took me right back home," he continues. "Then during sous chef training, they did another round of recipe tasting. You know how translating recipes to sous chefs is like a game of telephone? You have to make sure that it will come out the same when the next person is cooking it. I came in for another taste, and they all had big smiles on their faces when I got to the kitchen. 'Is this right?' they asked. 'Yes!' I said. 'You did it again!'

"They just broke out laughing and showed me a Hellmann's mayonnaise jar with the exact recipe printed on the side. I'll never know if that's where she got it, or if it was just one of those staple Midwestern recipes that became well established and passed around."

"I've heard other stories like that," I say. "A person's secret recipe for macaroni and cheese or cornbread came right off the package. But that taste and memory stayed with you and will forever be tied to your grandmother. And ultimately, don't you think a large part of why it tasted so good was the love that went into making it?"

"Oh, absolutely," agrees Danny.

Right-Off-the-Jar Potato Salad

This creamy, classic potato salad has been served at many a family gathering over the years.

2 lbs. potatoes (5 or 6 medium), peeled and cut into ¾-inch chunks

1 cup Hellmann's mayonnaise

2 tablespoons vinegar

1½ teaspoons salt

1 teaspoon sugar

¼ teaspoon ground black pepper

1 cup thinly sliced celery

½ cup chopped onion

2 hard-cooked eggs, chopped (optional)

In a 4-quart saucepot, cover potatoes with water; bring to a boil over medium-high heat. Reduce heat and simmer 10 minutes or until potatoes are tender. Drain and cool slightly.

In large bowl, combine mayonnaise, vinegar, salt, sugar, and pepper. Add potatoes, celery, onion, and eggs and toss gently. Serve chilled or at room temperature.

SERVES 8

Blue Smoke Deviled Eggs

Spending time in a professional kitchen was really a treat for me. I liked seeing how they set up the kitchen and getting ideas to make my own line work more smoothly.

Watching them develop their recipes was also fascinating. My cooking style is based on what I learned from Mama Faye. I watched one cook go through no fewer than 36 dozen eggs while coming up with the deviled eggs recipe. Back home, that would just be considered downright wasteful. And Mama Faye would wonder why I couldn't get it right in two or three tries. I just love deviled eggs, though, so I was happy to help taste-test each batch. Everyone I know simply mashes the yolks with a fork. Instead, this cook ran the yolks over a fine-mesh screen so they were powdered. He used champagne vinegar instead of apple cider vinegar. And rather than spooning the mixture into the egg white, he piped it in with a pastry bag. At the restaurant, they serve four deviled eggs with a bit of watercress tossed with vinaigrette and topped with almonds as a simple appetizer.

12 large eggs	¼ teaspoon cayenne (or to taste)
⅔ cup mayonnaise	½ teaspoon curry powder
1½ teaspoons tarragon-infused champagne vinegar	Finely ground kosher salt and ground black pepper
2½ teaspoons Dijon mustard	Magic Dust (see page 67) or your favorite dry rub
¾ teaspoon mustard powder (they use Colman's)	

Place the eggs in a saucepan, cover with cold water, and bring to a boil over high heat. Reduce the heat and simmer for exactly 9 minutes. Pour off most of the water and immediately run cold water over the eggs.

Crack the eggshells and peel the eggs under running water. Cut a small sliver off both ends of each egg and halve them through the equator, forming round cups.

Remove the yolks and pass them through a fine sieve into a bowl. Add the mayonnaise, vinegar, mustards, cayenne, and curry powder to the bowl and mix together with a rubber spatula until smooth. Season to taste with salt and pepper.

Spoon the egg-yolk paste into a pastry bag fitted with a star tip and pipe the mixture into the egg whites to form rosettes. (Or use a teaspoon to mound the yolk into the egg whites.) Sprinkle the top of the eggs with Magic Dust. Refrigerate until you're ready to serve.

MAKES 24

Blue Smoke's Iceberg Wedges with Roquefort Dressing

I get a kick out of seeing old foods come back into vogue. "Retro," they call it. Iceberg lettuce wedges used to be on the menu of every steakhouse. At Blue Smoke, they top this simple, crisp salad with homemade crumbled bacon.

1 cup sour cream	1/2 cup chopped parsley
1 cup mayonnaise	Finely ground kosher salt and ground black pepper
1/2 teaspoon Worcestershire sauce	
1 teaspoon chopped garlic	1 head iceberg lettuce, chilled and cut into 8 wedges
3 tablespoons red wine vinegar	Crisp crumbled bacon (optional)
1/2 cup crumbled Roquefort cheese	

Whisk together the sour cream, mayonnaise, Worcestershire sauce, garlic, and vinegar in a bowl. Using a rubber spatula, fold in the Roquefort cheese and parsley until well incorporated. Season to taste with salt and pepper.

Put a wedge of lettuce on each of 8 salad plates. Pour the dressing over the lettuce and garnish with the bacon, if desired.

SERVES 8

I have a sweet spot in my heart for Blue Smoke pastry chef Jen Giblin.

Blue Smoke Strawberry-Rhubarb Cobbler

Most barbecue restaurants don't have an official pastry chef, but Blue Smoke has the talented Jen Giblin. I spent a lot of time in her area of the kitchen during my extended stay in New York. She needed my help to taste-test just about everything she made. Believe me, I was happy to oblige. Try this fresh and fruity cobbler at the height of strawberry season.

BISCUIT TOPPING

- 3 cups all-purpose flour
- ¼ cup packed light brown sugar
- 3 tablespoons granulated sugar, plus additional for sprinkling
- 1 teaspoon ground ginger
- 3½ teaspoons baking powder
- ¾ teaspoon kosher salt, finely ground
- 12 tablespoons (1½ sticks) butter
- 1½ cups heavy cream, plus additional for brushing

FRUIT MIXTURE

- 1 pound strawberries, sliced
- 1 pound rhubarb, chopped
- 1 cup granulated sugar
- ½ vanilla bean
- 1 tablespoon cornstarch
- 1 tablespoon vanilla extract

FOR SERVING

Vanilla or buttermilk ice cream

Make the biscuit topping: Mix together the flour, brown sugar, 3 tablespoons granulated sugar, ginger, baking powder, and salt in a large bowl. Cut the butter into small pieces and rub into the flour mixture until it resembles coarse meal. Add about 1½ cups heavy cream and mix until it forms a dough (you might not need all the cream). Wrap the dough in plastic wrap and chill for at least 1 hour.

Make the fruit mixture: Combine the strawberries, rhubarb, granulated sugar, and vanilla bean in a large bowl. Let stand for 1 hour. Remove the vanilla bean and pour off half of the liquid, then stir in the cornstarch and vanilla extract. Pour the fruit into a 13 × 9-inch baking dish.

Preheat the oven to 350 degrees.

Roll the dough out on a floured surface to ¼ inch thick and cut into circles or any desired shape. Place the dough on the fruit mixture without overlapping any pieces. Brush the top of the dough with heavy cream and sprinkle with granulated sugar. Bake the cobbler for about 25 minutes or until the dough is golden brown and the fruit is bubbling in the center.

Serve warm with ice cream.

SERVES 6 TO 8

Continuing Education

I convinced Kenny Callaghan and Michael Romano that their barbecue education wasn't complete until they'd competed in a cook-off. They are fixtures in Murphysboro now, and they've taken to competing like a pig takes to Oreos.

When they arrived that first year, they were a little surprised when they saw the pit I had borrowed for them to use. I think they assumed they'd be cooking on one of my extra Ole Hickory pits, since that's what they're used to. But I thought working with a new pit would be a good learning experience.

"That first cook-off was really a remarkable experience," remembers Michael. "To go in as the total novice with everything to prove. To place fourth was totally mind-blowing. Winning a culinary award in Paris would not have been as gratifying as that."

I just smile. I know exactly how it feels to be handed a trophy. These boys are my protégés, and I was every bit as proud as they were when they won their first trophy.

The other competitors made the Blue Smoke crew feel right at home.

"These people would give you the shirt off their backs," says Kenny. "This is small-town America at its finest."

"There's an immediate connection," Michael reminisces. "You cut, season, cook, watch, serve, and then the ribs are judged. It's very direct. No games. Just us and the fire. We watched over that pit like a mother hen."

There were some embarrassing moments, Michael recalls. "Like at about four in the morning when we didn't have any matches. Garry Roark came over and started our fire with a blow torch—we didn't even know those were legal!"

Garry gets pretty tickled watching them compete. "These fancy chefs have all that training, but a good ole boy with a Weber and a rack of ribs can whup their butts," he says with a grin.

Dale Pierson, a good ole boy who's worked for me for years, comes over to visit, and he lifts the smoker's lid to take a look. The fire is burning hot and the shoulders are cooking fast.

"You goin' to serve this burned-up meat to them judges?" he asks Kenny.

Kenny does not know quite what to make of Dale. He might not look like he knows barbecue, but trust me, he does.

Dale is so concerned about this novice Blue Smoke crew that he comes back at 3:30 in the morning to check on them. When he doesn't see Kenny around, he goes ahead and puts all the ribs on the pit.

Kenny pulls in about 20 minutes later, and he is not appreciative of Dale's efforts.

"I made him take all the meat off," Kenny tells me later. "And I told him, 'Dale, don't you know you're never supposed to mess with another man's meat?'"

City slickers at their first cook-off

Perfecting Urban Barbecue

Kenny learned that there is a vast difference between running barbecue and fine-dining kitchens.

"In fine dining, you can plan anything within a day's notice and order on a day's notice. If a cook burns a steak, you can throw it away and start over again," he explains.

"Barbecue is way more planning and projection and preparedness. You have to order four or five days in advance so it can thaw and be rubbed and marinated for a day or so. And then you cook it for 7 to 12 to 15 hours, and then you let it rest. If it's overcooked or something happens, you're four days in the hole with no way to recover."

By virtue of being a Danny Meyer operation, Blue Smoke was under intense scrutiny from the get-go. Reading the first harsh Blue Smoke reviews was just as painful for me because I knew how hard they worked and researched and just how knowledgeable these boys are.

"Being so visible is a mixed blessing," I comment to Danny. "This experience has thickened your skin some, hasn't it?"

He nods solemnly. "I've developed some scar tissue."

Danny's also quick to point out that much of the early criticism was legitimate. He likens it to sports fans paying their money to see their favorite team play. "If you go to see the Mets play and the team is underperforming, there's a sense of letdown, and some of the people boo. As long as the fans keep coming back, because the loyalties are there, some of those boos will motivate the Mets to get their act together and win more games. If they succeed, they'll get cheered."

"And everybody wants to hear the cheer," I agree.

"I told our team that you can collapse or you can use it as additional motivation to get your act together. Of course, you have to figure out which criticism is constructive and which is a bunch of noise."

The number of Southern expatriates living in New York is astounding. Droves of them came to Blue Smoke, each looking for his own barbecue tradition. If they didn't find it, they were sure vocal about it.

Blue Smoke tried to do some different things on the menu in the beginning. Smoked foie gras with jalapeño marmalade, for example.

"The foodies loved it," says Michael. "And the barbecue purists scoffed at it."

"What we've learned is that we have to tip our hat to many different barbecue cultures. Like New York tips its hat to many different world cultures. As a manner of hospitality to our guests, I have to speak one language with several different accents," explains Danny.

"Hopefully you can lead them along and get them to try some different tastes as well," I add.

"A lot of people are not interested in being educated," Danny points out. "They just want their specific taste. For example, we also had a problem with people who were upset that the meat doesn't fall off the bones. The first thing I learned when I went to judging school to judge at Memphis in May and Jack Daniel's is that if the meat falls off the bone, it's a loser."

"I have some of those exact same customers," I tell him. "People who are used to eating ribs at chain restaurants where they boil them and bake them in the oven. And you're right, some of those people are convinced that's barbecue. They don't want to hear the truth. And then you have the people who send their meat back to the kitchen because it's pink and they think it's undercooked. I don't have that problem in Murphysboro, but I sure do in Vegas."

Another thing that is so impressive about an operation like Blue Smoke is their ability to hand-make virtually everything on the menu. They make their own buns; they churn the ice cream for the shakes and desserts; they make their own graham crackers for the pie crust. They smoke their own tomatoes for tomato sauce; they even make their own bacon. This is a reflection of Kenny's fine-dining background.

"Is doing this all from scratch just expected in New York?" I ask Kenny.

"No, it's not expected," he answers. "But New Yorkers do have very savvy palates, and they can tell when something comes from scratch. But we do this because it feels good. It's what I believe in."

I asked Michael what the most gratifying part of the Blue Smoke experience has been for him. "I was brought into something that is not natural to me, not a part of my heritage," he says thoughtfully. "And not only brought into it but allowed to participate at a very high level. But that's so much the nature of barbecue. It's all-inclusive. It's an opportunity to tap into the lore of America, and that's truly been a privilege."

Danny elaborates. "It's been a fun challenge. Barbecue has become a much more discussed and highly appreciated culinary item in the food chain."

Kenny adds his two cents. "There will always be challenges. I want to step it up—keep doing new things and keep elevating the level of what we're doing. New barbecue places are opening, competition is coming in. We laid the groundwork for barbecue in New York. Barbecue will eventually become another ethnic food category in New York City."

"I'll never forget," Danny reminds me, "that time I was sitting down with you in one of those early meetings we had, and there was this concern that New Yorkers would not be willing to pick up something with their hands and eat it. I will tell you right now that I had no idea that was a potential problem. In fact, for some people, the early criticism was that the ribs weren't messy enough. People in New York City are such experts at dining out. Blue Smoke is about eating, not dining.

"It's fun for New Yorkers to roll up their sleeves and take a break from dining. Too much dining is not a good thing. Sometimes you've just got to eat."

Big Apple Barbecue Block Party

One thing about Danny Meyer and those Blue Smoke boys: They don't do anything in a small way. They decided to start a yearly event called the "Big Apple Barbecue Block Party." I knew it would be a success, but no one had any idea just what a sensation it would actually prove to be.

Here's the premise: Highly regarded pitmasters from all corners of the country, each cooking his regional specialty, set up on one street in the middle of the city. Barbecue-starved New Yorkers buy coupons to use as currency and line up to sample different styles of barbecue. A variety of blues, jazz, and bluegrass bands play continuously throughout the two days. Noted food writers and experts hold seminars about all things barbecue. The proceeds from the event benefit various music philanthropies.

Nobody really knew exactly what to expect in the first year, 2003. The event took place on East 27th Street, in front of Blue Smoke. The street was blocked off for the weekend, and six of us fired up our pits and started cooking on Friday night. We each prepared enough food to feed 6,000 people over the course of the weekend. The response was staggering. Even in the pouring-down rain, and with not a lot of publicity, thousands of New Yorkers stood patiently and happily for upward of an hour and a half at some stands. There wasn't a scrap of meat left by the end of the day. In fact, most of us ran out early both days. People got smart the second day: The lines started forming an hour prior to opening, and people showed up with plastic containers, plastic bags, and even pizza boxes so they could take their food home.

Even though I'm deeply involved in the barbecue world on a daily basis, I don't really sit around and think deep thoughts about barbecue. That's the job of food writers, and some of the best were on hand to discuss various barbecue topics. In 2003 these discussions were held at Jazz Standard (the jazz club below Blue Smoke). Dozens of New Yorkers listened intently as well-known food writers, experts on Southern cuisine, and even some filmmakers held highbrow discussions about various aspects of barbecue.

"It's not often that a group like this gets together. I kept thinking, morbidly, that if someone had taken out the Jazz Standard that day it would be a far more tragic loss to American culture than, say, the same thing happening to the U.S. Congress," Steven Shaw, founder and culinary director, eGullet, commented.

What's most unusual is the caliber of the pitmasters involved. I am both humbled and honored to be part of this group. We pitmasters are a unique breed. Some of us have never eaten other styles of barbecue. Some don't compete or even attend the major barbecue competitions. Some rarely leave their own towns. A few of us might be together for restaurant conventions or other food events. Or maybe we visit each other's

Thousands of people crowd the street at the Big Apple Barbecue Block Party. "Attendance at the event has exceeded the expectations of even those who said it would exceed expectations. The general feeling was being at an end-of-the-world party catered by the nation's greatest pitmasters," said Steven Shaw, founder and culinary director of eGullet.

restaurants. But we've never all actually cooked in the same place at the same time. Somehow, though, those Blue Smoke boys convinced these top-notch barbecuers, from all corners of the barbecue belt, to travel to New York City for this soiree. And it is really something.

Due to the first year's success, in 2004 the event moved to a much larger location at Madison Square Park. There must be something magical about the smell of smoke in the streets of New York City. We fed 30,000 people, and a total of 75,000 came through the park to hear the live jazz, blues, and bluegrass bands and attend the seminars. As Danny says, "Everyone was there to smile."

The All-Star Team of barbecue: Me, Chris Lilly, Don McLemore, and Rick Schmidt

Stevie Mitchell
unloads whole hogs.

Theodore Sanders of Mitchell's shows off a smoking hog.

2004 All-Star Team (left to right): Front row: Kenny Callaghan, Ed Mitchell, Paul Kirk, Chris Lilly. Back row: David Swinghamer, Stevie Mitchell, Michael Rodriguez, Otis Walker, me, Danny Meyer

One of the most humbling moments for me was standing in front of Blue Smoke when Ed Mitchell turned the corner in his 18-wheeler with his picture and logo painted on the sides. My eyes got real big. I looked over at my little pit on its plain trailer. Then I looked at Amy and our crew and said, "Jethro! Elly May! We're going to help Mr. Mitchell unload and then we're pulling out of here!" Of course, it's all about your food, not your rig. But we all know that you stand a little straighter when you're all dressed up. So I went home and ordered myself a nicer rig for the next year. It's not an 18-wheeler, but it makes a statement.

Shooting the Bull at Midnight

I can't believe the number of people out walking around at midnight. But then again, this is New York City. Once my ribs are loaded on the pit, I walk down to talk some trash and lies with Paul Kirk, a.k.a. the Kansas City Baron of Barbecue. He starts telling me about a guy on the Barbecue Forum who said he could do a whole hog in five hours. A guy who builds barbecue pits. A guy who ought to know better.

"How's he gonna do that?" I ask.

"I don't know, but he got challenged quite a few times. Everybody was laughing at him. I don't think I'd want to eat it. Now a suckling pig I could do in five hours easy."

Kenny Callaghan and Otis Walker of Smoki O's in St. Louis join us.

"You need to get in on this conversation," I tell them. "We're talking about the biggest secrets, tall tales, and lies we've ever heard."

"You've barely told me any secrets, and I don't know if I can handle all of these tall tales," laughs Kenny. "And I don't know any lies, either!"

Otis chimes in, "I don't have any tall tales to tell today. I'll give you one tomorrow. But the biggest lie I've ever heard? People talk about 10-hour ribs and 15-hour chickens. I don't know how you'd cook a chicken for 15 hours. I just don't see it." He shakes his head.

"That's how you make charcoal!" says Paul.

"How about you, Mike?" Kenny asks me. "What's the biggest lie you've ever told?"

I think for a minute. "You know, I thought I caught myself telling a lie one time but come to find out I really wasn't. Might've been exaggerating a little bit, but it wasn't a 100 percent lie."

Paul rolls his eyes. "Well, there's a lie right there!"

"C'mon, really. What's the biggest lie you ever heard a barbecuer tell?" asks Otis.

Kenny glances over at me. "Someone told me, 'It's easy!'"

"You think that was a lie?" I laugh. "I think one of the biggest lies I've ever heard was some guy from New Jersey telling me he picked up his love of barbecue by traveling through the South as a kid."

"Ahhh, shit," Kenny groans. "I did go south! I went to Disney World when I was a kid!"

I laugh and laugh. I've gotten a lot of mileage out of that one.

We turn our attention to Paul's brisket. "Whatcha got there, Paul?"

"These are aged Angus briskets. On these pits, they'll take about 16 to 18 hours. I'm cooking right at 230 degrees."

I ask him about the beef. "Do you feel like the aging really helps, Paul?"

"Gives you much better flavor," he says. "I usually get 'em at 30 to 35 days aged, packed in Cryovac. My distributor does it for me. I can freeze them, too.

All of a sudden, this guy comes flying through on a bicycle. He has long, flowing, curly hair and looks like a wild man. He starts yelling, "Carnivores, go home! Carnivores, go home!" He hollers it all the way down the street. That dude is moving. We all look at each other and shake our heads in disbelief. Then we bust out laughing. Only in New York City.

Paul Kirk's Kansas City Brisket

Paul served this succulent brisket to much acclaim at the 2004 Big Apple Barbecue Block Party. Be sure to request Certified Angus Beef brisket; it will make a noticeable difference in the final product. And if you can, start this the day before you're going to smoke it. Best smoked with a combination of oak, hickory, and apple woods on a charcoal base.

1 Certified Angus Beef brisket (9 to 12 pounds)

BRISKET RUB

1 cup granulated sugar

½ cup dried dark brown sugar (see page 64)

⅓ cup seasoned salt (Paul uses Lawry's)

⅓ cup garlic salt

¼ cup celery salt

¼ cup onion salt

½ cup paprika

3 tablespoons chili powder

2 tablespoons ground black pepper

1 tablespoon lemon pepper

2 teaspoons ground sage

1 teaspoon mustard powder

1 teaspoon ground chipotle powder

½ teaspoon ground thyme

MUSTARD SLATHER

½ cup prepared yellow mustard

¼ cup apple cider vinegar

¼ cup good beer

Make the rub: Combine all the ingredients and blend well. Decant into a shaker. Set aside.

Make the slather: Whisk the mustard, vinegar, and beer together until incorporated. Set aside.

Trim the brisket, leaving a ⅛- to ¼-inch fat cap on the fat side; this is enough fat to keep the brisket moist. Coat the brisket with the mustard slather, using a pastry brush or just your hands, covering it all over with the slather. Season the brisket with the rub. You'll need about ½ cup of the rub for the brisket. Store leftover rub in a zippered plastic bag in the freezer if you're not going to use it right away. Marinate overnight if possible.

Smoke at 230 to 250 degrees for about 1½ hours per pound, turning the brisket at each half time. So, if you have to cook for 15 hours (as you would for a 10-pound brisket), turn it at 7½ hours and again after 3¾ hours more and again after about another 1 hour and 20 minutes. Cook to an internal temperature of 185 to 190 degrees.

SERVES 8 TO 10

Elizabeth Karmel

Elizabeth Karmel was raised on barbecue growing up in Greensboro, North Carolina. After years of working in corporate America, she finally figured out a way to turn her love of smoke and fire into a business. She created GirlsattheGrill.com and wrote her own cookbook on grilling and barbecue. She also spends a great deal of time teaching people how to grill and barbecue.

In the early 1990s, one of Elizabeth's clients was the Weber-Stephen Products Co. You know, Weber grills? She was instrumental in organizing their sponsorship of the Patio Porkers, the amateur division at Memphis in May (the teams cook ribs only and the judging is blind, except for the finals). Spending time at Memphis in May, the Kansas City Royal, and the Jack Daniel's Invitational were job requirements at first and then became a passion. Being around all that barbecue lured her right back to her roots.

She even competed at Memphis in May with her own Patio Porkers team, Bubba Meets Bacchus. But now she's an official member of the Memphis-based team Swine and Dine.

"That's a barbecue dream come true," Elizabeth says. "I always wanted to be a Swine and Dine member. They have the best team name, cool T-shirts, a double-decker booth on the river. Plus they have great barbecue, great parties, and lots of fun personalities. They have about 80 members, and someone has to "age-out" or quit before a new member is added. Being on their team is truly a privilege."

Elizabeth learned to barbecue out of necessity. She got hungry.

"Growing up, I took barbecue for granted because I was around it all the time," Elizabeth says. "When I moved away, if I was going to have real barbecue, which I perceived and still believe is North Carolina pulled pork, then I was going to have to figure out how to make it myself."

Elizabeth learned the secrets of smoke not only through the contests but also on culinary vacations on the barbecue trail.

"I've traveled the barbecue belt and the Texas Hill Country, on many occasions," Elizabeth tells me. "I always hung around the guy who was working the pit.

"Men will tell you their secrets." She looks at me slyly. "I just look at them and ask them about their barbecue. They think I'll never use those secrets for anything. I'm one of those girls who look girlie on the outside. So these guys don't think I'll get my hands dirty, until they get to know me. Sometimes it takes them awhile to figure out that I know what I'm talking about."

I know about that. Elizabeth has been part of our crew at every Big Apple Barbecue Block Party. She liked my baked beans so much that she wanted to use the recipe for one of her weekly GirlsattheGrill.com e-newsletters. Until I started working on this book, none of my recipes were written down. I had never given out the baked bean recipe, but she charmed me into writing it down for her.

The next year, a journalist named Fred Thompson came right up to me at the Block Party. "I've got a bone to pick with you," he told me. "I asked you for that baked bean recipe a number of times, and you told me you didn't have it written down. And then the next thing I know, you've given it to Elizabeth!"

"Sorry about that, buddy," I told him. "But you don't look like Elizabeth!"

About half of Elizabeth's teaching focuses on grilling, the other half on "authentic" Southern barbecue. She has a unique ability to take authentic methods and translate them for the home cook.

"The goal is to replicate the taste, even if I don't authenticate the method," she explains.

Knowing, for example, that many city dwellers don't have the space for a grill, much less a smoker, she's come up with methods to get excellent results from equipment like the Camerons Stovetop Smoker.

"Actually," she tells me, "for some things, like fish, cheese, salt, and butter, it's better than using a bigger smoker. It's only three inches deep, and it creates a better environment for flavoring food with smoke. Those are fragile foods. Fish, especially, dries out quickly in a larger smoker. This is a faster method, too. You can smoke fish in 20 or 30 minutes."

What a lot of people don't know about Elizabeth is that she is the gal who taught a number of very visible chefs and food writers how to grill and smoke.

"So who've you taught?" I ask. "Anyone I know?"

Elizabeth just smiles. "That's my barbecue secret."

Elizabeth Karmel's
Beer-Brined Smoked Catfish

This is one of Elizabeth's most requested recipes. She developed it when she was giving a smoking and barbecue training class for John T. Edge, whom you'll read about in Chapter 7. When Elizabeth was visiting John T. in Oxford, Mississippi, he introduced her to the Taylor Grocery, where she ate the finest catfish she ever had.

"I'd met Lynn Hewitt, the owner, on the barbecue circuit, and as an homage to him and his catfish, I created a recipe for beer-brined catfish. As John T. and I were cooking, we looked around at all this food, and he decided to have an impromptu party. So I took the beer-brined catfish and made a pâté out of it to use as an appetizer (see recipe on the opposite page).

"The pâté knocked everyone's socks off—including mine. Now it's a standard in my classes. Everyone loves it. And it works equally well with trout or bluefish. You can use a Camerons Stovetop Smoker for this recipe."

1 cup kosher salt, finely ground

½ cup packed brown sugar

1 cup hot water

3 cans cold beer (such as Budweiser)

1 tablespoon coarsely ground black pepper

6 bay leaves, crumbled

4 large catfish fillets (about ¾ pound each)

Olive oil

Dissolve the salt and sugar in the hot water in a large bowl. Add the cold beer, pepper, and bay leaves to make a brine. Whisk well to remove the carbonation.

Place the fish in a 13 × 9-inch baking dish and pour in the brine. Add cold water or ice cubes if more liquid is necessary to cover all the fillets. Brine the fish in the refrigerator for a minimum of 4 hours or overnight. Remove the fish from the brine, rinse in cold water, and air-dry on a rack for 10 minutes before smoking.

When you're ready to smoke, brush the fish lightly with oil.

If smoking on a charcoal kettle or gas grill, place the fish in the center of the cooking grate, skin side down, and smoke for 1 hour or until the fish is cooked through and smoked. My preference is to use a Camerons Stovetop Smoker. In the Camerons smoker, it will take 20 to 30 minutes. The fish will be moist and flaky, with a dark caramel color.

Serve directly from the smoker or, better yet, make into the smoked catfish pâté on the next page.

SERVES 4

Smoked Catfish Pâté

You'll notice there's no salt in this dish. That's because the brine and the smoking have already salted the fish.

4 Beer-Brined Smoked Catfish fillets (see the opposite page)

1 package (8 ounces) cream cheese, softened

½ to ¾ cup sour cream

2 large shallots, minced

2 tablespoons capers

2 teaspoons caper juice

¼ teaspoon granulated garlic

5 shakes hot sauce (such as Tabasco)

Ground black pepper

FOR SERVING

1 loaf French bread (or your favorite crackers)

Sour cream (optional)

While the fish is still warm, peel off the skin, break the fillets into pieces, and remove any bones. Put the fish into a medium bowl, add the cream cheese, and mix well. Add ½ cup of the sour cream and mix well. Add the shallots, capers, caper juice, garlic, and hot sauce. Add more sour cream at this point if the pâté is a little dry or tastes a little salty. Taste for seasoning, adjust the hot sauce, and add pepper to taste.

Let chill for at least 3 hours or preferably overnight.

Preheat the oven to 250 degrees. Slice the French bread into thin rounds, spread them out on a baking sheet, and bake for about 20 minutes, turning once, until dried through.

Taste the pâté once more before serving and adjust the seasonings if necessary. Serve on the cold side of room temperature on the toasted bread or your favorite crackers. Top with a dollop of sour cream, if desired.

SERVES 4 TO 6 AS AN APPETIZER

Elizabeth's Black-Tie Cole Slaw

You certainly won't see a cole slaw like this on the menu of any traditional barbecue joint. But Elizabeth's job is to take old-fashioned foods and make them seem a little more exciting and upscale.

This cole slaw recipe was adapted from Elizabeth's good friend Georgia caterer Marti Schimmel. It made the finals in the first (and most likely only) Southern Foodways Alliance Cole Slaw and Potato Salad Contest, curated by Elizabeth. Although it didn't win the top prize, it was Elizabeth's favorite.

I medium green cabbage, cored and shredded in a food processor

I large red onion, finely chopped

⅓ cup apple cider vinegar

3 tablespoons superfine sugar

⅔ cup mayonnaise (she uses Hellmann's)

⅔ cup sour cream

2 cups crumbled best-quality blue cheese (or more to taste)

Finely ground kosher salt and ground black pepper

Combine the cabbage and onion in a large bowl and set aside.

Combine the vinegar and sugar in a saucepan and bring to a boil. Pour the hot dressing over the vegetables and let sit 15 minutes to wilt. Drain the cabbage and onion well and return them to the bowl.

Combine the mayonnaise, sour cream, and blue cheese in a small bowl; stir until creamy. Add to the cabbage and onions, season well with salt and pepper, and toss. Let sit at least 2 hours or overnight, covered, in the refrigerator before serving. Adjust the seasonings and add more cheese if necessary before serving.

SERVES 8 TO 10

Elizabeth's Smoked Salsa

Fresh and simple flavors are Elizabeth's trademark, and she gives a modern update to some heavier barbecue side dishes. This thick, highly seasoned smoked salsa can be eaten with chips, spooned over grilled shrimp or chicken, or eaten cold like gazpacho.

1 head garlic

6 large ripe tomatoes (about 3 pounds), cored but left whole

2 cucumbers, peeled, halved lengthwise, and seeded

1 large sweet onion (like a Vidalia), peeled and cut in half across the equator

2 bunches scallions, trimmed

1 yellow bell pepper

1 red bell pepper

½ to ¾ cup olive oil, plus more for brushing on vegetables

2 tablespoons red wine vinegar

2 tablespoons chopped fresh herbs (including basil, mint, parsley, and oregano)

2 teaspoons Spanish smoked hot paprika (see Note)

Finely ground kosher salt and ground black pepper

Hot sauce (like Tabasco)

FOR SERVING

Tortilla chips

Set up a gas or charcoal grill for smoking.

Prepare the garlic for roasting by cutting about ⅛ inch off the top. Brush the garlic all over with oil, sprinkle with salt, and place in a square of aluminum foil. Close the foil around the head of garlic. Place the garlic on the warming rack of the grill or away from any direct heat to roast (this can be done in advance and will take about 45 minutes to roast and caramelize).

When you're ready to smoke the vegetables, brush them all with oil. Place the tomatoes, cucumbers, onion, and scallions in the center of the cooking grate, off direct heat. Place the peppers directly over the heat to blacken. Keep an eye on them and turn them as the skin blackens.

Cook the tomatoes, cucumbers, onion, and scallions until marked and soft but not mushy, about 20 minutes (the vegetables will take different lengths of time to cook). Transfer the vegetables to a platter to cool. When the peppers are blackened, place them in a closed container or paper bag until the steam loosens the skin. Remove the skin and seeds and set aside. Check to make sure the garlic is done and remove from the grill.

Puree the smoked vegetables and garlic in a food processor or blender. Slowly add the oil, vinegar, herbs, paprika, salt, pepper, and hot sauce until smooth and very thick. Adjust the oil, vinegar, salt, pepper, and hot sauce to taste. Chill until serving time. Serve with tortilla chips.

SERVES 6

NOTE: Find Spanish smoked hot paprika in specialty stores or online from thespicehouse.com.

Carolina BarBQ Society

When I hear that William McKinney is from South Carolina, the first question I have to ask is, "Tell me about that hash."

Now I'll try anything, and I really gave hash my best shot. I always try a taste at every restaurant when I travel to South Carolina. But this is one barbecue delicacy I just can't get my taste buds wrapped around.

My first encounter with hash was at a place in Columbia called Mr. T's. The hotel front desk clerk recommended the restaurant, and it was packed. Always a good sign. I noticed that lots of people going through the buffet line ordered hash as one of their two side dishes. So I thought it must be pretty good. I took a bite. Then I took another.

"You need to try this," I said to Amy.

She tried it and quickly reached for her ice tea. "What'd you do that for?" she asked.

"I just thought you ought to try it," I told her.

William smiles. "Hash is a beautiful, fragrant offal meat stew. There's good hash and there's not-so-good hash. I can see how it might be an acquired taste if you didn't grow up with it."

William was born in Columbia, South Carolina, and he grew up in Greenville. He spent his college years in North Carolina at Chapel Hill. During his junior year, he formed the Carolina BarBQ Society at the University of North Carolina. That's a fancy name for a bar-becue club, and its first meeting drew a crowd of 60 students, faculty, staff, and other folks who are keenly interested in eating good barbecue.

"We also have the distinction of having the largest number of Jewish members in a pork-based club," he tells me.

Many members are from out of state or from large cities. "The club introduces people to different cultures and communities around the state," William elaborates. "Even people

William McKinney and Stevie Mitchell at the Big Apple Barbecue Block Party

"The Big Apple Barbecue Block Party was like a barbecue outreach experience for New Yorkers—they got a little closer to understanding how good food can taste and how important it can be to the people and place from where it comes."

—WILLIAM MCKINNEY

who grew up in North Carolina might've come from metropolitan areas, and they just haven't experienced all of these wonderful types of barbecue."

William likes to talk about the link between politics, one of his passions, and barbecue. We pitmasters are always quick to point out that even George Washington had political barbecues.

"Barbecue is so intertwined with everything that happens in North Carolina, especially politics," William says. "When I was traveling in 2000, on a bus tour with the National Democratic Party, everywhere we stopped invariably was this barbecue restaurant, and you begin to realize that this is sort of the town hall of these places. Every time I go into Mitchell's, for example, I'll see a Supreme Court Justice or someone running for Congress. That's where people go to see and be seen."

It is long-established protocol for any Southern political candidate worthy of a spot on the ballot entertains potential voters with a barbecue. This is not the custom in Las Vegas, where some of my restaurants are located, but it's very much a custom in Southern Illinois. Ours are nonpartisan barbecue establishments, so we have catered many an event for politicians of all stripes. I certainly have my preferences, but I'm not out to convert anyone.

William had to pass on his barbecue club presidency once he graduated, but in his spare time, he's working on producing oral histories of Carolina barbecue for the Southern Foodways Alliance.

"What's your favorite place in South Carolina?" I ask. I always like to hear a new name to put on my list for future travels.

"One of my favorite places is Bub Sweatman's in Holly Hill. I sadly discovered that Bub—not Bob; it's an Orangeburg County thing—has been in a coma for the past few years. He was described to me as being a vegetable. That must be something like being in Dante's Inferno for someone who lives for pork."

East Coast Grill

Chris Schlesinger was ahead of the urban barbecue curve. Way back in the '80s, he operated Jake & Earl's Dixie BBQ right next door to his popular East Coast Grill in Cambridge, Massachusetts. Chris is a barbecue and grilling expert, and he's the author, along with John Willoughby, of some fine books on the subject. He closed Jake & Earl's in 1996, mostly because he needed the space for seating at East Coast. He kept his J & R pits, though, and pulled pork, brisket, and ribs remain fixtures on the menu.

Raised in Virginia, Chris's barbecue heritage is Eastern Carolina–style whole hog. He has vivid childhood memories of pig pickins in his own backyard.

"Four or five guys would come over and help dig a pit and put the hog on. They'd put me to bed at some point, and I'd look out the window and see them sitting in lawn chairs, drinking beers. And when I woke up the next morning and looked outside, they'd still be sitting in those same chairs, drinking beer!" he remembers.

"When I graduated from culinary school, I wanted to cook barbecue, but I didn't know how. The method isn't defined in terms of classic culinary technique. For me, being classically trained, I needed to understand and define it as a technique.

"And that's when my buddies and I started going down to Memphis in May. We went down three years in a row and hung out and talked to anybody we could. The people on barbecue teams aren't professional chefs. In an effort to understand barbecue, I had to decipher what the teams were doing. Everybody knows it now. It's smoked braising essentially. You have large, tough cuts of meat, and you cook them in a smoke resulting from a hardwood fire at a low temperature for a long period of time. Cook to the point of tenderness as opposed to doneness.

"Once I figured that out . . ."

"Then it was easy!" I laugh.

"Well, maybe not easy. But I understood. I already had the beer-drinking philosophy down pat. I just had to figure out the cooking part," Chris smiles.

"And the variables," I point out. "There are so many subtleties and so many nuances. That's what makes barbecue so fascinating, I think."

Chris and I agree that the ultimate barbecue may be the kind you find served on a street corner in the South. An old guy sets up, cooks all day, and starts selling. When it's gone, he packs up and goes home.

"That's the real expression of barbecue to me," Chris tells me.

"Yes," I agree. "But you can't make a living doing that these days."

Chris Schlesinger
of East Coast Grill

We both agree on that.

"You know," Chris adds, "yuppification is in some ways preserving the traditions of barbecue. In the Boston area alone, we have eight or nine places cooking with wood. People who love the craft and who are taking care to be authentic."

"Just because it's 'authentic' doesn't mean it's good," I'm quick to point out. "I've had a lot of barbecue that somebody's labored over and it wasn't too good."

"The importance of food, to me, is as a vehicle or a context for people to get together and share good fellowship and have good times," Chris says. "In Virginia, you ate barbecue. The idea of doing a whole pig and having a hundred of your best friends over and getting a keg of beer is the epitome of food serving as a context for people having a great time and being with each other. Barbecue is home."

Apple Cider Marinated Pork Loin

This is another one of those fancy chef recipes that uses herbs like rosemary and sage that you don't find in traditional barbecue. It's also one of the few recipes in this book that actually uses a marinade instead of a dry rub. The down-home side dishes for this moist and tender meat would include some type of apples—baked, fried— or even applesauce. For best results, smoke with apple or other fruit woods.

1 pork loin (4 to 6 pounds)	2 tablespoons Dijon mustard
1 can (6 ounces) frozen apple juice concentrate, thawed	2 tablespoons dried rosemary
⅓ cup apple jelly	1 teaspoon dried sage, crumbled
¼ cup vegetable oil	2 teaspoons kosher salt, finely ground
3 tablespoons apple cider vinegar	1 teaspoon ground black pepper
2 tablespoons Worcestershire sauce	

Set the loin in a shallow dish.

Combine the remaining ingredients in a blender and blend until creamy. Pour the marinade over the loin, coating thoroughly. Marinate, covered and chilled, overnight.

Discard the marinade and smoke at 200 to 225 degrees for about 3 hours or until the internal temperature measures 165 degrees.

SERVES 6

"Sometimes people say, 'Your barbecue is pretty good, but it's not real barbecue.' Real barbecue is the place where you grew up eating barbecue. It's good, but it's not real—that's a high compliment."

—CHRIS SCHLESINGER

Rouge

Andy Husbands and his wife, Gretchen, own a few fine restaurants in Boston and Providence, Rhode Island. Rouge, open since 2003 in Boston's South End, is his ode to Southern cooking and barbecue. Andy also offers barbecue catering all over New England.

A Seattle native and a Johnson & Wales–trained chef, Andy's first job was for Chris Schlesinger at East Coast Grill.

"Growing up, I might've had boiled ribs in a restaurant, but not real Southern barbecue. There weren't any barbecue joints in Seattle. East Coast Grill was my first true experience, back in 1991.

"I went to work for Chris Schlesinger, my mentor. Or de-mentor, I like to say. Chris was known for barbecue. One of my responsibilities was to manage Jake & Earl's. That was my job, and I knew nothing about barbecue. I was intrigued by the smoker, but I wanted to be this highfalutin chef and have nothing to do with barbecue. To me, it was stupid. Ridiculous."

"The other end of the food spectrum," I comment.

"Exactly, as far as I was concerned. Now, 15 years later, I've done a total 180. I own a barbecue joint.

"Chris taught me a lot of great stuff. But I would say my barbecue knowledge grew tenfold since we've seriously started competing in the last seven years."

Andy and his childhood friend Chris Hart are fixtures on the New England barbecue scene. Their team, UFO Social Club, was the 2002, 2003, and 2004 Team of the Year, and they consistently rack up top honors at area KCBS competitions.

"I have to give credit to Chris," says Andy. "He's the chief cook. I help out. He's developed most of our recipes. And he's not a professional chef or anything."

"What style do you guys cook?" I ask.

"We originally started off as sort of Memphis style. In the beginning, we lost a lot. We cooked what we liked. We like big, chunky, hot, spicy sauces. Chunky chunky. But that's not what the judges are looking for. I learned I can't win with sauces like that."

"No," I agree. "They're looking for more traditional flavors."

"Exactly. So we morphed into our style. It's not exactly Kansas City and it's not exactly Memphis. It's in between. Kind of a lightly glazed Memphis-style rib.

"Last year we placed 10th at Jack Daniel's," Andy tells me. "That was a thrill.

"In Boston proper, there is nobody doing the level of barbecue that I'm doing," Andy says. "Outside of Boston, you have Blue Ribbon in Newton, who were trained by me, Jake's over in Jamaica Plain, and Steve Euliss at Firefly's in Natick. They do a great job. But they're all out of town."

"What do you think is so emotionally appealing about barbecue?" I ask Andy. "Why the surge in popularity?"

"It's just so primal. It's salt of the earth. Just the simplicity of meat over fire. It's comfort food. Life is so stressful that people want comfort food. Takes you back."

"It's also very democratic," I point out. "You can appeal to every walk of life."

"Yeah, everybody likes ribs," agrees Andy. "But you know what I think is super kick-ass about it? It's American cuisine. It's ours. At the Jack, for four years, those European teams, they were all dead last."

"Really?" I question. "I judged last year and I remember being surprised by how many of them placed. I kept seeing that German team go up for trophies."

"Well, two years ago, they lost. They lost big.

"But you know what, it's our damn cuisine," he says. "Maybe that makes it extra-special, too. You can have your Frenchy French French stuff. Your Russian borscht. But we have our cuisine. Barbecue. Which is cool."

"Andy Husbands? You gonna put Andy Husbands in your book? I taught him everything he knows! You tell him I said that."
—JAKE JACOBS, JAKE'S BOSS BARBECUE

Andy's Hangover Hash

Andy packs 'em in for Sunday brunch, and this hearty dish is one of his most popular items. It is sure to cure what ails you. A Bloody Mary is the perfect complement.

4 tablespoons vegetable oil, plus additional for frying the eggs

½ medium onion, diced

½ green bell pepper, seeded and diced

3 large potatoes, diced

Finely ground kosher salt and ground black pepper

Magic Dust (see page 67), optional

2 cups pulled or chopped barbecue pork or beef

Hot sauce (like Tabasco), optional

4 to 8 large eggs

Heat 2 tablespoons oil in a medium cast-iron skillet over medium-high heat. Add the onion and green pepper and sauté until just tender. Don't overcook. Remove the onion and pepper from the skillet with a slotted spoon and set aside. Add 2 tablespoons oil and the potatoes to the skillet. Season with salt and pepper to taste and add a dash of Magic Dust, if you care to. Cook until the potatoes are almost tender. Return the onion and green pepper to the skillet and stir to combine with the potatoes. Add the meat and stir gently to combine. Cook for a few minutes more to heat the meat. Taste and add a few dashes of hot sauce, if desired. Cover and set aside.

Fry 1 or 2 eggs per person in a little vegetable oil.

Divide the hash among 4 plates. Top with the fried eggs; season with salt, pepper, and Magic Dust. Serve immediately.

SERVES 4

Barbecue on the Silver Screen

I never thought I'd see the day when an independent film about barbecue would be showing at film festivals—and winning awards. But that's exactly what's happened with two different films about Texas and North Carolina barbecue.

The young men who are made these films are still wet behind the ears. They aren't in the barbecue business, but they recognize the significance of barbecue to their respective cultures and childhoods. They've come up with two great films that really capture the flavor of barbeque culture.

Barbecue: A Texas Love Story

When I asked independent filmmaker Chris Elley about his previous films, he told me one is about NASA taking a cow pasture and turning it into the center of the technological universe and one is about Texas during the Depression.

"So *Barbecue: A Texas Love Story* is a departure for you," I say.

"No," he explains. "Each film is about Texas."

Of course they are. I'm just focusing on food.

"How did you come to choose this subject?" I ask.

"I've always loved barbecue, and there's lots to love around here. But I had two specific inspirational moments. One I didn't even know I was having," he tells me. "Six years ago when the famous Kreuz/Smitty's split took place, the Kreuz folks made a big show of ceremoniously carting the coals down the main street in Lockhart. People were lining the sides of the road like it was a parade route, and they even had a police escort. They'd tied chains to a metal container containing the coals, and they were dragging it by the chains.

"That image was all over the national new, and I remember thinking, 'This is what the rest of the world thinks about Texas.' And yet I was proud that people had that level of pride and support . . . to show up like it was a parade. Now, that's passion.

"Then in December of '02, I was driving in the Hill Country and the Robert Earl Keen song 'Barbeque' came on, and that Kreuz/Lockhart image popped immediately into my mind. I could see the images of all the different barbecue stories coming to life with the song. It was time to hit the road. I just knew I had to make the film."

Elley's film is less about the food than it is about how people relate around barbecue in Texas.

"Jesus loved barbecue."

—KINKY FRIEDMAN, WRITER, MUSICIAN, AND FREQUENT CANDIDATE FOR GOVERNOR OF TEXAS

"We didn't go into recipes; we went into hearts," explains Chris. The most heart-warming stop on the film's tour was the small town of Denton, a community that hangs its hat on civic pride. Steve Logan's barbecue place burned down after 22 years in business in Denton. The people of Denton were rallying together to put Steve and his institution back in business.

"It was tough to shoot that scene," Chris says. "We were standing there watching this grown man cry about the disappointment he feels late at night when he realizes he can't get up and pull meat because there's no meat anymore. No insurance. No business. This man's life was changed forever, and that community came together to rebuild it."

The film crew even joined the effort by holding fund-raisers across the state and contacting media on Steve's behalf.

As Herbie Lynn, one of the barbecue cooks featured in the film, says, "Ya gotta have the love."

That love has stretched its arms out wide from Texas to all corners of the globe, even the Oval Office.

"LBJ was the first guy to popularize barbecue as a diplomatic tool," says Chris. "He brought foreign dignitaries to the ranch for barbecue because he thought he could get more done that way, rather than sitting in the Oval Office."

Chris is a bit young, and I figure maybe he doesn't know that barbecue has been used as a political tool and reward for over 200 years. So I remind him: "George Washington had barbecues, too."

"Well, yeah, but LBJ turned it into a circus. He brought out the red-and-white checkered cloths and put everyone in cowboy hats and chaps. He used it for all it was worth. One phrase should say it all: monkeys on dogs, herding cattle."

One of the most compelling parts of the film shows LBJ's White House press secretary, Liz Carpenter, and then-presidential-entertainer Cactus Pryor recalling the events of the day JFK was assassinated. They were at the ranch that fateful day, putting the final touches on the barbecue that LBJ was hosting for President and Mrs. Kennedy. That barbecue never took place.

Cactus was one of the first people to know JFK had died. "A Secret Service agent came to the door and said, 'You're now standing in the house of the president of the United States,'" Cactus reflects solemnly.

I ask Chris if he cooks barbecue himself.

"Oh, no," he shakes his head. "I only eat it. I just can't even aspire to the level of expertise of what I really enjoy. I feel more like a critic. Someone who can eat it and have an opinion but not do it myself. After traveling and filming and eating our way through 10,000 miles of Texas, we have become experts at figuring out what is good and what is not. Of course, just having a Texas citizenship card seems to qualify you just as well," he says with a grin.

Barbecue Is a Noun

Hawes Bostic and Austin McKenna are good Southern boys and filmmakers in their early 30s. They now live in Brooklyn, but they were raised in North Carolina and met during their college years at the University of Virginia.

In 2000, they found themselves with buyout packages from their employers. Instead doing something sensible like investing in a house or a car or travel, they decided to use their money to make a film about the culture of barbecue in the Carolinas. Their wonderful documentary, *Barbecue Is a Noun,* is the result.

"When you grow up in North Carolina, you have zero idea that the same level of barbecue isn't available everywhere. That's one of the reasons we started making the film. The idea is that what we took for granted in North Carolina and what we talk about all the time, even with our own very strict regional differences, doesn't really have a lot to do with the rest of the world. The food's cooked a certain way with a certain sauce. You don't deviate from that. People take it seriously. And people get fired up to talk about it. That's the point. You have a regional discussion and love for and dependence on barbecue that we don't really get anywhere else in the country," Hawes tells me.

During the filming, they also gained an appreciation for the backbreaking work that goes into barbecue.

"One of the little ironies about our filmmaking process is that we actually funded portions of the film by cooking hogs and selling the barbecue," Austin tells me. "So it became

Filmmakers Austin McKenna and Hawes Bostic discuss their film, Barbecue Is a Noun.

a film about men who cook hogs for a living made by men who were cooking hogs to make the film about men who cook hogs for a living.

"We did our first hog at a bachelor party, and we burned the better part of an acre of scrub brush to get enough heat to cook two hogs," Austin continues. "It took 16½ hours and a crew of about 40 guys and several thousand beers, and I was exhausted. It took me a week to recover. There's no way I'd do that for a living. It takes so much effort to split the wood and dress the hog. Cut the hooves off and remove the lymph nodes. It's pretty serious stuff.

"A lot of places'll tell you they're doing it the faster way and they're still cooking with wood and it's hickory barbecue. But there's a difference between hickory flavor and hickory cooked, and that's part of the reason we wanted to make the film—because it's not going to be around in another 20 years."

We talked some about the characters they chose to include in the film. "There were an unlimited number of people we could've talked to," says Hawes. "We started by going to some of the more famous places." But Austin and Hawes are quick to point out that not everybody in the film is famous or smokes the best barbecue. Some just have a unique style about them.

"Blue Ox, over in Carpenter, North Carolina, cooks with a beer in hand the whole time. James Green, over on Farrow Road in Columbia, South Carolina, is a real character. It comes out in the film that he had been dealing coke and shooting people, and barbecue saved him. That's his story and it's pretty compelling. He's feeding the children and hooking up everybody in Columbia with jobs. His barbecue is not very good, but that didn't keep him from being in the film."

These boys learned more about hogs than they probably ever wanted or needed to know. I got a kick out of hearing about their visits to hog farms.

"I was surprised to learn that hogs'll eat anything," said Austin. "We filmed a guy, Mr. Henry in Hopkins, South Carolina; he's 80-plus years old and he's kind of one of the centerpieces of the film. He's an incredibly fascinating character. He's got a hog sty behind his property, and we went back there to watch Henry feed the hogs. We selected one, and Henry killed it and cooked it for us. This was while we were filming the soup-to-nuts process piece. Henry was feeding his hogs phone books and whatever he had laying around. I learned, from hanging around with Bob Garner—that journalist and expert on North Carolina barbecue—that in the western part of the state, pigs used to just run wild and eat acorns, which actually produces a very nutty meat. I can tell you we ate this hog that we cooked that was raised on phone books and refuse and whatnot and it was an inferior hog. You do have to pay attention to what these things are eating.

"But having spent a lot of time around them, they are nasty creatures, and everybody asks how do you feel about it, like it's gross, and we had some issues with showing some of this because it's pretty intense when you cut one of these guys open and dress it. So we're sorta looking at an NC-17 rating."

Chapter Seven

BAR
POLICE
EVANG

BECUE
and
ELISTS

ere are my three favorite things in the world: 1) eating barbecue, 2) cooking barbecue, and 3) talking about barbecue. Day to day, I mostly talk about the mechanics of cooking barbecue. People want to know very specific details about the process, and I can talk about that all day long.

Talking to food writers about barbecue is a whole other ball game. We talk about philosophy and history and evolution and all kinds of highbrow topics. Issues of race and politics and creeping regionalism. Things I don't necessarily think about on a day-to-day basis. That's their job: to keep the history, legend, and lore alive while evolution proceeds. I always learn from these fascinating conversations.

Barbecue Police

A number of people are known for helping form public opinion about barbecue—for better or worse, I might add. I'm going to turn the tables a bit on those experts I call the "barbecue police."

Personally, I have always wondered how white men from New York City could possibly be experts on barbecue. Some of these people have written real nice things about me over the years. Now I get to interview *them*. This is a diverse group of men and women from several corners of the country. They may have some differing views, but they're all united in the cause of promoting the tradition and culture of barbecue.

Calvin Trillin

When I called Calvin Trillin to ask him for some comments for this book, he said, "I'm happy to talk to you, but I think you've got the wrong guy. I don't barbecue, I don't cook food of any sort. Food writing in general is sort of a sideline. I enjoy barbecue, but I sometimes go for months and years without eating it."

I register my surprise. "You do?"

"Yeah, I live in New York. If I'm in a barbecue town, I eat barbecue. I'm not in a barbecue town very often," he says wistfully. "I'm going to San Francisco next week."

There's a place in San Francisco called Memphis Minnie's that I could recommend. But I don't bother because I know his thought process, and sure enough he tells me, "For me, barbecue is something you eat where the tradition is to eat it."

That's one way to be assured of getting some decent barbecue.

Way back in the 1970s, when food writing was mostly about foo-foo food, Calvin Trillin caused a sensation when he wrote that, generally speaking, "Everybody knows the best restaurants in the world are in Kansas City. Or at least the top four or so." He went on to elaborate on his childhood favorite, Arthur Bryant's.

"Did you have any idea," I ask him, "what a sensation that was going to cause?"

"None," he answers humbly. "It was purely a fluke.

"I originally wrote about Bryant's barbecue in *Life* magazine. The line about how the best restaurants in the world are in Kansas City comes from that piece I did in *Playboy* in about 1970 or 1971. Sort of a takeoff on the kind of food writing that was being done at that time. You know, 'Sophia Loren's Rome.' Originally I'd written the article as a sort of gourmet tour of Kansas City. But the magazine changed the thrust because of a companion article written by some sort of count, Roy Andries de Groot. He'd written an article about some foie gras restaurant in Paris, and the title was 'Have I Found the Best Restaurant in the World?'

"They ran my piece right alongside his, and the lead was: 'No. The best restaurants in the world are of course in Kansas City.'"

"And the rest is history," I say.

"Well, yes, I guess," Calvin says. "Some people took it too seriously, and some didn't take it seriously enough. People were calling and saying, 'We really *do* have the best restaurants . . .' and I'd tell them, 'I said they were the best in the world. What do you want from me?'

"And then there were people who called Bryant's to make a reservation. They just didn't understand. It's counter service."

Calvin Trillin tests some of my ribs at the Big Apple Barbecue Block Party. They don't measure up to Arthur Bryant's, but he eats almost a full rack just to see if they'll do in a pinch.

He keeps trying to convince me he hasn't written much else about barbecue.

"I think I wrote another piece about talking to Mr. Bryant after coming back from South America and eating what was called barbecue there. And I wrote about Memphis in May, probably in the early '80s, and I wrote a chapter of *Feeding a Yen* about barbecue and contests.

"Oh, and I went to the summit, of course," he says, referring to the Southern Food-ways Alliance barbecue symposium. Every year the SFA has a fall symposium devoted to a specific Southern food topic or theme. In 2002, the theme was barbecue.

"Don't you think that's funny," I ask, "that people gather to talk so seriously about barbecue?"

"Yes, it is funny," he agrees. "What's funnier is that I enjoyed the speeches. I usually tune out during seminars and fall asleep during those speeches. These were very interesting. I gave sort of the summing-up speech at the end.

"There was a really interesting talk by a woman named Marcie Cohen Ferris called 'We Didn't Know from Fatback' about growing up Jewish in Arkansas and loving barbecue. I stated in my talk that apparently the people in Arkansas hadn't heard of the 'barbecue easement' that was granted by the Joplin rebbe who was a distinguished Talmudist and pitmaster. He said that for Jews in the South and Midwest, it was kosher to eat any animal that was subjected to at least four hours of slow cooking and that had four hooves and no scales."

I laugh and tell him about a customer I have in Murphysboro. We don't have too many Jewish people in Southern Illinois, and all the ones I know love barbecue. There's one guy who comes into 17th Street regularly to order some "chopped beef." A new girl was helping him one day, and she told him we don't serve what he was looking for. Finally he asked for me, and I filled up a container with pulled pork. "Here's your beef," I said, and he looked at the waitress as if to say, "See, I told you so."

Calvin gets a kick out of that story. "See," he nods. "He knows about the easement."

Jeffrey Steingarten

I described my first meeting with Jeffrey Steingarten in Chapter 1. Little did I know that our chance encounter would develop into a professional and personal friendship. What impressed me immediately about Jeffrey was his intense focus and interest in learning about all things barbecue. For more than a decade, we have talked for hours and hours about barbecue, and Jeffrey has dreamed up questions and investigated details I'd never even considered.

"I was the first person to write about you," Jeffrey asserts.

"You definitely were," I assure him.

By the time I met Jeffrey, I'd been interviewed a number of times by regional reporters. Most focused on the competition circuit, but they saw only the caricature. Jeffrey wrote about our team and about the barbecue world with respect for its culture and the dedica-

Jeffrey Steingarten and I discuss the finer points of pork at the 2004 Big Apple Barbecue Block Party.

tion that teams show for the sport. He was first invited to Memphis in May as a "celebrity" judge, and he brought that same level of respect to his judging duties.

"I took judging very seriously," Jeffrey confirms. "I thought it would be wrong to have an ignorant person judge barbecue, because these people devote their lives to it. I went to the judging class and learned everything I could about what the meat should be. I learned later that there were other 'celebrity' judges who had no idea there was a class. I asked one a question about ribs, and she had the exact opposite view."

"She wanted the meat falling off the bone, didn't she?" I ask.

"Yes. And I knew from the class about white bone and how that was not a good thing. And how the ribs were supposed to separate right down the middle but not fall off the bone.

"You can certainly tell the difference between bad and good, but you may not be able to tell the difference between good and good. That was my fear. What if you have really bad first-round judges and good people are eliminated?" Jeffrey asks.

"That's why you have both live and blind judging," I explain. "If you don't get good marks outside, then you probably won't do well. But even if you get all great marks in live judging, you still have to win the blind judging to win the contest."

"One year I judged shoulder, and Big Bob Gibson was in the finals. I didn't know it was

255

Big Bob's shoulder at that time, but I did know that it was good," Jeffrey remembers. "I was amazed that the judges weren't allowed to talk to each other. I could've used a little conversation."

"It's supposed to be your own opinion, not colored by someone else's," I remind him.

"Yes, I understand," Jeffrey replies. "But I would've liked to hear what others had to say. We didn't talk, but we all pigged out on that shoulder, and it was obvious that team was going to win."

"The Memphis in May people have become very serious about making sure that the judges are trained and qualified. They used to let the judges drink and they got a lot of complaints because some judges would be totally sloshed by their last assignment, and that's just not fair to the teams," I add.

"That's good," Jeffrey says. "Because if someone says, 'These are the best ones,' how would you know? It's all subjective, but you have to have educated subjectivity.

"That's true of all food," he goes on. "If you've never eaten Indian food with Indian people, for example, then you're just going to apply American standards to their food. But if you eat a meal with Indians once or twice, they help you tune up your taste buds. That's why I was so looking forward to our first barbecue meal together."

Our first barbecue meal was nothing to write home about, I'm sorry to say. We planned to get together in Memphis on Sunday, after the contest. We drove around to three or four of my favorite places, but even in a barbecue epicenter like Memphis, most barbecue places are closed on Sundays. That's the Lord's day and family day. We ended up at a pretty famous place, and we had a not-so-good meal. It was memorable, though. Unfortunately, we remember how bad it was.

"It was just terrible," Jeffrey recalls. "And you wouldn't denigrate the food."

"No," I admit. "I don't like to criticize another pitmaster's food."

Present Perfect

Jeffrey pulled a fast one on me in the December 1993 issue of *Vogue*, when he named ribs from 17th Street Bar & Grill one of the top 10 food gifts to send for the holidays. I wasn't exactly set up for mail order, and I had no idea that the article was being published. Suddenly, the phone started ringing off the hook, and we scrambled for the entire month of December to fill the orders.

I distinctly remember one of our early conversations. Jeffrey called to ask my opinion about a pretty well-known barbecue restaurant. He phrased his questions every which way, but he couldn't get me to tell him what he wanted to hear. "Well, they've got good rolls," I finally broke down. "That's exactly what I wrote!" Jeffrey exclaimed.

For someone who came to barbecue relatively late in life, Jeffrey has tasted some of the best, I'd say.

"In 2002, I was in Mississippi for the Southern Foodways Alliance barbecue symposium. I flew in and out of Memphis, and Lolis Elie told me I had to go to Hawkins Grill on my way home, to eat some of J. C. Hardaway's barbecue. Turns out he had changed his location to a place called The Big S Grill, and it was going to be open Sunday. I changed my flight time so I'd be able to go there before leaving Memphis.

"It was located in a part of Memphis I'd never been in, along the railroad tracks. The poorest part of Memphis I've ever seen. J. C. Hardaway was standing in the backyard, a tiny little backyard, where they made their barbecue. He was doing it on a grill. It was fantastically good. One of the best sandwiches I've had.

"You could say he broke all the rules, but he didn't know there were rules. He didn't have a long time to talk, but he told me how he did his barbecue. He smoked it outside and then put it in the oven wrapped in aluminum foil. He took it out of the oven, one portion at a time, and fried it a little so the fat got crispy. I wish I'd known about him when we were driving around that day. They were open on Sundays, too."

"Do you know J. C. Hardaway died?" I ask.

"Yes," Jeffrey answers. "I'm so glad I got to eat his barbecue.

"I think I've tasted the pinnacle of barbecue," Jeffrey continues. "I've had your ribs and Big Bob Gibson's shoulder. I ate J. C. Hardaway's barbecue sandwich. And there's this place in Houston called Thelma's that I really liked. They had incredible brisket."

"There is more good barbecue out there," I assure him. "That's what I love about barbecue. There's room for everybody at the table." "Well, maybe not everybody," Jeffrey says, ever the discerning critic. "I'd say just about three people."

Lolis Eric Elie

Knowing Lolis is an honor and a pleasure, and I've discovered he's pretty knowledgeable about a variety of different subjects. I am continually impressed by his deep understanding of and commitment to the culture and tradition of barbecue. His book *Smokestack Lightning* is one of the most highly regarded books about the subject.

Lolis is intensely interested in how food and culture work together, and barbecue, to him, is one of the best illustrations of that.

"Barbecue begins to really tie in with identity, and even more so than most foods, barbecue tells you who you are, how you grew up, and where you grew up," Lolis tells me. "There are many national American foods—hot dogs, pizza, hamburgers. But nobody debates these foods as hotly as they do barbecue.

"My point is that we all like to have good food, and I think it deserves as much attention and analysis as any of the other cultural activities that we hold dear. Like art and architecture, for example."

We talk about the spread of barbecue and its increasing popularity in places like New York City and other Northern regions. Lolis believes that an interesting evolution in American food has taken place in the last 20 to 30 years.

"As we've become more interested in our own food and less interested in the food culture of Europe, we've been forced to recognize Southern cooking as among the most original, the most important, and most lasting traditions of American food," he asserts.

"That's the food I grew up with," I tell him. "I love barbecue, but I'm really surprised by the way New Yorkers embraced it. I still can't get over all those people who stood so patiently in the pouring-down rain at that first Block Party."

Smokestack Lightning: The Documentary

After writing the book, Lolis retraced some of his steps and filmed a documentary. His goal was to spotlight the devotion to the art and craft of barbecue shown by some legendary pitmasters, including J. C. Hardaway of the Big S Grill and Raymond Robinson of Cozy Corner. Raymond passed away in 2000; J. C. in 2002. Through Lolis's book and film, the stories of these men and their legacy will continue to be passed down over time. The film airs periodically on public television.

My ribs don't taste like Cozy Corner's, but Lolis managed to eat his fill.

Lolis agrees. "And for Southerners, the idea that people in places like New York and Seattle and Connecticut are gonna try to do barbecue is laughable."

"They'll eventually come up with their own traditions," I predict. "Just as New York is a melting pot of people, it'll probably become a melting pot of barbecue as well. If the trend takes hold."

"In order for a city or region to produce good barbecue, you need more than a few people doing it," Lolis reminds me. "And then you end up with friendly competition, and that's how it becomes part of the culture. You get a lot of people doing a lot of mediocre barbecue. And you get a few people who actually get good at it."

I ask Lolis about his own barbecue heritage.

"Writing that book was an education for me," Lolis explains. "Being from New Orleans, I never really experienced a pervasive barbecue culture such as they have in the Carolinas or Kansas City or Texas. A big part of the book was about me learning about what I was writing about. My thinking changed and evolved during the process.

"When you talk about barbecue and the differences between the styles in South and North Carolina and Georgia, for example, these are all neighboring states, but they have totally different types of barbecue. With that difference comes a kind of chauvinism that on one hand is a kind of boosterism—everybody trying to say they're the greatest. On the other hand, it adds political implications that go far beyond that. For example, why is it that some barbecue traditions cross state lines, while others remain largely in their region of origin? The barbecue dip in Owensboro, Kentucky, is similar to the Worcestershire sauce–style dip in parts of North Carolina. How did that happen? The mustard-based sauce of South Carolina seems to exist in only one place outside that state, in Phenix City, Alabama. How did that happen?"

"Let's talk about region for a moment. Some folks who are born and bred in the Northeast may not want to hear this, but there is this sort of sense that everything in the Northeast is somehow smarter, somehow better, somehow more sophisticated. And that ultimately means that you look down on Southerners as people who are somehow . . . kind of backward. People will say things like, 'I don't mean to sound prejudiced, but you've got to admit they're not real bright . . .'

"But this increasing national interest in barbecue and all foods American may go a long way toward reversing that stereotype," Lolis continues. "After all, as soon as more Northeasterners put away the hamburgers and hot dogs and try to do some real barbecue on those grills of theirs, more of them will realize that this Southern food requires techniques that are not easily mastered."

"It's not as easy as it looks, is it?" I smile.

Lolis and his coauthor, photographer Frank Stewart, began and ended their *Smokestack Lightning* journey at Cozy Corner, and Lolis has a warm spot in his heart for the place.

"If you pin me down, I'd have to say Cozy Corner in Memphis is my favorite place. It embodies a perfect balance of ideals. You don't want a barbecue place to appear too refined, or too antiseptic. Then it seems to be more about the image than the food. Cozy Corner is clean and imperfect and delicious. Plus, they play great jazz all day long.

"As for the food, my favorite is their ribs. They're so well seasoned that the sauce is an afterthought. I also love their barbecued Cornish game hens and an off-the-menu special: the brisket sandwich with slaw dressing and raw onion."

He feels so at home at Cozy Corner that in August of 2004, when Hurricane Ivan threatened New Orleans, Lolis evacuated to the Cozy Corner to ride out the storm.

"Tell me, what was the most profound thing you learned while writing your book?"

"The power of listening, of listening to pitmasters who may be unlettered but who are not untutored in the art of barbecue. I learned to get out of the way and let them speak in the book. The more I listened to these people, the more I realized that their knowledge extends far beyond the barbecue pit. And once you understand that, it becomes very difficult to dismiss them."

Lunchtime scene at the Cozy Corner

Jim Auchmutey

I had the pleasure of making Jim Auchmutey's acquaintance at a National Barbecue Association Convention held in Atlanta. Unfortunately, we met over a rubber chicken luncheon while watching a slide show about grilling. Nonetheless, we recognized a kindred spirit in one another.

Since 1980, Jim has been a reporter at the *Atlanta Journal-Constitution*. He is also coauthor of *The Ultimate Barbecue Sauce Cookbook*.

"To be a Southern journalist, you have to be able to write and debate about barbecue, same as you have to be able to sip bourbon and tell stories," he says. "I've always been interested in food as another way of looking at our culture. Given my location in the South, I couldn't resist writing about barbecue."

And he is well qualified to discuss the subject. Jim's barbecue heritage is long and distinguished. His mother's side of the family runs a slaughterhouse in rural Georgia and specializes in hot country sausage. His father's side includes a long line of pitmasters and Brunswick stew makers. His great-grandfather, James Robert Auchmutey, for whom he's named, used to smoke pork and mutton and make Brunswick stew for one of Georgia's oldest barbecues, one put on by the Euharlee Farmers Club. His grandfather followed in his footsteps and was featured in a 1954 article in the *Saturday Evening Post* titled "Dixie's Most Disputed Dish."

"How could I turn my back on all that?" Jim asks me. "I guess it's in my blood."

We talk about the notion of Northerners writing about barbecue. "Northerners are entitled to opine about barbecue all they want. But I am entitled to regard their opinions the way they would if I started holding forth on bagels," he says with a wink. "My only complaint has to do with terminology. I'm amused by the way many outlanders regard anything cooked on a grill, from wieners to mushrooms, as 'barbecue.' I say, welcome these folks to the fold, then quietly explain the difference between grilling and barbecuing. As a person who uses words for a living, I think the distinction is worth keeping."

In 1998, Jim was instrumental in forming the Southern Foodways Alliance, along with John T. Edge, John Egerton, Nathalie Dupree, Louis Osteen, and a couple dozen other chefs and lovers of food and history.

Barbecue was the subject of the SFA's fall symposium in 2002, and Jim was invited to speak about the long tradition of politics and barbecue in the South.

"I got to repeat one of my favorite barbecue quotes. A gubernatorial candidate in Georgia once lost an election he thought he was going to win, in part because his campaign rallies, usually barbecues, were so well attended. Analyzing his defeat afterward, he said, 'Everybody that ate my barbecue I don't believe voted for me.'"

"Politicians used to believe they could sway votes with a dram of whiskey or a plate of pork. Now they do it with tax cuts and state lotteries. The barbecue was cheaper."

—JIM AUCHMUTEY, AT THE SOUTHERN FOODWAYS ALLIANCE BARBECUE SYMPOSIUM

Auchmutey Family Brunswick Stew (Domesticus)

Not only can he write about barbecue and Southern food, Jim can talk the talk. He makes an outstanding Brunswick stew, and he generously shares that recipe here. This is a domesticated, kitchen-friendly version of the stew his family has been making for generations. "Domesticated" because it isn't a big batch made in a huge black kettle over a hardwood fire. It's still made that way at his family reunion every September in Bartow County, Georgia, but he wanted a family-size recipe that he could make year-round without starting a fire outside, which is actually illegal in most of metro Atlanta. So his father came up with this recipe, which can be made in a Crockpot.

1 pound ground sirloin	1 tablespoon butter
1 pound chicken parts	⅓ cup apple cider vinegar
½ pound pulled pork barbecue	½ teaspoon kosher salt, finely ground (or to taste)
1 can (28 ounces) tomatoes, coarsely chopped, with juice	1½ teaspoons coarsely ground black pepper
1 can (16½ ounces) creamed corn	1 teaspoon cayenne
¼ cup ketchup	

Cook the ground sirloin in a large skillet until it's barely gray. Skim off the grease. Leave the meat in the skillet.

Remove the excess fat and skin from the chicken parts. Place in a large saucepan, cover with water, and bring to a boil. Lower the heat, cover, and simmer until the chicken falls off the bones, 20 to 30 minutes. When the chicken cools, remove the bones and tear the meat into small pieces by pulling and pinching it.

Add the chicken and the pork barbecue to the skillet with the cooked meat. Cook over low heat, stirring often with a wooden spoon, until the meats are thoroughly mixed.

Put the meats into a Crockpot. Add the remaining ingredients and stir well. Cook at the high setting for 3 hours, then at the low setting for another 2 to 3 hours. Monitor the taste, adding vinegar, pepper, and salt as needed. The stew won't be ready until it turns muddy red—the color of Georgia clay.

SERVES 4

John T. Edge

Whenever I ask a Southerner about barbecue in his childhood, the memories just come tumbling out.

"I used to ride my Schwinn five-speed bike—a bright-yellow Lemon Peeler model with a banana seat—down to Old Clinton Barbecue. I'd always have a barbecue sandwich, Brunswick stew, and either an Orange Crush or a Mountain Dew," John T. Edge remembers. "My family had a charge account there, so I went often.

"There was a community that called that place home, and for me, it was the beginning of an obsession with barbecue."

John T. is the director of the Southern Foodways Alliance at the University of Mississippi in Oxford. The SFA's mission is to celebrate, preserve, promote, and nurture the traditional and developing food culture of the American South. And yes, he gets paid to do that. He also writes for food magazines, and he's written a number of books. My personal favorite is *Southern Belly.*

As someone whose job is to preserve culture, John T. makes a number of wise observations about barbecue. "One of the salient features of great barbecue is that it's local. It emanates from one place. What I call barbecue, growing up in middle Georgia, somebody else says is crap. The difference could be infinitesimal. People are so passionate and localized in their passion of barbecue. It becomes this very provincial culinary art form."

One of John T.'s roles at the SFA is to serve as a source of information for people who write about Southern food.

"When people call from outside the barbecue belt, what are the common misconceptions that you have to educate them about?" I ask him.

"There are so many generalizations about barbecue perpetuated by the press," he answers. "Most people are attempting to get an understanding of what barbecue is all about."

I try to stir up a little controversy and ask what he thinks about the Northern media elite who write about barbecue, but John T. doesn't bite.

"There are a number of Northerners who've written well about barbecue," he points out. "I don't think one needs to be born in the South or Midwest or Texas to understand barbecue. Someone needs to spend a good deal of time with the mouth shut, listening, and a good deal of time with the mouth open, eating barbecue. Once they've done those two things, *then* they begin to be qualified to write about barbecue."

"Barbecue exists in the margins. That's where the great stories are. And that's where the great barbecue is."

—JOHN T. EDGE

I would agree with that.

Turnabout is fair play, so John T. tells me some of his concerns about barbecue cook-offs.

"The competition circuit is interesting and great, and people make fabulous barbecue. But because it's focused on grand prizes and it's well merchandised and well publicized, there's a possibility of losing sight of all of these old-line pitmasters who have been working in smoky restaurants for generations. Let's not forget them when we valorize the competition circuit."

I understand his concern. "Cook-offs are newsworthy. They're a spectacle. People like to come out and see the show," I point out. "And let's face it. Newspapers are looking for news. Barbecue contests are fun and easy to write about. Local teams, like Apple City, for example, become hometown heroes. That good old barbecue joint down the street that's just cooking good food day in and day out, they might get written up a few times, but if there's not something new to write about, they won't get any press.

I met John T. Edge at the first Big Apple Barbecue Block Party. One of my favorite memories of that event is John T. (right) and Jeffrey Steingarten sitting side by side on an Igloo cooler. Two of the country's most celebrated food writers; one from the South and one from the North. And they were getting along just fine.

"The old-timers, the legends, the shrines. Someone is always writing about them. They're consistently doing a good job," I continue. "The newer places who are trying to establish a reputation might be the ones who have the hardest time. No one takes them seriously for years. How many years do you have to be in business before you're legitimate in the eyes of the barbecue police?"

"At what point do you pass muster? Five, seven, ten years? It's difficult to give hard-and-fast rules about that," John T. acknowledges.

"To me, that's what this new breed of barbecuer is all about," I say. "The best ones are figuring out a way to get the ultimate barbecue taste and flavor. If they don't do it the back-breaking way, does that make it any less authentic? There are lots of people who do it the old way and their barbecue doesn't taste too good."

"One of the factors in great barbecue is the back story," he says thoughtfully. "And it can be a differentiating factor. When you head out on the road in search of barbecue, if you're a barbecue pilgrim, you're looking for that great smoky punch in pork and beef, but you're also looking to meet the pitmaster. You're looking for an encounter with someone who is real and honest and forthright. Years from now, the person you encounter may be a person who's been working over that newfangled pit for 40 years. Our expectations of what barbecue is will change. Barbecue is not static. Southern culture is not static. For me, the real thing of import is dedication to the craft."

What John T. is passionate about is preserving the art. And what I am passionate about is preserving the art while figuring out how to feed a whole lot of people the very best barbecue I can cook. I deeply respect tradition. My job, as I see it, is to create a new tradition. We agree that there's a place for all of us at the table.

Barbecue played an integral role in John T.'s courtship with his wife, Blair. "When we were courting, sometimes we'd break the law and get a barbecue and a 'tall boy' and drive down the road."

"What if you'd discovered she didn't like barbecue?" I ask. "Would you have married her anyway?"

"Of course I would have!" John T. tells me, barely hesitating. "I would've married her and then worked hard to convert her."

"That's the right answer," I laugh. "Good thing you didn't have to worry about it."

"Exactly," he says. "I don't like having to make choices like that."

Shout Hallelujah Potato Salad

"John T. and I fell in love over food," says Blair. "And after we had our son, I started to think serious thoughts about potato salad. I wanted to cook like a good Mississippi mama and raise our son on certain foods of which he'd one day be proud. He could only say a few words when I came up with this recipe. But in my dream, he would take a bite of potato salad, rip off his bib, hoist his hands into the hallelujah air as if addressing all of humankind, and shout, 'My mama makes the best potato salad in the whole wide world!'"

5 pounds small Yukon Gold potatoes

6 large eggs, hard-cooked and peeled

4 celery stalks, chopped

1 jar (4 ounces) diced pimentos, drained and topped with about 4 fat drops of Louisiana hot sauce

2 teaspoons celery salt

¼ cup seasoned rice wine vinegar

1 cup diced sweet pickles (sweet salad cubes, if you live in the South)

1 tablespoon olive oil

1 cup plus 2 tablespoons mayonnaise

¼ cup prepared yellow mustard (don't go fancy or Creole or grainy)

1 or 2 jalapeño peppers, seeded and minced

Heaping ½ cup chopped red onion

Heaping ½ cup chopped green bell pepper

¼ cup chopped parsley

Finely ground kosher salt and ground black pepper

Smoked hot paprika for garnish

Boil the potatoes, skin on, for about 20 minutes or until a sharp knife easily pierces them. Drain the potatoes and peel them with your fingers, under running water (as if you were peeling a hard-cooked egg). Put the potatoes and eggs into a chilled bowl, then chop. Add the other ingredients except the paprika garnish. Don't stir. Dive in with your hands, mashing some of the potatoes to bond the intact golden chunks. Taste it for salt and shape into a pretty mound with a spoon or spatula. Dust the top with the smoked paprika. Cover with plastic wrap and chill. Serve cold.

SERVES ABOUT 15

Barbecue Spaghetti

"Mutant" barbecue is the term John T. uses to refer to dishes like barbecue nachos, barbecue salad, barbecue pizza, and barbecue hash. But nothing, for sheer oddity, compares with barbecue spaghetti, he says. His favorite comes from Bar-B-Que Shop in Memphis. My recipe is different from what I've eaten at the Bar-B-Que Shop, but it is good. We serve this as a special at 17th Street, and it's always a sellout.

½ cup olive oil

2 large onions, diced

1 clove garlic, chopped

1 can (4 ounces) diced tomatoes

1 can (3 ounces) tomato paste

¼ cup sugar

1 tablespoon finely chopped fresh oregano

1 tablespoon chopped fresh basil

¾ to 1 cup barbecue sauce (Apple City Barbecue Sauce on page 54 or your favorite)

1½ teaspoons kosher salt, finely ground

1 cup pulled pork (optional)

1 box (16 ounces) spaghetti

Heat the olive oil in a medium skillet over medium-high heat. Add the onions and garlic and cook for 3 to 5 minutes, until the onions are translucent. Add the tomatoes and tomato paste and simmer for 5 minutes or so. Add the sugar, oregano, and basil. Simmer for another 5 minutes and remove from the heat. Stir in the barbecue sauce and salt to taste. Blend with a hand mixer until smooth. Add the pulled pork, if desired, and stir to combine.

Cook the spaghetti according to the directions on the box. Al dente is preferred. Pour into a colander and drain well, but do not rinse.

Pour the drained spaghetti into a large bowl and toss with the sauce. Serve immediately.

SERVES 6

Doug Worgul

Growing up in Michigan, *Kansas City Star* reporter Doug Worgul never had barbecue.

"You were deprived," I say.

"Totally! I'm thinking of filing a lawsuit against my parents for deprivation of basic needs!"

"Today that might be considered child abuse," I tell him.

He was converted around the age of 30, when he visited a friend in Chicago and they went out for some barbecue.

"He took me to Robinson's Ribs, and I got a sandwich. And then I had another one. It was awesome. It was unlike any I'd ever had, and I was transfixed," he remembers.

When Doug moved to Kansas City, his cousin was determined to baptize him in all things Kansas City. "He took me to the Grand Emporium to listen to the blues, and we went to Arthur Bryant's. Both the blues and barbecue have been driving passions for me ever since. Of course, blues and barbecue have a shared heritage, so that makes sense. I'm the self-appointed blues and barbecue writer for the *Star*."

We talk a little bit about the fascination with ethnic food and food traditions.

"The more our culture is homogenized and manufactured and diluted by mass marketing, more people hunger for something real. And this is one of those things."

"Barbecue is the most real food I know," I agree. "You can't hurry it. It's personal. When you eat barbecue, you know that you are eating something that has been personally prepared by hand. Someone has touched and tended that meat and watched it every step of the way."

"Just like fine wines and sushi are part of that trend," Doug adds. "Those things take time."

"I don't know much about that," I laugh. "I don't drink too much wine, and where I'm from, we use sushi as bait."

In June of 2004, Paul Kirk's $18,000 custom-built Klose rig was stolen, along with his van, right out of his driveway while he slept. Paul frantically posted a cry for help on the BBQ Forum message board. Doug is a regular reader, and when he saw that message, he kicked into gear and alerted the appropriate department at the *Star*. A story was immediately posted on the paper's Web site, and the Associated Press picked it up and ran it all over the country. Luckily, the grill was recovered within a day.

"Now that's a friend," I comment.

"Well, I knew we had to help get that back," Doug says. "That would've been a real barbecue tragedy."

John Shelton Reed

John Shelton Reed, noted sociologist and expert on all things Southern, grew up in Kingsport, Tennessee. Closer to Canada than to Memphis, he explains. During his 30-odd years in teaching at the University of North Carolina–Chapel Hill, he was schooled in the two very different styles of North Carolina barbecue.

"Honestly, I never thought about barbecue much until I moved to North Carolina, where it's a cult. The Eastern versus Western styles. In Chapel Hill, we lived on the fault line," he tells me.

"So which style do you prefer?" I ask.

"Actually, I like both styles," he says diplomatically.

"So you're bipartisan?"

"Yes, and people in North Carolina think that's heretical," he laughs. "Truth is I like the Memphis style. I didn't get to Memphis until I was 30, and my first Memphis experience was the Rendezvous."

The beauty of barbecue, John points out, is that by and large, if you're buying barbecue you're buying it from someone local. In some subtle way, it's different everywhere.

"I've never met a smoked pig I didn't like. I can remember a few disappointing barbecue experiences, but not any truly awful ones," he says thoughtfully.

"Even bad barbecue is better than fast food, isn't it?" I laugh.

"Oh, absolutely," he agrees.

"Southern barbecue is the closest
thing we have in the United States to Europe's
wines or cheeses; drive a hundred miles
and the barbecue changes."
—JOHN SHELTON REED

Mock Ridgewood Barbecue Sauce

The Ridgewood, a modest-looking barbecue joint that has served barbecue since 1948, is located in Bluff City, midway between Johnson City and Bristol in upper East Tennessee, not far from where John and his wife grew up. As with many great barbecue places, the hours at Ridgewood are iffy at best. People flock to the Ridgewood for the barbecue: good pork, well smoked, and served with an incomparable sauce, according to John.

"Let me tell you about that sauce. Like most sauces west of the mountains, the Ridgewood's is sweet, thick, and red. But the flavor is marvelously complex—what ketchup will taste like in heaven. This nectar is poured over the pork sandwiches before they are served, and the management has definite ideas about how much sauce to use: a lot. There are no squeeze bottles of sauce on the tables. You eat what's put before you.

"Naturally," John continues, "the sauce ingredients are a closely guarded secret, but a few years ago some ladies in Kingsport, no doubt tired of driving 30 miles to find the place closed, set out to duplicate the sauce. The recipe they came up with is a reasonable facsimile, and I will share it with you."

1 bottle (24 ounces) ketchup	1 large clove garlic, minced
¼ cup Worcestershire sauce	3 tablespoons unsulfured molasses (Grandma's preferred)
1 tablespoon prepared yellow mustard	1 tablespoon Kitchen Bouquet
¼ cup apple cider vinegar	1 tablespoon hot sauce (like Tabasco)
½ cup vegetable oil	Finely ground kosher salt and ground black pepper (to taste; start with ¼ teaspoon)
5 tablespoons sugar	
1 medium onion, finely chopped	

Mix the ingredients in a bowl, then blend the sauce in a blender. Put the goop into a pot and heat it to the boiling point, then simmer it for 15 to 20 minutes. This sauce freezes well.

MAKES ABOUT 1 QUART

JOHN'S HINTS: You probably don't want to baste with this sauce, because the sugar in it makes it turn black and ugly looking (although it still tastes good). It makes a fine dipping sauce for ribs, and—don't tell anybody I told you this—it's also great on beef brisket or chicken. Shoot, I've been known to eat it with a spoon. But it's best the way the Ridgewood serves it: Just pour it on some sliced or pulled pork, heaped on a big, warm, white-bread bun.

Fred Thompson

Fred Thompson is a culinary jack-of-many-trades. He has trained at the Culinary Institute of America, works as a food stylist, and writes articles and books about food. He divides his time between Raleigh, North Carolina, and New York City. Fred is an expert on ice tea and he's come up with a whole book on the subject.

Ice tea, also known as the "house wine of the South," complements barbecue perfectly. Some people order it unsweetened, but the standard is sweet, often pronounced "sweetea," as one word, with a bit of a twang. Please note: The spelling *is* "ice tea," without the "d" here in Southern Illinois and throughout the South. Fred tells me that adding a "d" on the end has become so accepted that he was forced to use it in the title of his book.

Tea was a precious commodity in the old days, and a popular theory about the addition of sugar to ice tea is based on frugality. Sugar was less expensive and could be used to "stretch" a pitcher of ice tea.

Sweet tea became a foil for the vinegar base in many barbecue sauces. In the South and especially in North Carolina, there seem to be a lot of vinegar tendencies in barbecue sauce.

Even Danny Meyer tells me how much he likes ice tea with barbecue. "But you're always talking about pairing wine and barbecue?" I ask him.

"I'm trying to *sell* wine with barbecue," he explains. "But I *drink* ice tea with my barbecue."

True ice tea is brewed fresh daily on the premises. I've seen fancier restaurants serving prepared ice tea purchased from a food service vendor. They actually dispense it from the same type of "gun" used to dispense soda. This kind of tea tastes terrible. Avoid at all costs.

Fred prefers Luzianne brand tea, and he packs several boxes in his suitcase before spending part of each year in Manhattan, "to ensure that I have quality tea."

"I tend to distrust any barbecue restaurant that doesn't have sweet tea."
—FRED THOMPSON

Fred Thompson's Southern-Style Ice Tea

According to Fred Thompson, there are as many ways to brew ice tea as there are Southern grandmothers. He admits to being biased toward this method, and I can vouch that it definitely makes good tea. The baking soda might seem strange, but it softens the natural tannins that cause an acid or bitter taste.

6 regular-size tea bags

$\frac{1}{8}$ teaspoon baking soda (a good pinch)

2 cups boiling water

6 cups cold water

Sugar or other sweetener to taste (optional)

Place the tea bags and baking soda in a glass measuring cup or ceramic teapot large enough to accommodate the boiling water. Pour the boiling water over the tea bags. Cover and let steep for 15 minutes.

Remove the tea bags, being careful not to squeeze them (squeezing the bags will add bitterness).

Pour the concentrate into a 2-quart pitcher and add the cold water. Sweeten, if desired.

Let cool, then chill and serve over ice.

MAKES 2 QUARTS

TIP: Granulated sugar will not dissolve in a cold glass of tea. If you're making a whole pitcher of sweet tea, add the sugar while the tea is still hot. To avoid this problem, fancy restaurants will serve a small pitcher of simple syrup (equal parts sugar and water, boiled to dissolve the sugar) to sweeten tea.

Excerpted from *Iced Tea*, by Fred Thompson, Copyright © 2002, with permission from Harvard Common Press, 535 Albany Street, Boston, MA 02118, www.harvardcommonpress.com

The Evangelists

There are also barbecue lovers who don't own restaurants but who actually make a real good living out of barbecue. By "living," I don't necessarily mean making piles of money. What I do mean is the ability to do what they love and still pay the bills. Following is some friendly conversation with a few of the real behind-the-scenes champions of the barbecue world. These people are like evangelists, spreading the word about all things barbecue.

The Phelps Family: Carlene, Joe, and Kell

Joe Phelps got involved in barbecue in 1987 when he and his favorite fishing buddy and local dentist, Donald "Doc" Gillis, entered a barbecue contest and were immediately bitten by the barbecue bug. Over the next few months, they kept cooking and experimenting, and their barbecue kept improving. They traded in the bass boat for a barbecue smoker and hit the Memphis in May–sanctioned cook-off trail. Both of their extended families got involved, and there would often be upward of 23 Phelps and Gillis family members at any given contest.

As much as they were enjoying the barbecue world, Joe and Doc found themselves frustrated by the lack of centralized information about what was happening. Where were the upcoming contests? What new and different things were people doing? One day, Doc made the comment, "You'd think somebody would put out a paper or something about what's going on."

Joe Phelps and Kell Phelps, founding publisher and current publisher of the National Barbecue News

A lightbulb went on in Joe's head. His wife, Carlene, owned a publishing company that printed shopping guides and local weekly newspapers. The two men formed a partnership and put out their first issue in January 1990. Carlene, of course, helped 'em out a little; soon she sold her other papers in order to concentrate on the *National Barbecue News*, which has become the local community newspaper of the barbecue world. "We're just out to spread the gospel," says Carlene.

I first met Joe Phelps at Memphis in May of 1990. Joe was a judge, and I was there competing for the first time. I was a bit bewildered about exactly what would happen during competition. In order to get water at your booth, you had to take buckets and walk a mile or so uphill to a fireplug. At the bottom of the hill was a log and there sat Joe, catching his breath. I was a bit winded myself, so I sat down next to him. We got to talking, and he asked about our team and our prior wins.

As we wrapped up the conversation, Joe said, "Well, it's rare that anyone places on their first time out, but I want to wish you luck." He reached into his pocket and pulled out a silver-dollar-sized sterling coin with a horse on it. "This here's a good luck charm, and I hope it'll bring some your way."

Carlene Phelps and me at Memphis in May 2002

I thanked him and put it in my pocket. Later the next day, after Apple City Barbecue won World Champion in ribs and Grand World Championship overall, Joe and Carlene made their way over to our team. He handed out silver pieces to my teammates, and they joined us as we celebrated at the Peabody Hotel.

I have worn that silver coin every day since. Much good luck has come my way.

In 2003 Carlene and Joe's son, Kell, took over as publisher of the paper. Kell has jumped into his new job with great enthusiasm.

"What's the best piece of advice your mama and daddy gave you about your new career?" I ask Kell.

"When I decided to buy the paper, Mama and Daddy told me, 'You might not make a lot of money, but if you go away hungry, it's your own fault.'"

"We were in Vegas for a publishing convention, and we invited some friends to go with us to Memphis Championship Barbecue. The group got so big that Joe decided to rent a limo so we could arrive in style. That was the first and only time we ever rented a limo, and there we were, redneck barbecuers arriving in style."

—CARLENE PHELPS, NATIONAL BARBECUE NEWS

Mike's Comforting Bread Pudding

One of Carlene's favorite desserts is our bread pudding. "Once we gave our son and daughter-in-law a trip to Vegas for Christmas. Naturally, we had to go along to show them the ropes. You were practicing on some bread pudding, and it was the best I've ever eaten," Carlene reminds me. For the best bread pudding, the bread needs to be very dry so it can absorb more of the liquid. You can experiment with a combination of whole milk, half-and-half, and heavy cream. I like to add different sauces for variety and I've included recipes for my three favorites on page 278.

1¼ pounds dry (to the point of crumbling) white bread, cut into ½-inch cubes (about 8 cups; see Note)

8 large eggs

3 tablespoons butter, melted

1½ cups plus 1 teaspoon sugar

4 cups, in any combination, whole milk, half-and-half, and/or heavy cream

1 tablespoon vanilla extract

2 teaspoons ground cinnamon, divided

Honey Butter, Praline Sauce, or Lemon Sauce (see page 278)

Preheat the oven to 350 degrees.

Fill a 13 × 9-inch baking dish with the bread cubes—they should pile up in the dish.

Whisk the eggs, butter, 1½ cups sugar, milk, vanilla, and 1 teaspoon cinnamon in a large bowl until frothy.

Pour the mixture over the bread and push the cubes down with your fingertips or the back of a large spoon. All of the cubes should be moist. You should see some of the liquid mixture around the inside edge of the pan. If you don't, add more milk, half-and-half, or cream.

Mix 1 teaspoon cinnamon and 1 teaspoon sugar together and sprinkle over the top of the pudding. Bake for 1 to 1½ hours or until golden brown on top and a knife inserted in the center comes out clean.

Remove the pan from the oven and allow to sit for 5 minutes, then cut into squares and place in individual serving bowls. Serve with a healthy amount of Honey Butter, Praline Sauce, or Lemon Sauce. Leftover bread pudding will keep in the refrigerator for up to 4 days. Microwave individual servings to reheat.

SERVES 10 TO 12

NOTE: If the bread isn't already dried, place the pieces of bread on a cookie sheet and dry them in a 200-degree oven for about 20 minutes. The bread shouldn't be browned or toasted, just dry.

Honey Butter

8 tablespoons (1 stick) butter, softened

1/4 cup honey

2 tablespoons confectioners' sugar

1/8 teaspoon ground cinnamon

Whip the butter, honey, sugar, and cinnamon with an electric mixer for about 10 minutes, or until very light and frothy. Spoon a healthy amount on individual servings of warm bread pudding.

Refrigerate leftover honey butter in a covered container. Keeps up to 4 days.

MAKES ABOUT 1 CUP

Praline Sauce

1/2 cup packed brown sugar

1/2 cup granulated sugar

2 tablespoons all-purpose flour

1 cup water

4 tablespoons (1/2 stick) butter

1 teaspoon vanilla extract

Put the brown sugar, granulated sugar, flour, and water into a medium saucepan and whisk together. Cook over medium heat, stirring often, until clear, about 20 minutes. Add the butter and stir until melted. Stir in the vanilla.

Serve immediately, spooning hot praline sauce over individual servings of warm bread pudding. Refrigerate leftover sauce in a covered container. Can be reheated in the microwave.

MAKES ABOUT 1 1/2 CUPS

Lemon Sauce

1/2 cup sugar

1 tablespoon cornstarch

1/2 teaspoon grated lemon zest

3/4 cup orange juice

2 tablespoons lemon juice

4 tablespoons (1/2 stick) butter

Combine the sugar, cornstarch, and lemon zest in a small saucepan. Stir in the orange and lemon juices. Cook over medium-high heat, stirring constantly, until thickened and bubbly. Cook for 2 more minutes, stirring constantly. Remove from the heat and stir in the butter.

Immediately spoon hot lemon sauce over individual servings of warm bread pudding. Refrigerate leftover sauce in a covered container. Can be reheated in the microwave.

MAKES ABOUT 1 CUP

Carolyn Wells

I'm always reading quotes from Carolyn Wells in articles about barbecue, but I don't read much about Carolyn herself.

"That's because my role is to promote barbecue," Carolyn reminds me. "And to help other people get what they need. I prefer to think of myself as the 'glue that holds the community together.'"

The Kansas City Barbeque Society was founded in 1986 and boasts over 5,000 members. That's a pretty remarkable feat. Carolyn presides as executive director.

"When we started, the rule was that nothing could be taken seriously," Carolyn says. "That would be grounds for immediate ejection from the Society. But somewhere along the way, people started taking barbecue seriously."

"This is just a part-time job for you, right?" I ask with a wink.

"No, it's a full-time job with a vow of poverty," she says firmly. "It was a full-time, non-paying job for about the first eight years."

"I know about these deals," I tell her.

What I do know about Carolyn is that she was born in Nashville and used to work for Wicker's Barbecue Products. I tell her about my conversation with Woody Wood (see page 61).

"He worked on and off for years to come up with a pretty close rendition of that sauce," I say.

"Any food company could've broken down the chemistry of that for him," she replies.

"But trying to figure it out for yourself is part of the fun," I remind her.

"Did he use Far West chili powder?" she asks.

"Far West? I'm not sure about that," I make a note. "Is that from a specific place or is it a brand?"

"It's a specific brand," she informs me. "We always used to say that's what made it taste so distinct."

"Is that the truth?" I question.

"Of course," she says with a smile.

As with all barbecue people, we have to spend some time talking about our barbecue travels.

"I can't believe some of the places I've gone because of barbecue," I tell Carolyn. "From coast to coast, it's been beyond my wildest imagination."

"It's real America," Carolyn agrees. "Tryon, North Carolina, for example. I would never have discovered that beautiful place.

"One of my most bittersweet memories is going to Decatur, Alabama, three days after

9/11. Everyone was shell-shocked, and people were trying to pick up the pieces of their lives and go on. It was wonderful to see the children playing on the playground and hear music playing. Actually, it was very healing to see that sense of community and people leaning on each other for support."

"Our contest was that weekend, too," I remember. "Flags were flying everywhere, and the Vienna Firefighters team was competing. They built a shrine and had some boots set up to collect money to send to New York. People were looking at that display with tears in their eyes and stuffing money in those boots. I'll never forget the feeling of loss and hope of that weekend. That stays with you forever."

Steven Shaw and Jason Perlow

I met Steven Shaw and Jason Perlow at the Big Apple Barbecue Block Party. Both men are lifelong New Yorkers and are quick to tell me that they have no real barbecue heritage, but they've been happy to jump on the bandwagon.

Steven, also known as "Fat Guy," is an attorney who wrote about his experiences with food and the New York dining scene on the Internet and eventually chucked the rat-race life as an attorney to become a full-time freelance food journalist. Jason is a computer systems analyst and food fanatic. Steven and Jason met on the Internet in 1999, and a few years into their food-oriented friendship, they founded eGullet.org, an Internet community devoted to all things food. This is a labor of love and a public service, they're quick to tell me—eGullet is not a money-making venture.

"One of those all-fame, no-fortune deals," I nod. "I've been involved in a number of those."

"A number of core groups were already active in Internet food chatter," says Steven. "We combined forces, and through word of mouth and media mentions, people started joining. In 2003, it reached a critical mass."

eGullet is the single most comprehensive Internet food site. There are discussion boards that reach every corner of the globe, feature articles, recipes, and question-and-answer sessions. The *Washington Post* called the site "the next Food Network."

I'll admit that I'm not too computer-savvy. Fortunately, there are people around me who keep up to date on this sort of thing. I first learned about eGullet in 2003 when Amy showed me some of the site's coverage of the first Big Apple Barbecue Block Party. I told Jason and Steven how impressed I was with the pictures and the commentary.

Steven thinks part of the success of the Block Party is due to the fact that barbecue is one American thing that New York doesn't really have.

"The spectacle of the thing is so bizarrely appealing. Roasting whole hogs in the middle of Manhattan. The first year, it was not really promoted. Kind of low-key. But when I got there and saw what was going on, I *knew* it was something really special. The reaction was tremendous. So the next year, we were ready for it. Word got out. And the only place to go for real-time updates, commentary, and photos was eGullet."

Jason and Steven think that barbecue and the Internet have a lot in common. I couldn't quite draw the parallel until they explained.

"Barbecue in particular is a populist food. The Internet is the ultimate populist medium. No middleman, no economic force," they tell me.

"We can create a living documentary history," Steven says. "eGullet is a new medium that doesn't have to make money. We have the time and space and flexibility to cover issues in depth, and we don't care if people want to read about it or not. We can post as many pictures and as many paragraphs as we want, just because we think it's right and good and worth doing. We're allowed to go out ahead of the curve."

Jason feels that New York is going to be the site of a barbecue renaissance. And he will happily be right in the middle of it.

"There's a very focused interest in providing high-quality barbecue in a limited fashion. In the next 10 years, there will be 5 to 10 really hard-core barbecue places in New York City," he predicts. "Not at the scale of those other major barbecue centers like North Carolina. There'll be outposts that will have some very good stuff. That's a good thing."

"Kenny Callaghan thinks that barbecue is going to be another ethnic food group," I say.

"He's right," agrees Steven.

> **"**The way I figure it, it would take me something like 70 hours' driving over a period of a week, at a cost of $560 in gas, to get to all these different barbecue places. So I've got to say to anybody who complains about waiting an hour for a taste, 'You just haven't thought it through.' Regardless of what you think about the mechanics of crowd control, those lines were actually moving really fast. Some of these booths were serving, I am sure, in excess of 5,000 people in six hours. And every one of them that I saw did it with a smile, took the time to chat with whoever wanted to strike up a conversation, and maintained a very, very, very high standard of 'cue. It's a monumental accomplishment.**"**
>
> —Steven Shaw, founder and culinary director, eGullet

Watermelon Ice Cream with Chocolate Seeds

Jason Perlow and his wife, Rachel, are developing their own barbecue traditions, and this recipe has been one of their contributions to a barbecue potluck. The recipe was inspired by Joyce White's recipe for Watermelon Ice Cream from her book *Brown Sugar: Soul Food Desserts from Family and Friends,* then further developed by Rachel Perlow on eGullet.

4 cups pureed watermelon

1 cup sugar

1 tablespoon corn syrup

⅛ teaspoon kosher salt, finely ground

⅓ cup Passoã passion fruit liqueur (or substitute another liqueur, like Chambord or port)

1 teaspoon vanilla extract

2 cups light cream

2 ounces dark chocolate, shaved

Place 2 cups watermelon puree, the sugar, corn syrup, and salt in a saucepan and bring to a boil. Reduce the heat to low and simmer for about 20 minutes. Remove from the heat, add the liqueur and vanilla, then mix into the remaining 2 cups watermelon puree. Chill thoroughly. Stir in the cream and allow to sit in the fridge for several hours or overnight to chill and allow the flavors to blend.

Freeze in an ice cream maker until of soft consistency. Spoon into an airtight container, adding a sprinkling of chocolate shavings to each spoonful as you go. Allow to harden in the freezer for several hours before serving.

MAKES ABOUT 1½ QUARTS

Gerry Dawes

Gerry Dawes is a home-grown Southern Illinois boy made good. He grew up in Anna and Alto Pass, small towns just a few miles south of Murphysboro. Alto Pass is actually a village, Gerry reminds me. Its population was 400 or so in my and Gerry's youth. "It's still about 400; more, if you count cats and dogs," he likes to say. Gerry lives just outside New York City now; he's gone upscale. He's known as "Mr. Spain" because he's a writer and a noted authority on Spanish food, wine, and travel.

Unlike some people who move to the city and get too big for their britches, Gerry has never forgotten his roots. "That's Southern Illinois with a capital 'S,'" he's quick to point out. "When I go back home, I notice that my accent gets thicker as I'm driving down Interstate 57, and it comes back full force after my first bite of one of 17th Street Bar & Grill's barbecue sandwiches."

Gerry and I didn't know one another until the mid 1990s. He subscribes to a weekly hometown paper, and back in the late 1980s and early '90s, he read a lot about Southern Illinois barbecue teams. Great Boars of Fire out of Anna and our team, Apple City Barbecue, got a lot of local press coverage because of all the contests we were winning. Those articles confirmed that the barbecue he ate during his youth must've been as good as he remembered. Gerry's uncle, Bob Minton, is a friend of my cooking partner, Pat Burke. When Gerry came home to visit, Bob made arrangements for us to meet at 17th Street so he could see what all of the fuss was about. The rest is history.

Ever true to his upbringing, Gerry decided to write an article about the Murphysboro Barbecue Cook-Off, 17th Street Bar & Grill, and me.

Gerry and I traveled many of the same paths during our youth—particularly the road to Whitt's barbecue. When we were growing up, families didn't travel around to different restaurants the way they do now. In fact, we barely got to eat in restaurants at all. Going to Whitt's was a big treat. If you visited family or friends in another town, you might have gotten lucky enough to be exposed to other barbecue.

"My Uncle Bob lived in Cairo, and his former wife worked at Mack's Barbecue. He still makes that style of sandwich for me when I come home. Over the years, I would also go to hang out at Southern Barbecue in Anna and go to Pulley's in Marion, but my favorite barbecue was Whitt's.

"I don't remember how old I was when I first ate barbecue, but it was probably around the time my teeth came in," he says.

Gerry has an interesting theory about the way Pat Burke and I developed our distinct barbecue flavor.

"Just as all great wines have a real palate behind them, one that's subtly refined from generation to generation, I think you must have learned about good barbecue from your dad when you were very young, and then you and Pat Burke further fine-tuned your barbecue palates at Whitt's. That was fabulous barbecue. You grew up knowing what truly great barbecue tasted like, then you guys took your long-term, cumulative memory of that taste and put your own twist to it. Now you've defined Southern Illinois barbecue, and your version is a benchmark for the whole country, so people try to copy *your* style and taste. That is something incredibly special."

"That's very flattering," I tell him. "But by and large, I'd agree with that."

One day Gerry shows up from New York at 17th Street Bar & Grill for a pulled pork barbecue sandwich, which he accompanies with a glass of ice tea. We get to talking about beverages to serve with barbecue. Gerry takes his ice tea unsweetened, but sweet tea is the national barbecue beverage; it just goes perfectly with barbecue. Soft drinks and ice-cold beer are the runners-up. There's been a lot of publicity about pairing wine and barbecue, and I don't know anything about wine, so I ask Gerry's opinion about some wines to add to my menu.

Though he was in the wine business for 20 years and even sold some to a barbecue joint in New York, he rolls his eyes at the notion of barbecue and wine—except for when he goes to Alto Vineyards' music festivals and has their wines with 17th Street's pulled pork sandwiches. He does however recommend that we support local Southern Illinois wineries on our wine list. Otherwise, he says, he never drinks wine with barbecue, but he thinks there are some other "adult beverages" that might be very good with barbecue. Specifically real Spanish sangría.

"Well, you think maybe we'd better mix up a test batch?" I ask.

So we stake out a spot at the end of 17th Street's bar, where Gerry instructs the bartender which ingredients he needs to make the sangría.

Gerry Dawes's Down-Home Andalusian Sangría

Gerry's right: The fresh and fruity flavors of real Spanish sangria go great with barbecue.

I bottle white wine (the wine should be of decent quality but relatively neutral and not loaded with oak, like a California Chablis or a Spanish Viura grape-based white wine from Rioja)

I shot brandy, preferably good Spanish Brandy de Jerez (may substitute cognac or other brandy)

I orange, sliced

I lemon, sliced

I peach, sliced (from Southern Illinois, if possible)

¼ teaspoon ground cinnamon

I cinnamon stick

Simple syrup (see Tip)

½ pint strawberries, sliced

Sparkling water to taste

Pour the wine and brandy into a large pitcher (or punch bowl). Add the orange, lemon, peach, ground cinnamon, and cinnamon stick, stirring to combine. Sweeten with simple syrup to taste (Gerry likes his sangría on the dry side), then add the strawberries. Leave in the refrigerator to chill.

When ready to serve, add sparkling water (or even orange soda) to the pitcher to taste and serve. On a hot day, Gerry prefers it over cube ice, never chopped ice. Garnish the rim of glasses with an orange or lemon slice and float a piece of cinnamon stick on top.

SERVES 6

TIP: To make simple syrup, combine I cup water and I cup sugar in a small saucepan and bring to a boil. Stir until the sugar dissolves completely. Let cool and store in the refrigerator.

VARIATION: Substitute a bottle of good inexpensive red wine, such as a Spanish wine from La Mancha or Jumilla or a joven (young, unoaked wine) from La Rioja.

Gerry's World's Finest Barbecue-Friendly Margaritas

After we mixed up the batch of sangria, Gerry decides he can't leave without showing me that he makes the best margaritas in the world.

GARNISH

Kosher or sea salt

1 lime

DRINK

2 cups tequila (Cuervo Gold or Sauza Gold—save the good stuff for shots)

½ cup Torres Licor de Naranja (Torres Valencia Orange Liqueur; or substitute Cointreau or Triple Sec)

2 limes, cut into quarters

1½ cups fresh grapefruit juice (you can substitute juice from cartons, but no bottled or canned shelf juice, please)

Make the garnish: Sprinkle a layer of kosher or sea salt (never table salt) on a small flat dish. Cut the lime in half. Slice 1 half for garnishing glasses. Cut the other half into 2 pieces; rub the pieces over the rim of each glass, then turn the rim in the salt (Gerry likes only half the rim salted). Put the glasses in the freezer to chill.

Make the drink: Have ready a strainer and a large pitcher filled with cube ice, not crushed ice. Put the tequila, orange liqueur, and limes into a blender and blend until the limes are chopped into small pieces but not pulverized. Strain the liquid into the pitcher filled with ice; reserve the chopped lime in the strainer. Add the grapefruit juice to the pitcher and stir to mix. Put at least a tablespoon or more of the chopped lime into the pitcher—or if desired, add a little dollop to each margarita glass. Pour into your chilled margarita glasses (Gerry likes his on the rocks), garnish each glass with a half-slice of lime, and serve.

SERVES 6

Gerry adheres to a strict dress code wherever he eats barbecue: at least one, if not more, of his 17th Street Bar & Grill clothing items, blue jeans, and his beloved cowboy boots. He has six pairs of Tony Lama and Lucchese boots that he buys mostly at the Rusty Spur in Marion, Illinois.

"These 17th Street shirts are for hard-core aficionados," he tells me, patting his chest. "The real barbecue dudes know where these shirts come from. I get a lot of comments and questions from people. At the Eastern barbecue festivals, they think I'm part of your crew. I would be proud if I was, but I wear them because it supports you and it supports Southern Illinois. Besides, it gets me in the right down-home frame of mind to eat barbecue."

I appreciate Gerry's support, and I send him a new supply of shirts every so often. He just about wears them out, and I wouldn't want him to go around looking too sloppy. That reflects poorly on me, as well as on him.

"If I go down to Blue Smoke, I wear these clothes. Danny Meyer gets a big kick out of it. In fact, I wore these shirts on Blue Smoke's opening night, and Danny said, 'God bless you, Gerry, I knew you'd come dressed right.'"

Gerry, wearing his trademark 17th Street shirt, and me, at Sakonnet Vineyard in June 2003

Chapter Eight

PLAY WITH

A Few Things to Get Yourself

ING FIRE:
You Need
Started

'm always looking for new information. Whenever I visit a new barbecue joint or visit with a team on the competition circuit, I keep my eyes open and I ask lots of questions. I look at equipment. I want to know about spices and seasonings, cooking methods, and what kind of wood they're burning. New products and suppliers are of interest to me, too.

I've filled this chapter with lots of very simple suggestions and secrets, because this is the kind of information people ask me about all the time. Whether you're just getting started or you've been cooking for a long time, you'll find some pearls of wisdom to put to good use. You don't need a lot of fancy equipment to make good barbecue. However—and here's where the women will likely roll their eyes—there are some things that will make the job easier and more enjoyable. This is one of the reasons barbecue is often compared to a sport. You know how you start out with one simple fishing pole and a little boat or a cheap set of golf clubs? Then, as you get more serious about the activity, you start upgrading? Next thing you know, you've got a boat outfitted with thousands of dollars of fishing rods and lures, or you've got a country club membership, fancy golfing clothes, and the best clubs you can afford. For some people, barbecue is the same way.

Tools of the Trade

All kinds of clever things have been invented for barbecuing. Some are necessary; others are a waste of money. Here's my list of essentials.

CHIMNEY STARTER I think this is one of the best inventions ever. Requires nothing but matches and a couple of pieces of paper. And charcoal, of course.

SMALL CHARCOAL GRILL (TABLETOP SIZE) OR METAL BUCKET (OPTIONAL) You can use either of these to hold extra coals while you're starting a new batch in the chimney starter.

MATCHES OR PROPANE TORCH I can't believe how any people show up at a barbecue cook-off with no matches.

TONGS Don't use a fork or any tool that will pierce or puncture the meat. The juices will leak, and the meat will dry out. I'm always surprised when I see experienced cooks stabbing their meat.

HEAVY-DUTY RUBBER GLOVES AND A BOX OF DISPOSABLE GLOVES You'll need the heavy gloves to move and unload the meat on the pit. You can't move an 18-pound shoulder with a pair of tongs; you'll have to use your hands. That meat is hot, and you don't want your hands to blister. You can use the thin plastic gloves while you're handling the ribs.

DISPOSABLE ALUMINUM ROASTING PANS OR PIE PANS To capture the grease and prevent the coals from catching on fire, particularly when you're using a charcoal grill.

SMALL SHOVEL OR TROWEL You'll want this for adding or moving hot coals.

FIRE EXTINGUISHER As you may have read in Chapter 5, you can never be too safe.

THERMOMETER I prefer a dial thermometer, but I'm old-fashioned. Digital models are too fancy for me. You can buy a dial thermometer for $2.98 to $20. I always buy one that I can calibrate. Put the thermometer in a glass of ice water and swish it around. Use the little nut right on the stem to turn the dial and calibrate it to 32 degrees. It'll be accurate plus or minus 1 degree.

GRILL BRUSH I can't believe how many people cook on a dirty grate. Please keep yours clean.

APRON Do I have to tell you why?

RAGS AND A TUB OF BLEACH WATER You'll want to wipe and sanitize your prep area as you go. Use one capful of bleach to one gallon of water.

SPRAY BOTTLE For spritzing. I keep apple juice in mine.

SHAKER OR DREDGE (LARGE SHAKER) Fill it with dry rub.

PLASTIC WRAP I wrap barbecue in plastic as it comes off the pit; this is not to keep it warm but to seal it off and protect it from the air. Plastic wrap seals tighter than foil. Also, you can't punch holes in it as easily, and it's less expensive.

ALUMINUM FOIL Use heavy-duty foil. Lightweight foil is a waste of time and money. I might wrap product in foil, but I'll always wrap it in plastic wrap first.

MOP Use a barbecue mop (which looks like a miniature floor mop) to baste during the cooking process. Some people use a new paintbrush, about three inches wide, to brush barbecue sauce on ribs right before they come off the pit.

COOLER Actually, make that two coolers: one to hold the meat, and one to hold the beverages of your choice.

COMFORTABLE PORTABLE CHAIR You'll have to babysit the pit, so you might as well be comfortable. At a cook-off, you'll want to be sure to have some chairs for company, too. Those portable, collapsible chairs that fit in a carrying case work real well.

WORK SURFACE A folding table is fine, but make sure it's a sturdy one.

CUTTING BOARD Disposable cutting boards don't work well at all for barbecue. I prefer large wood cutting boards; they're easier on your knives. Acrylic boards tend to dull your knives.

Pits and Smokers

Your biggest barbecue expense will be a good pit or smoker.

More expensive smokers are pretty well insulated, but it doesn't hurt for a pit to leak. In a well-insulated pit, you have to learn to control the smoke with the draw and flue. In order to get your smoke value, you have to have air coming in and smoke going out.

The best way to decide which pit to purchase is to ask for advice, especially at a cook-off or home show. Sample some food cooked on that pit, if possible. You can post questions on barbecue message boards, and people will happily give their opinions. Think about how much and how often you want to cook, so you don't buy a piece of equipment that's too big or too small. You know how you feel when you buy a new car and then you see the next year's model and it seems just a little better than what you just bought? Be

Apple City Barbecue's Secret Weapon

Pat Burke and I built this pit out of a 1,000-gallon propane tank. You can load and unload this pit from both the front and back. You can cook using indirect and direct heat, and there's a flue on either end. The rotisserie keeps the meat moving, and you can remove the racks and install a rod so you can smoke a whole hog on it.

There are no hot spots. We worked on perfecting this pit on and off for a year. We cut holes in the shield for indirect heat and just kept experimenting until we got it right. Every now and then, we'd have to go back and fill in some holes.

prepared, because new models of smokers come out all the time. You'll notice that the real aficionados have more than one. You can use the *National Barbecue News* to sell a pit you no longer need, or you might just find the smoker of your dreams at a real good price.

There are many smokers on the market for backyard and competition use. They'll all work, some better than others. Here are a few of my personal favorites.

CHARCOAL GRILL The least expensive way to get started is to rig your charcoal grill for smoking. Remember, you don't want to cook your meat directly over the flame. Some people arrange the coals around the outside edge and cook the meat in the middle. This will create even heat, and you won't have to turn your meat as often. If you choose this method, you'll need about 15 to 20 pieces of charcoal to go around the perimeter of the grill.

I prefer to make a little pile of charcoal over to one side of the grill. This keeps the meat farther away from the heat source and gives you more leverage in moving the meat to a warmer or cooler spot on the grill. If you use this method, you'll only need 8 to 10 lumps of charcoal.

Use a drip pan or water pan if you're using this type of grill, to capture the grease during the cooking process. This will help with cleanup and prevent the coals from catching on fire.

55-GALLON BARREL When I was in high school, I made extra money by building barbecue pits and grills out of 55-gallon oil barrels. Today, these are still a popular style of pit for home and competition use. If you're handy, you can make your own. Various instructions are available on the Internet. These pits will eventually rust out, but the price is right.

Designing and building your own pit can be very satisfying. As long as you understand the mechanics, the sky's the limit. Barbecue forums and message boards are filled with tips and conversations. Lots of people post pictures of the final results.

With this type of pit, you'll also need to create an indirect heat situation. You can build an external firebox down at one end or in the back. Or you can make a mound of coals on the inside. You'll need about 1½ to 2 pounds of charcoal at one end and a few more coals scattered throughout the bottom of the barrel.

Use a drip pan or water pan, if you're using this type of pit, to capture the grease during the cooking process. This will help with cleanup and prevent the coals from catching on fire.

REFRIGERATOR An old refrigerator makes an excellent pit. What I'm referring to is an old, pot-bellied-door refrigerator, nothing that's been manufactured in the last 10 to 15 years. They're easy to find, well insulated, and long lasting. A do-it-yourself type of guy can convert one of these pretty easily. You'll need a heavy metal pan so you can burn charcoal and wood in the bottom. Cover that with a shield. Make an air source at the bottom and install a damper at the top for exhaust purposes. Air needs to be drawn in, up, and out to keep the fuel burning.

BROILMASTER Folks who simply won't or can't fuss with charcoal and fire might want to consider a Broilmaster grill. These are professional-grade gas grills with a smoker shutter that converts the grill into an indirect cooker. The bow tie–shaped burner helps distribute heat uniformly. There are some skeptics who think you couldn't possibly turn out barbecue on a gas grill, but I know someone who does. Her name is Elizabeth Karmel; read about her in Chapter 6.

PRIMO KAMADO This egg-shaped ceramic cooker works kind of like a clay oven. Ceramic smokers seal in the heat and keep air out, resulting in moister meat. They don't lose heat, and, therefore, they use less charcoal. A Primo Kamado can be used as a grill and smoker, and it is excellent for home use. You'll see a few on the competition circuit, too.

Ceramic smokers originated in Asia, and Primo Kamado is the only ceramic model designed and manufactured in the United States.

BACKWOODS SMOKER These are real popular with a lot of teams and backyard cookers. They're easy to use, easy to move, and affordable. The internal chimney and double-wall design allow smoke to flow by "downdraft" throughout the smoker. The rectangular design makes them easy to store and provides easy access to food and fire.

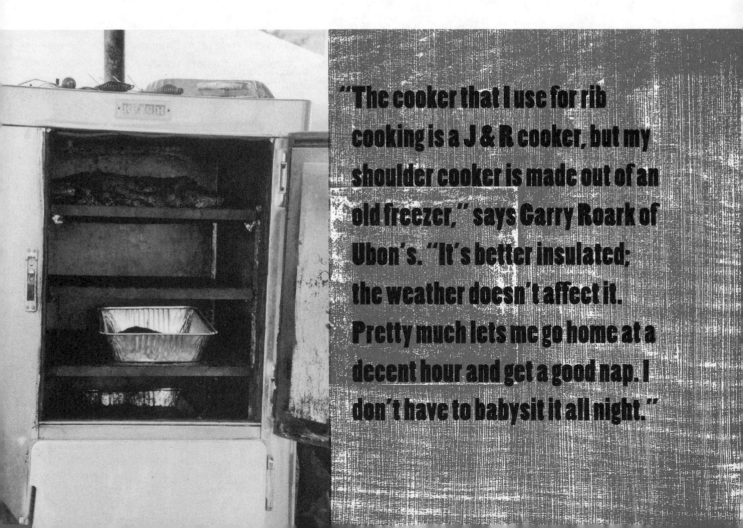

"The cooker that I use for rib cooking is a J & R cooker, but my shoulder cooker is made out of an old freezer," says Garry Roark of Ubon's. "It's better insulated; the weather doesn't affect it. Pretty much lets me go home at a decent hour and get a good nap. I don't have to babysit it all night."

JEDMASTER Chris Lilly of Big Bob Gibson is partial to the Jedmaster. He likes to put his charcoal in the firebox in the shape of a snake and trail it off. As it burns down the trail, the fire keeps going for several hours at a time.

KLOSE PITS David Klose (pronounced "Claus") down in Houston custom-builds bullet-type pits in any shape or size, from beer bottles to chuck wagons. If you can dream it, he can build it. You're limited only by your imagination and wallet. Klose pits are crafted by hand and guaranteed for life. At last count, John Stage of Dinosaur Bar-B-Que owned seven different models of Klose pits. The legendary Paul Kirk is a fan as well, and there's even a Chef Paul Kirk Mobile Wagon designed especially for him.

"When I bought my first mobile pit down in Texas," says John Stage, " I didn't even know how to drive with a trailer attached. I drove the whole way from Texas to New York going straight. I never put it in reverse."

W'HAM TURBO COOKER The famed John Willingham of Memphis invented the W'ham Turbo Cooker. *Today* show weatherman and barbecue lover Al Roker has one of these pits. The W'ham uses wood, charcoal, or pellets. A unique feature of this cooker is that the meat cooks vertically, hanging from hooks. Even the rotisserie is vertical.

THE LEGEND, BY OLE HICKORY I'm especially proud of this pit; it's called "The Legend," after me. I teamed up with Ole Hickory Pits to develop this small smoker for both home use and for restaurants that want to add just a little barbecue to the menu. I brought the prototype to the first Big Apple Barbecue Block Party in New York City in 2003 and gave it to Tom Viertel and Pat Daily, whom you've read about in Chapter 6. Jeffrey Steingarten was sitting on a cooler in my tent and getting his fill of ribs. He watched Pat and Tom go crazy over their gift, and he said, loudly, "Huh. I wonder just how good a friend you have to be to get a gift like that?" I quickly assured him that this was a prototype and it just wasn't as *perfect* as the one I'd want him to have. The serial number on Jeffrey's new smoker reads #000001.

The beauty of this compact smoker is that it operates and will cook exactly the same as any other large Ole Hickory pit. It's well insulated and takes a small amount of wood or

Here I am with John Willingham in front of his unique invention. This particular pit was built for Al Roker.

charcoal to keep up the heat. The heavy-duty wheels let you move it around if necessary. For commercial use, it can easily be installed indoors under a hood. You can order it with flat shelves, rotisserie shelves, or a combination of the two. You can order it with gas or electric assistance if desired. We really thought this part through: It's narrow enough to fit through a standard door opening.

This pit will hold 20 butts, 20-plus racks of ribs, 32 half chickens, or 24 whole chickens at one time. Remove the rotisserie and insert the flat shelves, and you can cook a 40- to 50-pound suckling pig.

The Legend will really make a statement on your patio. Properly maintained, it'll last a lifetime.

PELLET SMOKER This is a kind of high-tech, electric-powered pit or smoker, with an auger—to feed the fuel into the firepot—and a draft-induction fan. The fuel is pellets made from a variety of hardwoods: hickory, mesquite, alder, apple, and so on.

I think pellet smokers are a great concept, and I know a lot of people really like them. They burn clean with very little ash. However, I don't think that the flavor is the same as it is when using regular wood. But that's just my opinion.

The Mike Mills Legend model from Ole Hickory can be used at home, for competition, or as an ancillary pit in a restaurant.

More Secrets

Let me tell you the secret to any pit, whether it's a homemade 55-gallon barrel or a premier smoker: You have to learn what that pit is capable of doing. And the only way to learn is by trial and error and lots of practice.

The difference between barbecue and grilling is the heat source. Grilling is directly cooking over live coals at a fairly high temperature. Barbecuing is indirect. The heat source is far away from the meat.

A novice barbecue cook may not realize that the major heat source in barbecue should be the charcoal. People who get all of their heat directly from wood will oversmoke their meat. You can make your own charcoal by burning down your wood, but just using wood will not result in great barbecue. Smoke should be an ingredient, not the main taste you notice when you take a bite. This is one of the biggest mistakes people make.

Smoking requires that you constantly check the temperature inside the grill or smoker. If yours doesn't have a built-in thermometer, you can use a regular meat thermometer. Just poke it through the vent on the top of the grill or drill a hole in the lid for this purpose.

How to Light a Fire

As I've mentioned, I think the chimney starter is one of the best inventions ever. All you'll need is the charcoal, a few sheets of newspaper or a paper towel, and a match. A chimney starter will hold about 2 to 2½ pounds of charcoal—half of a 5-pound bag.

Determine how many coals you think you'll need at one time. This will depend on your pit, and it'll require some trial and error. Put the charcoal in the chimney, wad up a piece of newspaper or a paper towel, stuff it underneath the chimney, and light the paper. Set the chimney on the ground next to your pit. Your charcoal will be ready to transfer to the grill in the time it takes to drink one beer—about 15 minutes.

Again, anticipating when you'll need that next batch of coals takes some practice.

When you transfer your coals to the pit, leave one or two lumps in the bottom of the chimney starter and then add some more charcoal on top of that. The smoldering coals will start burning the fresh charcoal. You won't need to use any more paper. This batch of charcoal will take a little longer to burn down, maybe 20 to 30 minutes, but typically you have the time. You won't need this next batch of coals that quickly.

If you're competing and you're using two or more pits, you'll want to have two or three chimney starters to keep up with the amount of charcoal you'll need.

If you're using natural lump charcoal, which I highly recommend, you could add a few raw lumps directly to the fire, once it gets going. In a pinch, I might add two, three, or four raw lumps, but I'd never add 30 at a time. It takes too long for 'em to catch on fire. I'd never add raw briquettes. Not only do they take too long to catch on fire, but even good briquettes seem to put off a fume. Something to do with the binder and compression of wood.

Most people overfire. By that I mean that they start off with too much charcoal, thus starting out at too high a temperature, I suggest starting off with fewer pieces of charcoal and increasing the temperature as necessary. It's easier to increase the temperature than to try to bring it down.

Another common mistake is opening the lid to bring the temperature down. This does allow the heat at the top of the pit to escape, but it also lets the fire get all of the oxygen it wants, so the fire picks up. If you do need to bring the temperature down, you need to shut off the air source to the fire. Shut off both the draw (bottom vent) and the top vent to smother the fire.

CHARCOAL Charcoal is what you use for heat. Be sure to use a natural lump charcoal. Charcoal briquettes have additives such as carbon, coal dust, lime, binders, and other chemicals that make them easy to light but that throw off an unpleasant taste. Never use lighter fluid, either. Briquettes and lighter fluid will leave your meat with a noticeable chemical taste.

There are many good natural lump charcoals on the market. Be sure to look for the words "all natural" and "no additives" on the label. On the competition circuit, I used charcoal by Hickory Specialties, now called Royal Oak. Peoples Woods' "Nature's Own" from Cumberland, Rhode Island, is another one of my favorite brands. Barbecue legend Billy Bones has his own private label charcoal made by Sugartown Products for sale on his Web site.

WOOD Wood is used in barbecue to get smoke value, not heat value. Heat comes from charcoal; smoke flavor comes from wood.

When you use wood chips, you'll need to wet them before adding them to the pit. In a charcoal grill, you simply sprinkle them over the charcoal. Wetting them allows the

FLAVOR COMES FROM WOOD.

WOOD	FLAVOR	USES
Alder	Light	Traditionally used with fish.
Apple	Mild, sweet, and fruity	Use with pork, poultry, and beef.
Cherry	Distinct, sweet, and fruity	Use with pork and poultry.
Hickory	Rich, strong, and hearty	Use with pork, beef, and poultry.
Maple	Smooth, mild, and sweet	Use with poultry, seafood, and pork.
Mesquite	Distinct, robust, and smoky	Use with beef.
Oak*	Strong and distinct	Use with beef, poultry, and seafood.
Peach	Light and fruity	Use with pork and poultry.
Pecan	Earthy and not overly pungent	Use with pork, poultry, and beef.

WARNING: Don't use citrus woods. I made this mistake so you don't have to. I once got the bright idea to try some orange wood, thinking it would give my meat a nice tangy flavor. I obviously didn't think this idea through. All citrus fruit is acidic, and the meat came off bitter and black.

*Oak makes great charcoal; that's what my mentor, Mr. Whitt, burned. But I'm probably one of the only people out there who don't like using raw oak alone for smoke flavor. If push comes to shove, I'm going to use it. But I'll use less of it.

wood chips to smolder and create smoke instead of simply catching on fire and adding to the heat. If you add sticks of wood, you will get some heat from them when they eventually catch on fire. But again, the main purpose of the wood is to create smoke.

Some people—Rick Schmidt of Kreuz Market, for example—strictly burn wood, and they're using that for both the heat source and the smoke source. When the wood burns down, they're left with a bed of coals and that helps start the wood as it's added.

Different types of woods give different flavors to the things you smoke, but there's a time and reason to use each kind of wood. I'm partial to the sweet, smoky taste that comes from apple wood, and I use it for all meats, not just pork. I also like to combine apple wood with a few sticks of hickory or oak.

I don't like to brag too much, but here's some gosh-to-honest truth: Nobody on the circuit was smoking with apple wood when Pat Burke and I started using it. Being from Apple City, we came up with that idea as our angle. We spritzed our meat with apple juice, and we always served the judges a glass of chilled, freshly squeezed apple juice while they were tasting our meat. As we began to win trophies and get good press, all of sudden everybody was cooking with apple wood.

The Meat of the Matter

Simply buying meat is confusing for many people. The best meat comes straight from the source. If there is a local slaughterhouse, you're in luck; most will sell directly to individuals. If you're getting into competition or cooking large quantities, you might consider contacting a meat purveyor who supplies restaurants. Both price and quality may be better. You'll know by reputation which butcher shops in your area are good and reliable. If you don't have a good butcher or a slaughterhouse nearby, get to know the butcher at your local supermarket.

Taking any one of these sources a sample of your barbecue won't hurt. You'll surely be remembered in the future, and your service might improve, too.

Fresh-frozen meat is okay, but you want to know how long it's been frozen. Meat that's been loosely wrapped before freezing will have a tendency to have freezer burn, and you can taste that in the meat, even after it's been cooked. Ideally the meat has been sealed in Cryovac before freezing so air can't get to it.

Good meat is fresh. You don't want to buy old meat that's over in the special discounted section of any butcher shop or supermarket.

When buying pork, look at the color. Meat that is light pink usually means that it came off a younger hog. Meat from younger hogs is difficult to find anymore, but it's usually better tasting. If the meat is deep pink or real reddish in color, that can mean it's off an older, larger hog. Or it's been exposed to air and perhaps has been in the meat case longer. If you have a choice, go for the lightest pink you can find.

The amount of fat marbling is an indicator of quality beef. If there are no fat veins in

Sides of beef hang in the cooler
at Smitty's in Lockhart, Texas

301

it, it won't be as tender and flavorful. I must keep repeating that fat is flavor. Well-marbled meat is an indication that the cow was fed some grain. Prime meat, the best grade you can buy, is corn fed, and it's full of marbleization; it'll be the most flavorful and most tender.

As my buddy Rick Schmidt says, "If you start with a good piece of meat, you have a pretty good chance of winding up with a pretty good piece of barbecue. If you start with a sorry piece of meat, you have to be very creative—and you might get there, you might not. So take the easier route and buy a better piece of meat."

That's still not a guarantee that you'll end up with something great, but the odds will be in your favor.

Once you get your meat home, you'll need to prep it for barbecue.

Pork

BABY BACK OR LOIN BACK PORK RIBS These terms are used synonymously, but officially, the difference is in size. A baby back rib is around 1 to 1½ pounds. A loin back rib weighs 1¾ to 2¾ pounds. Most restaurants are serving loin back ribs because smaller hogs are not butchered as often. But the menu will list them as baby backs because that's the term the customer knows.

A full sparerib is the whole rib including the brisket, the bony piece with the gristle. The St. Louis cut is the sparerib with the brisket removed.

To prep ribs, all you have to do is trim any excess fat and remove the skinlike membrane on the back of the ribs. The easiest way to remove it is to start in the middle of the rack and work a table knife or a screwdriver underneath the skin, going all the way across and teasing it up. Slide your forefinger in there and bring your thumb across, holding the rib down and pulling the membrane straight up. It'll peel from the middle.

Or you can start near the first or second bone. Then take a dishtowel or paper towel and pull the membrane from one end toward the other. It'll slip out of your hand if you don't have something to grip it with.

Season the ribs top and bottom with Magic Dust (see page 67) or your favorite dry rub. You can prep meat up to 24 hours in advance and let it marinate in the refrigerator, or you can season the meat while you're waiting for your charcoal to burn down. The decision is yours. If you're cooking in a contest, your meat may only get to marinate for three to six hours because the meat must be raw and not treated in any way when you arrive at a competition. You can't begin to prep your meat until the contest officials have inspected it.

By necessity, I often dust meat and put it right on the pit, both in the restaurants and at home. Dusting in advance is optimal, but you can still produce a great piece of barbecue no matter how little time the meat has to marinate.

You can take the meat out of the refrigerator and bring it to room temperature before putting it on the pit, or you can transfer it directly from the refrigerator to the smoker.

PORK SHOULDER AND BOSTON BUTT When I choose shoulders and butts, I want young meat, not meat from old hogs. You'll find shoulders and butts both fresh and frozen, fresh being better. If you're using frozen meat, it must be completely thawed before you cook it.

When prepping shoulders, cut off any skin, except for the skin on the shank bone—leave that on.

On both shoulders and butts, it's important to remove the blood vein and any blood clots about one inch in on the inside of both cuts of meat, where the piece of meat would've attached to the hog. Otherwise, the meat next to that vein and blood clot will not taste as good.

Look the meat over carefully and remove any other blood clots or bruised areas that do not look appetizing. Trim any excess fat, but be sure to leave about $1/8$ to $1/4$ inch of fat on the meat. What I do is press down on any lumps of fat. If the lump is hard, I remove it, because I know that hard piece of fat won't render during smoking. During the cooking process, the fat that's left will render and absorb the spices, and it will taste just like an outside piece of meat or crunchy bark.

Season all over the shoulders and butts liberally with Magic Dust or your favorite dry rub. Again, you can do this up to a day in advance.

Here I am trimming excess fat and removing the membrane from the back of a rack of ribs.

WHOLE HOG Choosing a whole hog is kind of like choosing a girlfriend. I wouldn't presume to tell you where to go searching, but I do have some thoughts on what makes a good catch. I look for a woman with a little personality; one who stands up straight and is kind of proud. If you pick out a droopy, sickly female, she'll be like that her whole life; you can never straighten her out. I've always known to steer clear of the droopy ones, but I've watched a few friends deal with that kind of woman. Likewise, too much struttin' in a woman means she's too high maintenance.

Ideally, you can go to a hog farm, straight to the source, and look over the selection. You want a lively pig, one with the ears perked up. Don't choose a pig that's moping around the pen with its head hanging down. If the pig looks like she's leading the band, with her nose too high in the air, then that means that pig might give you trouble. You want a pig with a little pride, but not too proud. Just proud enough to become grand champion barbecue.

Make sure the pig doesn't have too many notches in its ears. Farmers do that to keep track of their ages and what litter they're from. Those notches never fill in, so a lot of them are an indication of an old pig—which you don't want for smoking.

For parties or for competition, people want to display the pig before it's eaten. I request that the slaughterhouse skin the hog and scald the head. I believe that if the skin is removed you get better flavor through the hog. The smoke penetrates the meat easier. Penetrating the skin is harder, but it can be done. During cooking, the baste, dry rub, smoke, and the hog's natural juices will color a skinless hog, and the bark will be like a new skin.

I have the head scalded and the skin left on because to me, a skinned head is ugly. A cooked whole hog with the ears perked up is a beautiful thing. If you're cooking purely for eating and not for show, you might want to saw off the head and the feet.

Beef

BEEF RIBS Beef ribs can be prepped using the same procedures outlined for pork ribs. They'll have more fat on the back side that you'll need to trim. You can season them, top and bottom, with salt and pepper or your favorite dry rub. The Holy Cow Dry Rub for Beef (see page 67) would be good, too. I, of course, use Magic Dust (see page 67).

BRISKET In most places outside Texas, brisket is considered a less desirable cut of meat because of the grain structure.

The most flavorful cut is the full brisket with deckle and nose on, but you have a lot of waste. If you're cooking the bottom flap only, you still need to have about a $\frac{1}{8}$-inch fat cap on the top.

Again, when prepping brisket, you want to trim the fat down to about $\frac{1}{8}$ to $\frac{1}{4}$ inch all over. Push on the fat and remove the hard lumps of fat. Just as with the pork shoulders and butts, the fat will render and form a very tasty piece of outside skin or bark.

Season liberally with your favorite dry rub, Holy Cow Dry Rub, or Magic Dust.

Trim excess fat from brisket.

BEEF TENDERLOIN When you're prepping beef tenderloin, you need to remove the silver skin and excess fat. Again, leave $\frac{1}{8}$ to $\frac{1}{4}$ inch of fat, removing any hard pieces that won't render. Tie the tenderloin closed with butcher's twine. Season with your favorite dry rub, Holy Cow Dry Rub, or Magic Dust.

SHOULDER CLOD AND TRI-TIP Shoulder clod and tri-tip don't require as much prep work because they don't have very much excess fat. Simply season them with your favorite dry rub, Holy Cow Dry Rub, or Magic Dust.

Chicken and Turkey

Remove the fat in the cavity of both birds. Remove the neck and any packages of giblets. Thoroughly rinse the poultry.

Unlike when you're roasting in the oven, you don't want to truss the chicken or turkey legs. This will make the bird harder to cook.

Splitting a chicken will help it cook quicker and more evenly. Use poultry shears to cut out the backbone, lay the bird bone side down on your cutting board, and press down on the breastbone to flatten the bird.

I sprinkle the birds liberally with garlic salt to add extra flavor and to help draw the fat and crisp up the skin. Then I lightly dust with Magic Dust (see page 55). You could use your favorite barbecue dry rub.

I prefer keeping turkeys whole for smoking. A tom turkey is going to be the largest (20 pounds and up); hen turkeys will be smaller. Here's one case where size really doesn't matter. Most people will smoke a 10- to 12-pound turkey or a 14- to 16-pound bird, depending on how many people are coming for Thanksgiving dinner. You can also smoke just the breast, prepped the same as described above. Be sure to cook the breast bone side down.

A Few More Barbecue Tips and Hints

■ Whenever possible, cook meat on the bone. The bone acts as a cooking agent, and it transfers heat down into the meat. This helps it cook faster and more evenly, and it acts as a shield for the meat near the surface.

■ Always start with the fat side up.

■ Turn your meat minimal times. Sometimes you need to turn or move it from a hot spot so it doesn't burn or cook unevenly. Sometimes you'll want to turn it to add color evenly to the product.

■ Don't sauce your meat too early in the process. Most sauces have a high sugar content, and the sauce will burn before the meat is finished cooking. If you need to apply moisture, spritz or lightly mop on a baste with a high vinegar or oil content.

■ Make sure your smoker has an accurate, easy-to-read thermometer. Chris Lilly of Big Bob Gibson says, "By the time the thermometer wears out, you will be a master of your pit and you'll be cooking by feel and intuition."

I agree with Chris. I can pretty much gauge the temperature just by touching the pit. But if you're not cooking professionally or on a regular basis, you'll always want to double-check the pit temperature with a thermometer.

Water Pans

A water pan is simply an aluminum pie pan or roasting pan filled with water to help add moisture to the pit. Whether or not you need a water pan depends on the type of pit you have and your own personal method of cooking. If you use a lot of direct heat, you can have coals underneath the water pan. The water pan will deflect the heat and heat the water to make steam and moisture in the pit. You'll notice that your meat doesn't dry out as quickly, so you won't have to baste as much.

The pan can also serve as a drip pan. If, for example, you're cooking a turkey on a charcoal grill rigged for indirect heat, you'll want to use a drip pan. Turkeys have a lot of

One of my secrets is very simple. Other books will tell you to cook at higher temperatures, but I'm truly low and slow. I keep the pit temperature at 210 to 225 degrees for everything I cook, with the exception of poultry. This gives me time to get a deep penetration of flavor, and there's less shrinkage of meat.

CUT	WEIGHT	TIME	INTERNAL TEMPERATURE
Baby back ribs[1]	1–1½ lb.	3–5 hr.	—
Loin back ribs	1¾–2 lb.	4–6 hr.	—
Spareribs	2¼–3+ lb.	5–7 hr.	—
St. Louis–style ribs	2¼–3+ lb.	5–7 hr.	—
Pork shoulder	12–16 lb.	18–20 hr.	165°–180° to slice, 185°–195° to pull
Boston butt	6–8 lb.	12–16 hr.	165°–180° to slice, 185°–195° to pull
Whole hog[2]	30–50 lb.	14–16 hr.	185°–190°
Whole hog[2]	50–85 lb.	16–18 hr.	185°–190°
Whole hog[2]	85–125 lb.	18–24 hr.	185°–190°
Pork tenderloin	1½–2 lb.	2–2½ hr.	160°–165°
Pork loin	4–6 lb.	3–3½ hr.	165°
Sausage	1½"–2½" diameter	1–2 hr.	165°
Beef ribs[3]	2¼–3+ lb.	5–7 hr.	—
Beef brisket flap	8–12 lb.	12–18 hr.	185°–195°
Beef brisket, nose on	12–16 lb.	14–18 hr.	185°–195°
Shoulder clod	14–16 lb.	10–12 hr.	160°–170° to slice
Tri–tip[4]	2–2½ lb.	1½–2 hr.	140°–155°
Beef tenderloin	3–4 lb.	3–4 hr.	130° for rare, 140° for medium-rare, 150° for medium, 160° for well-done
Prime rib	12–16 lb.	3–4 hr.	130° for rare, 140° for medium-rare, 150° for medium, 160° for well-done
Chicken (whole)[5]	2½–3 lb.	1½–2 hr.	170° in the thigh
Chicken (whole)[5]	3½–4½ lb.	3–4 hr.	170° in the thigh
Turkey	10–12 lb.	7–8 hr.	170° in the thigh
Bologna[6]	10–14 lb.	2½–3 hr.	140°

[1]The rack will bend when you pick up one end, and the meat will pull away from the bone. If your fire's too hot, the meat will shrink and expose bone on the sides. Maintain a pit temperature of 200 to 210 degrees.

[2]Whole hog will be cooked at 165 degrees, but it needs to be at 185 to 190 degrees for you to be able to pull the meat.

[3]Beef ribs won't feel as limp as pork ribs, and the meat won't be as tender, either. Beef has a different density than pork. I still determine doneness by feel. I just push on the meat. This takes practice.

[4]Tri-tip does not need to cook nearly as long as brisket; it's a better cut of meat, so it doesn't have to break down and tenderize. You want to serve the meat barely pink, between medium and medium-well. Slice it against the grain, like brisket.

[5]Maintain a pit temperature of 240 to 250 degrees for chicken. Split chickens will cook more quickly.

[6]Bologna is already cooked. You're just adding smoke to it and getting it hot.

fat, and if it drips down onto the coals, it'll make a mess in the bottom of the pit. Take an aluminum pie pan and fill it with a few inches of water to create moisture and catch the fat that drips down out of the turkey. Or just use the pan without water.

When Pat Burke and I were learning to cook on our homemade pit, we used a water pan a few times. But we practiced and practiced and practiced and learned how to get the end result we wanted without having to use the water pan. The Ole Hickory pits I use these days don't require water pans because the draw is from the bottom of the pit and the pit itself is tight enough and well-insulated enough that it holds the moisture in.

There's nothing wrong with using a water pan; it's just a personal preference to cook without it.

Pink Meat and the Pink Smoke Ring

Educating people about the characteristics of smoked meat is a full-time job.

Smoke gives the meat a pinkish hue. This isn't so much of an issue with pork and beef, but when people eat smoked chicken or turkey for the first time, they immediately think the meat isn't thoroughly cooked when they see that pink color. This can be confusing for first-time barbecuers, too. When you're cooking barbecue, don't focus on the color of the meat; look for other indicators. If the meat feels right and it's up to temperature, then it's done. You can tell when you're trying to cut into a piece of chicken whether or not it's cooked. Can you cut it easily and pull the leg off easily? Then it's done. But when in doubt, always use your thermometer to check the temperature. The USDA guidelines suggest a temperature of 170 degrees in the thigh.

When you slice a piece of meat that's been cooked with charcoal, wood, or a combination of the two, you'll notice that the meat closest to the edge, all the way around, will be a deep red or darker pink than the rest of the meat. That's called the smoke ring, and it's highly desirable. The depth of the ring can range from $1/4$ to $3/8$ inch. The deeper the ring, the more skilled you are as a cooker. In competition I would always pull apart the shoulder and say to the judges, "Look at that perfect $1/2$-inch smoke ring." Interestingly, you may have two pieces of meat that are almost identical in size, shape, and weight, both cooking on the same pit at the same time, and one will have a better smoke ring.

A smoke ring is sometimes called a heat ring. A piece of meat cooked in the oven or with gas will also form a ring, but it won't be pink. So don't be fooled. Only barbecue that's been cooked with charcoal, wood, or a combination of the two will have pink meat and a true smoke ring.

Help spread the word. Tell all of your friends—pink meat and the pink smoke ring are the marks of the real thing.

Characteristics of a Perfectly Cooked Rib

Knowing when ribs are done is an intuitive skill and takes lots of practice. Whatever you do, avoid poking the ribs, or any meat for that matter, with a fork. That punctures the "bark," the tasty, spicy coating formed on the outside of the meat, and allows juice and moisture to escape, resulting in dry meat. Instead, simply lift up one end of the rack with your finger. There should be a slight bend or give to the ribs, as though they're bending a bit in the middle. If they move up and down, straight as a board, they need to cook a little longer. Ribs should have some "pull" to them. Some meat should stick to the bone when you tear them apart. If the meat slips entirely away from the bone, then they are way overcooked.

You need to watch your temperature while cooking. If the pit gets too hot, the meat will start pulling away from the bone, exposing the tips. This is called "bone shine" or "shiners," and this is not a good thing. You don't want to see the bones poking up out of the meat around the edges.

Some of My Secrets for Moist and Delicious Chicken and Turkey

■ If I'm cooking a whole chicken, I cook it on its back. When I'm cooking a split chicken, which I prefer, I cook it bone side down. The bone acts as a shield and helps cook the chicken faster and more evenly.

■ Don't keep turning the chicken; you'll dry it out.

■ I like to eat the skin, so I put extra salt on it; that helps draw the fat out of the skin and crisps it up.

■ Baste when the skin looks dry throughout the cooking process, every 30 minutes or so.

■ Here's my recipe for a chicken basting liquid. Combine 2 cups of apple cider vinegar, 1 cup of water, and 4 tablespoons of butter or oil with some Magic Dust (see page 67) in a saucepan and bring it up to a simmer. I'll mop the chickens with this baste as needed throughout the cooking process. The vinegar tenderizes the meat and helps remove the fat from the skin so it crisps, and the butter helps the seasoning cling.

■ When you're cooking a whole bird, the cavity will fill up with juices. Remove the bird from the pit very carefully so the hot juices don't spill on you. What I do is put on my heavy rubber gloves and carefully lift the bird out onto a sheet pan so I can capture the juices. There is no finer stock than this liquid. I pour the stock into a container and keep it in the refrigerator for a few days or freeze it for future use. You can use this liquid in any dish where you want to add richness. We use it for soups, chicken and dumplings, and to moisten dressing (that's what some people call stuffing).

Whole Hog Tips

It may be easier to flavor a skinless hog, but it's easier to cook a hog and not burn it with the skin on it. You're using the skin as a heat shield to keep it from blackening and to help keep the meat moist. Your cooking temperature will make a difference, though. Ed Mitchell, whom you read about in Chapter 3, for example, could not cook a hog without the skin at the temperature at which he cooks. But remember that the North Carolina whole hog tradition is to chop and mix up all the different parts of the hog. Ed's not cooking for display. What he does do at one point is pull off the skin, throw it back on the heat, and really crisp it up. That's how he makes the cracklin's that get chopped up and mixed up with the meat and are really delicious.

■ When I prep a skinless hog, I sprinkle it liberally first with kosher salt, then with Magic Dust (see page 67).

■ There's no sense in putting seasoning on the skin itself; the flavoring won't penetrate. You can, however, oil the skin. That will make it easy to wipe down and clean up for display.

■ Cut the hog down the center so you can lay it flat. Season the entire belly side and turn it over. Cut some pockets in the shoulder and leg areas and put some seasoning down inside the hog. Remove some skin from the leg area and season that meat, too.

■ Most people who cook with the skin on start with the hog in a sprawled position, spread-eagle, legs straight out to the side. Start off belly side down first to get some smoke in it. You want the inside to be colored up but not burned. Cook on the tummy for two to three hours. You should still be able to flip it easily; the meat should not become too loose. Once you turn the hog over so the skin side is down, you can fill the body cavity with your baste and it'll seep through the meat. You can reach in and mop the areas that look dry.

> "Best way to kill a pig is to have somebody who knows how to butcher one. While he's alive, grab that son of a gun by the dadgum ear and twist his head around there and take a knife and just cut his throat. He'll bounce around like a chicken'll do. He'll run around and make you sicker than the devil because he'll bleed and blow. Blood'll be all over the place. But he'll bleed completely out. And get all of that blood and stuff out of there. And when you peel it, don't ever let your hand that touched the outside touch the meat. Just peel it off. You touch the hair and then touch the inside, that'll taint the meat."
>
> —Sarge Davis

Living the Barbecue Dream

Writing this book has been quite an experience. Over the past year, my daughter, Amy, and I tried to condense a lifetime into one book. We traveled almost 100,000 miles through 15 states, visiting old friends and making a few new ones. We'd land in one city and make our way to six others. And, of course, wherever there was a sign that said "Barbecue," we'd pull over for a snack—just to make sure we weren't missing something.

If this book shows you anything, it's that there's no such thing as a "typical" barbe-cuer. These people are simple yet complicated, humble yet confident. Many have culti-vated that "good ol' boy" persona, yet they're razor sharp underneath. Some were born into barbecue and others embraced it later in life. For many of us, barbecue has sent our children to college. And barbecue has even saved more than one man.

Through the years, here's what I've learned: Barbecue soothes the soul. It's simple in philosophy and rich in tradition. It's an art and a craft, a love and a passion. It's provided me with a life full of friendship and love.

As you've read in these pages, credit is given again and again to luck, but, as the old saying goes, "The harder I work, the luckier I get." It surely has been hard work, but we all feel pretty lucky to get paid to barbecue. And we feel lucky to be able to make a living doing what we love. For my friends and me, barbecue is much more than a job, it's a way of life. We're living our version of the great American Dream.

"This has been a great ride. And I plan to ride this horse as long as she'll go."
—MIKE MILLS

Resources

Films

Barbecue Is a Noun, barbecueisanoun.com
Barbecue: A Texas Love Story, www.bbqfilm.com

Books

Auchmutey, Jim, and Susan Puckett. *The Ultimate Barbecue Sauce Cookbook.* Atlanta, Georgia: Longstreet Press, 1995.

Dornenburg, Andrew, and Karen Page. *Culinary Artistry.* Hoboken, New Jersey: Wiley, 1996.

Early, Jim. *The Best Tar Heel Barbecue: Manteo to Murphy.* Winston-Salem, North Carolina, The Best Tar Heel Barbecue, Inc., 2002.

Edge, John T. *Southern Belly.* Athens, Georgia: Hill Street Press, 2000.

Egerton, John. *Cornbread Nation.* Chapel Hill, North Carolina: University of North Carolina Press, 2002.

———. *Southern Food.* Chapel Hill, North Carolina: University of North Carolina Press, 1993.

Elie, Lolis Eric. *Cornbread Nation 2.* Chapel Hill, North Carolina: University of North Carolina Press, 2004.

Elie, Lolis Eric, and Frank Stewart. *Smokestack Lightning: Adventures in the Heart of Barbecue Country.* New York: Farrar, Straus and Giroux, 1996.

Garner, Bob. *North Carolina Barbecue: Flavored by Time.* Winston-Salem, North Carolina: John F. Blair, 1996.

Griffith, Dotty. *Celebrating Barbecue.* New York: Simon & Schuster, 2002.

Jamison, Cheryl and Bill. *Smoke & Spice.* Boston, Massachusetts: Harvard Common Press, 2003.

Kirk, Paul. *Paul Kirk's Championship Barbecue.* Boston, Massachusetts: Harvard Common Press, 2004.

———. *Paul Kirk's Championship Barbecue Sauces.* Boston, Massachusetts: Harvard Common Press, 1998.

Stage, John, and Nancy Radke. *Dinosaur Bar-B-Que: An American Roadhouse.* Chicago, Illinois: Ten Speed Press, 2001.

Thompson, Fred. *Iced Tea.* Boston, Massachusetts: Harvard Common Press, 2002.

Trillin, Calvin. *Feeding a Yen.* New York: Random House, 2003.

———. *Tummy Trilogy.* New York: Farrar, Straus and Giroux, 1994.

Walsh, Robb. *Legends of Texas Barbecue Cookbook: Recipes and Recollections from the Pit Bosses.* San Francisco, California: Chronicle, 2002.

Worgul, Doug. *The Grand Barbecue.* Kansas City, Kansas: Star Books, 2001.

Publications

Bull Sheet
(Published by KCBS)
11514 Hickman Mills Drive
Kansas City, Missouri 64134
816-765-5891
kcbs.us

National Barbecue News
P.O. Box 981
Douglas, Georgia 31534-0981
800-385-0002
barbecuenews.com

The Big Boys

For a complete list of sanctioned cook-offs, visit the *National Barbecue News* Web site at barbecuenews.com.

The American Royal
1701 American Royal Court
Kansas City, Missouri 64102
816-221-9800
americanroyal.com

Houston Livestock Show and Rodeo
P.O. Box 20070
Houston, Texas 77225
832-667-1000
hlsr.com

Jack Daniel's World Championship
    Invitational Barbecue
Route 1
Lynchburg, Tennessee 37352
931-759-4221
jackdaniels.com

Memphis in May World Championship
    Barbecue Cooking Contest
88 Union Avenue, Suite 301
Memphis, Tennessee 38103
901-525-4611
memphisinmay.org

Organizations

International Barbeque Cookers Association
P.O. Box 200556
Arlington, Texas 76007
817-469-1579
ibcabbq.org

National Barbecue Association
8317 Cross Park Drive, Suite 150
P. O. Box 140647
Austin, Texas 78714-0647
888-909-2121
nbbqa.org

Kansas City Barbeque Society
11514 Hickman Mills Drive
Kansas City, Missouri 64134
816-765-5891
kcbs.us

Southern Foodways Alliance
Center for the Study of Southern Culture
Barnard Observatory
University, Mississippi 38677
662-915-5993
southernfoodways.com

Supplies

PITS AND SMOKERS

Backwoods Smoker
8245 Dixie-Shreveport Road
Shreveport, Louisiana 71107
318-220-0380 or 318-458-4131
backwoods-smoker.com

BBQ Pits by Klose
2216 West 34th Street
Houston, Texas 77018
713-686-8720
bbqpits.com

Broilmaster
918 Freeburg Avenue
Belleville, Illinois 62220
800-851-3153
broilmaster.com

Camerons Stovetop Smoker
CM International Inc.
P.O. Box 60220
Colorado Springs, Colorado 80960
888-563-0227
cameronssmoker.com

Jedmaster
22251 Diesel Drive
McCalla, Alabama 35111
866-568-8200
brittsbarbecue.com

Ole Hickory
333 North Main Street
Cape Girardeau, Missouri 63701
800-223-9667
573-334-3377
olehickorypits.com

Primo Grills and Smokers
5999 Goshen Springs Road
Suite C
Norcross, Georgia 30071
770-729-1110
primogrill.com

W'ham
P.O. Box 17312
Memphis, Tennessee 38187-0312
800-737-WHAM
willinghams.com

LUMP CHARCOAL AND WOOD

Peoples Woods
75 Mill Street
Cumberland, Rhode Island 02864
800-729-5800
peopleswoods.com

SPICES

Townsend Supplies, Inc.
8 East Main Street
P.O. Box 100
Oxford, Arkansas 72565
870-258-3523

The Spice House
1031 North Old World Third Street
Milwaukee, Wisconsin 53203
414-272-0977
thespicehouse.com [BE CAREFUL . . .
    spicehouse.com is a sex site]

Hatch Chile Express
P.O. Box 350
Hatch, New Mexico
800-292-4454
hatch-chile.com

Mexene Chile Powder
P.O. Drawer 1030
New Iberia, Louisiana 70562
800-299-9082
brucefoods.com

BARBECUE SAUCES

Many of the people and restaurants in this book sell their barbecue sauce locally, regionally, and nationally. In addition, here is information about two popular grocery store brands.

Maull's Barbecue Sauce
The Louis Maull Company
219 North Market
St. Louis, Missouri 63102
maull.com

Wicker's
501 Main Street
Hornersville, Missouri 63855
800-847-0032\
web.inetba.com/wickers

HUSH PUPPY MIX

Lakeside Mills
716 West Main Street
Spindale, North Carolina 28160
828-286-4866
lakesidemills.com

Mike Mills's Restaurants

17th Street Bar & Grill
32 North 17th Street
Murphysboro, Illinois 62966
618-684-3722 (restaurant)
618-684-8902 (catering)
17thstreetbarbecue.com

17th Street Bar & Grill
2700 17th Street
Marion, Illinois 62959
618-998-1114

Memphis Championship Barbecue
   (my Las Vegas outposts)
memphis-bbq.com
4379 North Las Vegas Boulevard
Las Vegas, Nevada 89115
702-644-0000

2250 East Warm Springs Road
Las Vegas, Nevada 89119
702-260-6909

4949 North Rancho Drive
   (inside the Santa Fe Station Hotel)
Las Vegas, Nevada 89109
702-396-6223

1401 South Rainbow Boulevard
Las Vegas, Nevada 89108
702-254-0520

My Stomping Grounds—Other Southern Illinois Barbecue You'll Enjoy

Dixie Barbecue
205 Broad Street
Jonesboro, Illinois 62952
618-833-6437

Giant City Lodge
About 10 miles south of Carbondale, Illinois,
   in Giant City State Park
618-457-4921
There a few barbecue items on the menu, and you can get a taste of Mr. Whitt's barbecue sauce, made from the original recipe. Most people, however, go for the family-style fried chicken suppers.

Mack's Barbecue Stand
3201 Sycamore Street
Cairo, Illinois 62914
618-734-9847

Shemwell's Bar-B-Q
1102 Washington Avenue
Cairo, Illinois 62914
618-734-0165

Shrines, Shacks, Joints, and
Right Respectable Restaurants Worth a Stop

Some of these places are mentioned in this book; others are places where
I've had a good meal over the years.

Alabama

Big Bob Gibson
1715 Sixth Avenue SE
Decatur, Alabama 35601
256-350-6969
and
2520 Danville Road SW
Decatur, Alabama 35603
256-350-0404
bigbobgibson.com

Bob Sykes Bar-B-Q
1724 Ninth Avenue
Bessemer, Alabama 35020
205-426-1400

Chuck's Bar-B-Q
905 Short Avenue
Opelika, Alabama 36801
334-749-4043

Dreamland (the original)
5535 15th Avenue East
Tuscaloosa, Alabama 35405
205-758-8135
dreamlandbbq.com

Arizona

Joe's Real BBQ
301 North Gilbert Road
Gilbert, Arizona 85234
480-503-3805
joesrealbbq.com

Thee Pits Again
5558 West Bell Road
Glendale, Arizona 85308
602-996-7488

Arkansas

Demo's Barbeque & Smokehouse
1851 South Church Street
Jonesboro, Arkansas 72401
870-935-6633

McClard's Bar-B-Q & Fine Foods
505 Albert Pike
Hot Springs, Arkansas 71901
501-623-9665
mcclards.com

Woody's Bar-B-Q
Highway 49
Waldenburg, Arkansas 72475
870-579-2251

Whole Hog Café
2516 Cantrell Road
Little Rock, Arkansas 72202
501-664-5025
wholehogcafe.com

California

Memphis Minnie's BBQ Joint
576 Haight Street
San Francisco, California 94117
415-864-7675

Shrines, Shacks, Joints, and
Right Respectable Restaurants Worth a Stop—*Continued*

Florida

Cross Creek Steakhouse & Ribs
850 Lane Avenue South
Jacksonville, Florida 32205
904-783-9579
crosscreeksteaks.com

Georgia

Fresh Air Barbecue
1164 Highway 42
Flovilla, Georgia 30216
770-775-3182

Jack's Old South Bar-B-Q
120 North Third Street
Vienna, Georgia 31092
229-268-1500
and
2010 Central Park Exit
Cordele, Georgia 31015
229-271-9144

Melear's Pit-Cooked Barbecue
Highway 85
Fayetteville, Georgia 30214
770-461-7180

OB's Barbecue
725 Industrial Boulevard
McDonough, Georgia 30253
678-432-6002

Old Clinton Barbecue
4214 Highway 129
Gray [Clinton], Georgia 31032
478-986-3225

Williamson Bros. Bar-B-Q
1425 Roswell Road
Marietta, Georgia 30062
770-971-3201

Kentucky

Moonlite Bar-B-Q Inn
2840 West Parrish Avenue
Owensboro, Kentucky 42301
800-322-8989
moonlite.com

Massachusetts

East Coast Grill
1271 Cambridge Street
Cambridge, Massachusetts 02139
617-491-6568

Firefly's Bodacious BBQ (multiple locations)
350 East Main Street
Marlborough, Massachusetts 01752
508-357-8883
fireflysbbq.com

Holy Smokes BBQ & Whole Hog House
9 Church Avenue
West Hatfield, Massachusetts 01088
413-247-5737
holysmokesbbq.com

Jake's Boss BBQ
3492 Washington Street
Jamaica Plain, Massachusetts 02130
617-983-3701

Rouge
480 Columbus Avenue
Boston, Massachusetts 02118
617-867-0600
rougeboston.com

Memphis Roadhouse
383 Washington Street
South Attleboro, Massachusetts 02703
508-761-5700

Minnesota

Roscoe's Root Beer & Ribs
603 Fourth Street SE
Rochester, Minnesota 55904
507-285-0501
roscoesbbq.com

Mississippi

Leatha's
6374 U.S. Highway 98
Hattiesburg, Mississippi 39402
601-271-6003

Ubon's
801 North Jerry Clower Boulevard
Yazoo City, Mississippi 39194
662-716-7100
and
1029 Highway 51
Madison, MI 39110
601-607-3322
ubonsbbq.com

Missouri

Arthur Bryant's (the original)
1727 Brooklyn Avenue
Kansas City, Missouri 64127
816-231-1123
arthurbryantsbbq.com

Fast Eddy's
9604 East U.S. 40
Independence, Missouri 64055
816-358-3278

Gates Bar-B-Q (the original)
1325 East Emanuel Cleaver Boulevard
Kansas City, Missouri 64110
816-531-7522
gatesbbq.com

Oklahoma Joe's
47th and Mission Road
Kansas City, Kansas 66103
913-722-3366
oklahomajoesbbq.com

Smoki O's
1545 North Broadway
St. Louis, Missouri 63102
314-621-8180

Super Smokers (multiple locations)
601 Stockell Drive
Eureka, Missouri 63025
636-938-9742
supersmokers.com

Nevada

BJ's Barbeque
754 North McCarran Boulevard
Sparks, Nevada 89431
775-355-1010

New York

Blue Smoke
116 East 27th Street
New York, New York 10016
212-447-7733
bluesmoke.com

Brother Jimmy's BBQ
1485 2nd Avenue
New York, New York 10021
212-288-0999

Dinosaur Bar-B-Que
246 West Willow Street
Syracuse, New York 13202
315-476-4937
and
99 Court Street
Rochester, New York 14604
585-325-7090
and
646 West 131st Street
New York, New York 10027
212-694-9777
dinosaurbarbque.com

North Carolina

Allen & Son
6203 Millhouse Road
Chapel Hill, North Carolina 27516
919-942-7576

Alston Bridges
620 East Grover Street
Shelby, North Carolina 28150
704-482-1998

BBQ & Ribs Company (multiple locations)
501 South Main Street
Graham, North Carolina 27253
336-223-9886

Bridges Barbecue Lodge
2000 East Dixon Boulevard
U.S. Highway 74
Shelby, North Carolina 28152
704-482-8567

King's
405 East New Bern Road
Kinston, North Carolina 28504
252-527-2101
kingsbbq.com

Lexington Barbecue
10 Highway 29-70 South/Business 85
Lexington, North Carolina 27295
336-249-9814

Mitchell's Bar-B-Q Ribs & Chicken
6228 South Ward Boulevard
Wilson, North Carolina 27893
252-291-3808
mitchellsbbq.com

Ole Time Barbeque
6309 Hillsborough Street
Raleigh, North Carolina 27606
919-859-2544

Stamey's Barbecue
2812 Battleground Avenue
Greensboro, North Carolina 27408
336-288-9275

Wilber's Barbecue
4172 U.S. Highway 70 East
Goldsboro, North Carolina 27534
919-778-5218

Oregon

Hole in the Wall Barbecue
3200 West 11th Avenue
Eugene, Oregon 97402
541-683-7378
holeinthewallbbq.com

Pennsylvania

Jack's Firehouse
2130 Fairmount Avenue
Philadelphia, Pennsylvania 19130
215-232-9000

South Carolina

Louis's at Pawley's
10880 Ocean Highway
U.S. 17
Pawley's Island, South Carolina 29585
843-237-8757
louisatpawleys.com
Barbecue served a few nights a week. You
might want to give a call in advance.

Maurice's BBQ/Piggie Park (the original)
1600 Charleston Highway
West Columbia, South Carolina 29171
803-796-0220
mauricesbbq.com

Mutt's Bar-B-Q (multiple locations)
Highway 14 and 101 West Road
Greer, South Carolina 29650
864-848-3999

Sweatman's
Route 453 North
Holly Hill, South Carolina
843-563-7574

Tennessee

A & R Bar-B-Q
1802 Elvis Presley Boulevard
Memphis, Tennessee 38109
901-774-7444

The Bar-B-Que Shop
1782 Madison Avenue
Memphis, Tennessee 38104
901-272-1277
dancingpigs.com

Corky's (the original)
5259 Poplar Avenue
Memphis, Tennessee 38119
901-685-9744
www.corkysbbq.com

Cozy Corner
745 North Parkway at Manassas
Memphis, Tennessee 38105
901-527-9158

Jim Neeley's Interstate Barbecue
2265 South Third Street
Memphis, Tennessee 38109
901-775-2304
jimneelysinterstatebarbecue.com

Payne's
1762 Lamar Avenue
Memphis, Tennessee 38114
901-272-1523

Pratt's Real Pit Barbecue
1225 East Stone Drive
Kingsport, Tennessee 37660
423-246-2500

Rendevous
52 South Second Street
Memphis, Tennessee 38103
901-523-2746
hogsfly.com

Ridgewood Barbecue
900 Elizabethton Highway
Bluff City, Tennessee 37618
423-538-7543

Three Little Pigs Bar-B-Q
5145 Quince Road
Memphis, Tennessee 38117
901-685-7094

Texas

Angelo's Barbecue
2533 White Settlement Road
Fort Worth, Texas 76107
817-332-0357
angelosbbq.com

Black's BBQ
215 North Main Street
Lockhart, Texas 78644
512-398-2712
blacksbbq.com

Blake's Bar-B-Q
2916 Jeanetta
Houston, Texas 77063
713-266-6860

City Market
633 East Davis Street
Luling, Texas 78648
830-875-9019

Crosstown Bar-B-Que
202 South Avenue C
Elgin, Texas 78621
512-281-5594

Cooper's Old Time Pit Bar-B-Que
505 West Dallas
Llano, Texas 78643
325-247-5713
coopersbbq.com

Drexler's World Famous BBQ & Grill
2300 Pierce
Houston, Texas 77003
713-752-0008
drexlersbbq.com

Shrines, Shacks, Joints, and
Right Respectable Restaurants Worth a Stop—*Continued*

Gonzales Food Market
311 St. Lawrence
Gonzales, Texas 78929
830-672-3156
www.gonzalesfoodmarket.com

Harlon's Bar-B-Q
11403 Martin Luther King
Houston, Texas 77048
713-230-0111
harlonsbbq.com

Kreuz Market
619 North Colorado Street
Lockhart, Texas 78644
512-398-2361
kreuzmarket.com

Louis Mueller's
206 West Second Street
Taylor, Texas 76574
512-352-6206

Luling City Market Bar-B-Q
4726 Richmond Avenue
Houston, Texas 77027
713-871-1903

Lyndon's Pit Bar-B-Q
13165 Northwest Freeway
Houston, Texas 77040
713-690-2112

New Zion Missionary Baptist Church
2601 Montgomery Road
Huntsville, Texas 77340
936-295-2349

Railhead Smokehouse
2900 Montgomery Street
Fort Worth, Texas 76107
817-738-9808

Rudy's Country Store & Bar-B-Q
24152 West IH 10
San Antonio, Texas 78257
210-698-2141
rudys.com

The Salt Lick
18001 FM 1826
Driftwood, Texas 78619
512-858-4959
saltlickbbq.com

Smitty's Market
208 South Commerce Street
Lockhart, Texas 78644
512-398-9344
smittysmarket.com

Sonny Bryan's Smokehouse
(the original location)
2202 Inwood Road
Dallas, Texas 75235
214-357-7120
sonnybryansbbq.com

Southside Market
1212 Highway 290 East
Elgin, Texas 78621
512-281-4650

The Swinging Door
3818 FM359 Road
Richmond, Texas 77469
281-342-4758

Taylor Café
101 North Main Street
Taylor, Texas 76574
512-352-2828

Thelma's Barbecue
1020 Live Oak at Lamar
Houston, Texas 77003
713-228-2262

Virginia

Pigs R Us
1014 Liberty Street
Martinsville, Virginia 24112
276-632-1161

Virginia Barbeque (multiple locations)
451 Jefferson Davis Highway
Fredericksburg, Virginia 22401
540-368-2800
virginiabbq.com

Wisconsin

Smoky Jon's #1 BBQ
2310 Packers Avenue
Madison, Wisconsin 53704
608-249-7427

Barbecue Caterers

Most restaurants cater as well. The following are strictly barbecue catering companies.

Billy Bones BBQ
751 Saginaw Road
Sanford, Michigan 48657
989-687-7880
billybonesbbq.com

Bonnie's Catering
Bonnie & Ruben Gomez
7820 Enchanted Hills, Suite A-131
Rio Rancho, New Mexico 87144
505-771-3145

Eddie Deen Ranch & Catering
944 South Lamar
Dallas, Texas 75202
214-741-4211
eddiedeen.com

Hogg Heaven Bar-B-Q Catering Services
411 West Ninth Street
Mount Carmel, Illinois 62863
618-262-7779

Paul Kirk/K.C. Baron of Barbecue
3625 West 50th Terrace
Roeland Park, Kansas 66205-1534
913-262-6029

Porky's Catering & Concessions
P.O. Box 5044
Lafayette, Indiana 47903
765-583-0286

Porky's Place
4223 Lincoln Highway East
York, Pennsylvania 17402
717-755-3101
porkysplacebbq.com

The Q Company
40 Serendipity Way
Atlanta, Georgia 30350
770-998-7287
theqcompany.com

Ranch Hands Barbeque Catering
3037 South Bristol
Santa Ana, California 92704
714-754-6397
ranchhandsbbq.com

The Rib Doctor
Eva and Hayward Harris Jr.
P.O. Box 51718
Riverside, California 92517
951-683-7427

Smokin' Joe's BBQ Express
Joe Jackson
510 Eastmore Boulevard
Columbus, Ohio 43209
614-235-2476

Recipe List

Index

Underscored page references indicate boxed text. **Boldface** references indicate photographs.

Barbecue
    as equalizer, 129
    experimenting with, 51
    films about, 246–49
    gaining legitimacy in, 266
    vs. grilling, 262, 298
    hints and tips for, 306–9, 311
    ingredients for, 53
    meaning of, 5, 77, 241, 244, 258
    memories of, 129
    new breed in, 134
    politics and, 239, 247, 262
    purity of, 77
    real, definition of, 50
    regional differences in, 43, 57–58,
        259–60
    temperature guide for, 307
    wrong ingredients in, 62
Barbecue: A Texas Love Story, 246–48
Barbecue competitions, **164**, **169–71**,
        202–3
    advice on, 168
    blind box in, 167
    camaraderie in, 74, 76
    categories in, 30
    community spirit in, 165, 173
    drawbacks of, 265
    drinking at, 176, 256
    Friday night meals before, 173
    judges at, 200–202
    judging processes in, 166–67
    sanctioning organizations in, 166, 314,
        323
    teams in, 180
        Apple City Barbecue, 29–30, **30**, 32,
            181–83
        Arizona Kid, the, 196, **197**
        Big Bob Gibson Bar-B-Q, 74, 76–77
        Flying Pigs, 190–91, **190**
        Jack's Old South, 186
        popularity of, 165
        Porky's IV, 193
        Rib Doctor, 188–89
        rivalry in, 167
        size of, 165
        smokers in, 172–73

    stories of, 50
    Super Smokers BBQ, 198, **198**
    Tower Rock Barbecue, 184, **184**
    Ubon's, 194
Barbecue evangelists
    Carolyn Wells, 279–80
    Gerry Dawes, 283–84, 287
    Jason Perlow, 280–81
    Phelps family, 274–76
    Steven Shaw, 280–81, 281
Barbecue Is a Noun, 248–49
Barbecue police, 252
    Calvin Trillin, 252–54, **253**
    Doug Worgul, 269
    Fred Thompson, 272, 273
    Jeffrey Steingarten, 254–57, **255**
    Jim Auchmutey, 261–62
    John Shelton Reed, 270, 271
    John T. Edge, 264–66, 265
    Lolis Eric Elie, 258–60
Barbecue recipes
    Apple Cider Marinated Pork Loin,
        242
    Apple City Barbecue Grand World
        Champion Ribs, 34–35
        in competitions, 30
        popularity of, 32–33
    Becky's Deep-Dish Barbecue Pie, 40
    Big Bob Gibson's Grand World
        Championship Pork Shoulder, 78
    Big Bob Gibson's Hickory-Smoked
        Chicken, 56
    Elizabeth Karmel's Beer-Brined Smoked
        Catfish, 234
    Homemade Sausage with Michigan
        Cherries, 85
    Kreuz Market Shoulder Clod, 91
    Paul Kirk's Kansas City Brisket, 231
    Smoked Canadian Loin Back Sausage,
        174
    Smoked Pork Butt, 6–7
    State Fair Sausage-and-Pepper
        Sandwiches, 149
    Super Smokers Sweet and Spicy Chicken
        Wings, 199
    Ubon's Smoked Prime Rib, 195

W

Wagner, Cheryl, 196, **197**
Wagner, Roger, 196, **197**
Walker, Otis, 230
Wall, Billy Bones, 83–84, **83**, 86–87, 299
Wall, Sharon, 87
Walsh, Rob, 89
Watermelon Ice Cream with Chocolate
    Seeds, 282
Water pans, 306, 308
Wells, Carolyn, 279–80
Wendt, George, 32
W'ham Turbo Cooker, 296
White, Joyce, 282
Whitt, Lionel, 22, 23
Whitt, Mr., 20, 22–23
Whitt's Corner, **21**, 284
Whole Hog Café, 143–44

Wicker's barbecue sauce, 61
Wilber's, 111–12, 114, 116–17, 131, **131**
Wilber's Hush Puppies, <u>115</u>
Willingham, John, <u>172</u>, 296, **296**
Willoughby, John, 240
Wilson, August, 209
Wisconsin, barbecue restaurant in, 322
Wood, 299–300, <u>299</u>
Wood, Cecelia, 61, 69, 140–41, **141**, 142
Wood, Woody, 61, 140, 141–42, **141**, 279
Woody's Barbecue, 140–42
Woody's Bar-B-Q Dip, 69
Worgul, Doug, 269
Work surface, 291

Y

Yelton's Best, <u>115</u>
Your Basic Dry Rub, 66

About the Authors

In the world of barbecue, champion pitmaster **MIKE MILLS** is affectionately known as "The Legend." He presides over the pits at his six nationally acclaimed barbecue joints: two 17th Street Bar & Grill restaurants in Southern Illinois and four Memphis Championship Barbecue restaurants in Las Vegas. In the early 1990s he was cocaptain of the Apple City Barbecue Team, one of the most celebrated teams ever on the circuit. He has the distinction of being the only three-time Grand World Champion at Memphis in May, otherwise known as the Super Bowl of Swine. He is also the barbecue guru and a partner at Blue Smoke restaurant in New York City.

AMY MILLS TUNNICLIFFE, daughter of Mike, is a writer and sought-after professional speaker. She lives near Boston with her two children. She always wanted to be a glamorous heiress. Little did she dream her fortune would lie in barbecue.